IMAGES
of America

WILL ROGERS COLISEUM

I0806316

On the Cover: This 1967 photograph shows the side of the Will Rogers Coliseum and Pioneer Memorial Tower. (Courtesy of the W.D. Smith Commercial Photography Collection, Special Collections, University of Texas at Arlington Library.)

IMAGES
of America

WILL ROGERS COLISEUM

Debbie M. Liles

ARCADIA
PUBLISHING

ISBN 978-0-7385-8548-2

Published by Arcadia Publishing
Charleston, South Carolina

Printed in the United States of America

Library of Congress Control Number: 2011945134

For all general information, please contact Arcadia Publishing:
Telephone 843-853-2070
Fax 843-853-0044
E-mail sales@arcadiapublishing.com
For customer service and orders:
Toll-Free 1-888-313-2665

Visit us on the Internet at www.arcadiapublishing.com

To my husband, Mike, who is the best thing that ever happened to me; to my mum, Rosemarie, who taught me to love history; and to my kids, Kelly and Chase, whom I love more than life

Contents

ACKNOWLEDGMENTS

A book is never just the work of the author; it is the combined efforts of so many. There are so many people to thank, but most of all Ruth Karbach, who made this project possible with her unceasing support and knowledge. Thanks are just not enough for Dalton Hoffman; Ben Guttery; Doug Harman; Max Hill; Scott Barker; Clara Ruddell; Jabari Jones and Betty Shankle at the Genealogical Department of the Fort Worth Public Library; Chris Harmon, Brenda McClurkin, and Cathy Spitzenberger at Special Collections, University of Texas at Arlington; Tiffany Schureman at the Fort Worth Museum of Science and History; Jonathan Frembling at the Amon Carter Museum; Tom Kellam; Pete Charlton; Randy Pruett; Jeanie Sharp at Texas Golden Gloves; Judith Cohen; Ames Fender; Mildred Bryant of the Fort Worth Kennel Club; Billy Joe Gabriel; Jack W. Graves; Tom B. Saunders IV; and Deborah Kilgore. Not only did they make this project possible with their support, but they made it a true pleasure with their friendship and sharing. Thank you so very much.

I would also like to thank Randolph B. Campbell and Richard B. McCaslin, my mentors at the University of North Texas, for all the opportunities they have made possible.

The images in this volume appear courtesy of the Fort Worth *Star-Telegram* Collection, Special Collections, University of Texas at Arlington Library (FWST); Jack White Advertising Collection, Special Collections, the University of Texas at Arlington Library (JWC); the Genealogy, History, and Archives Unit, Fort Worth Public Library (FWPL); Texas Christian University Special Collections (TCU); Fort Worth Stock Show and Rodeo Collection, Fort Worth Museum of Science and History (FWSS); W.D. Smith Commercial Photography Collection, Special Collections, University of Texas at Arlington Library (WDS); and the Amon Carter Museum of American Art (ACM.)

INTRODUCTION

Fort Worth originated as the northernmost in a line of federal forts established to protect frontier Texas from Indian invasions. Established on June 6, 1849, by Maj. R.A. Arnold, commander of Company F of the 2nd Dragoons, Fort Worth was composed of several rough-hewn log quarters, a hospital, a stable, a commissary store, a wheelwright shop, a blacksmith shop, a guardhouse, and a quartermaster's storehouse and was located in an area with plenty of grass for grazing. When the settlement line moved westward, the fort was decommissioned and a community developed.

The Texas & Pacific Railroad came to town in 1876, bringing settlers from all walks of life, including ranchers, bankers, and civic boosters. As the cattle industry grew in the region, meatpackers were convinced to move into town by savvy businessmen and city incentives, and "Cowtown" was born. By 1920, Fort Worth had a population of 106,482 and ranked as the 65th largest city in the nation.

The 1920s brought prosperity to many areas of Texas, as it was a time of economic growth spurred by oil money. Fort Worth became a major hub of activity, with manufacturing plants, oil refineries, and all of the residual businesses. By 1925, a new city charter was drawn up and a $100-million building plan, known as the "Five-Year Work Program," helped Fort Worth develop from a small outpost of the past into a city of the future. The program acted as a buffer against the full fury of the 1929 stock market crash until 1933. After the five-year plan ended, everything stopped. With the force of a tidal wave, the Depression hit Fort Worth.

On May 6, 1935, the Works Progress Administration (WPA) was established under President Roosevelt's New Deal. Designed to put unemployed citizens back to work in a way that would serve the public for years to come, WPA projects benefitted the country in immeasurable ways—and still do. One of these benefits was the financial aid that made the construction of Will Rogers Memorial Coliseum and Auditorium possible.

The story of these structures intertwines with the history of Fort Worth. Starting with the very ground they were built on, continuing with who was involved in the construction, and ending with an understanding of how the center has been used by so many, its significance is undeniable.

The Landmark Commission and Planning Department defines a building worthy for historic landmark designation as such: "A building or site of immeasurable value in preserving the cultural heritage, *or* an outstanding example of design *or* a site closely related to an important personage, act or event in history." Will Rogers Memorial Coliseum, Tower, and Auditorium fits each and every one of these categories, and yet it has no such designation or protection.

There is no way to document every event that has been held at the Coliseum and Auditorium in a book this size, or to take the story much further than the 1970s. As you read through the pages, do not look for what is left out; instead, look at what is included and supports any of the three historic designation categories. It would be quite a challenge to find another set of buildings in Fort Worth that contains as much of the city's history.

One

To Protect and Serve

The first recorded owner of the land, once the hunting grounds of Kiowa, Comanche, and bands of the Wichita Indian tribes, was John P. Montgomery on July 31, 1851. By the early 1870s, it was acquired by Civil War veteran Maj. Khleber Miller Van Zandt, who became a successful businessman, civic booster, and founder of the first Fort Worth newspaper, the *Democrat*. The parcel of land stretched from Penn Street to Montgomery Street and from Lancaster Avenue to Trinity Park. When America entered World War I, training camps were needed to prepare the men for war. Texas was the site of more training camps than any other state, due in part to the weather, which allowed for year-round training. Camp Bowie was established to train the Panther Division, later known as the 36th Infantry, and was located approximately three miles west of downtown Fort Worth. Parts of the camp included training grounds for specialized units and Auxiliary Remount Depot No. 328. Both were located on the land that Will Rogers Coliseum and Auditorium sits on today.

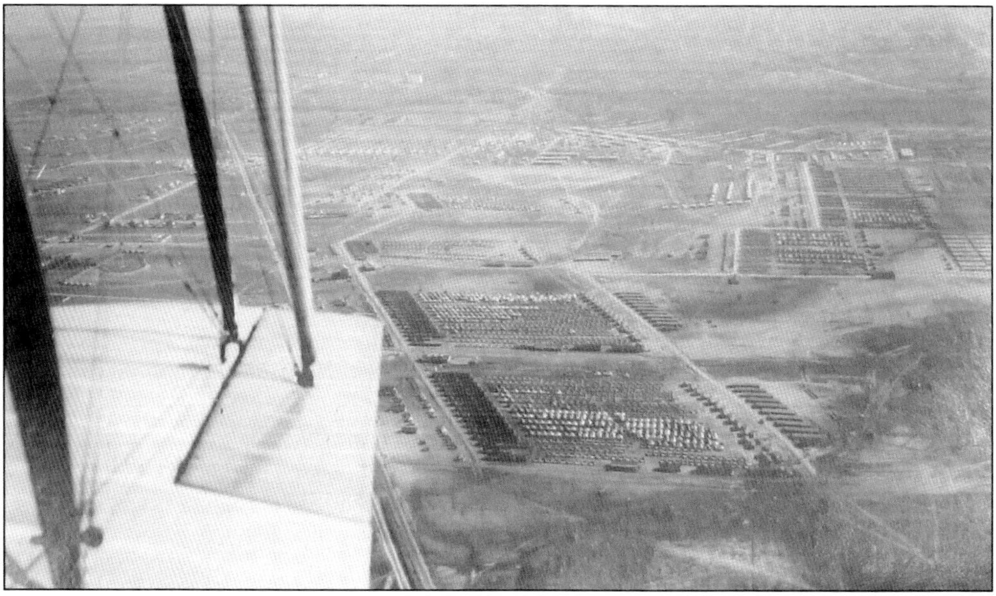

This aerial view of Camp Bowie shows its vast size. The main road (bottom center) is present-day Camp Bowie Boulevard (then Arlington Heights Boulevard). At the turn, it becomes Seventh Street. The two large blocks (center) are an infantry brigade camp composed of wooden buildings and tents. A row of white buildings (upper center) made up the grounds for the ammunition, supply, and sanitary trains. Extending to the far right of that area is Auxiliary Remount Depot No. 328. (Benbrook Public Library.)

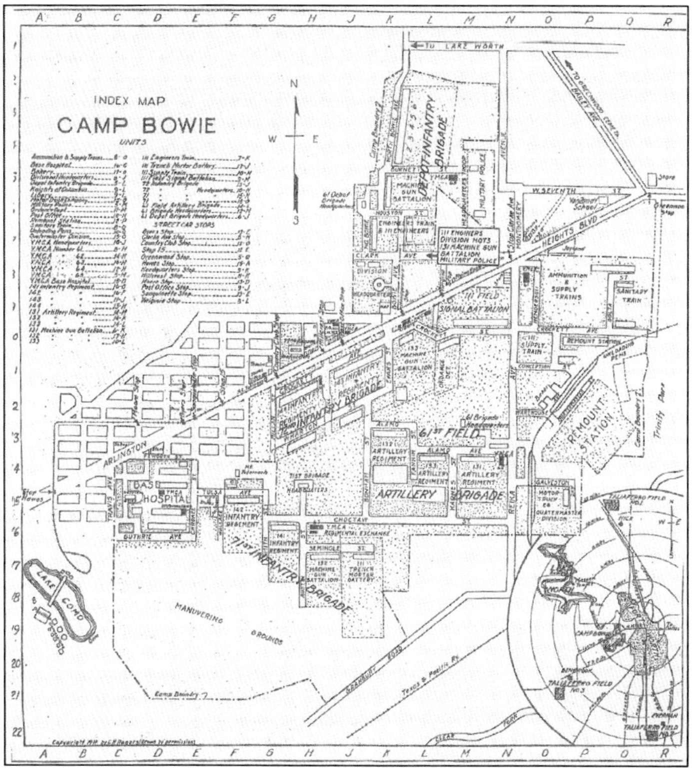

Camp Bowie, shown on this 1917 map, was built at a cost of more than $3 million. East of Reika Avenue (now Montgomery Street) and south of Arlington Heights Boulevard, on the land that is now the Will Rogers Memorial Complex, were the YMCA; the ammunition, sanitation, and supply train areas; the headquarters building; and the ambulance and field buildings. Just south of those is Auxiliary Remount Depot. (Doug Harman.)

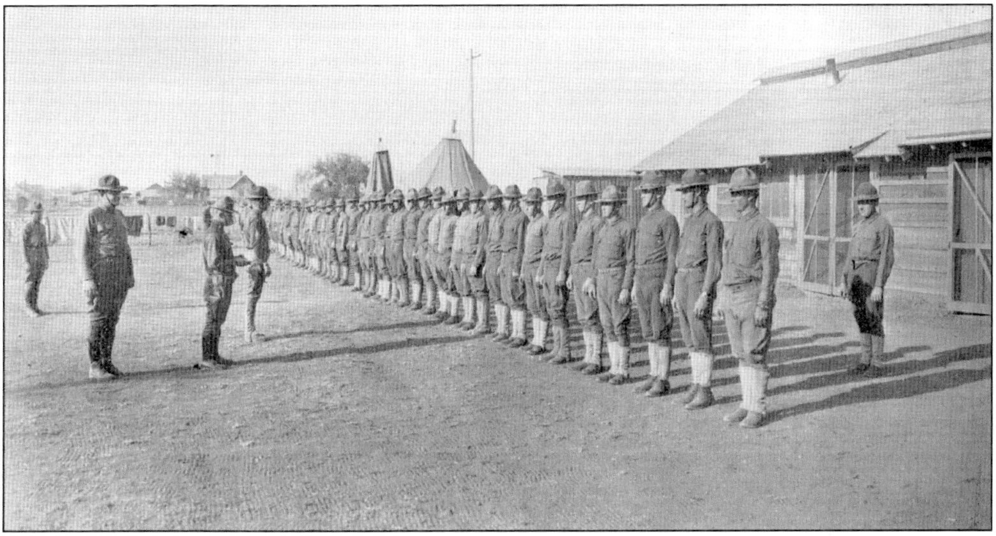

Train units were attached to combat divisions as support troops. The 111th Sanitary Train, commanded by John J. O'Reilly, was formed with a headquarters, two hospitals, and two ambulance companies on October 1, 1917. The sanitary train's purpose was to conduct matters generally dealing with health, such as water, sewerage, and first-aid in the war zones. Shown here is the ambulance section of the Corral Guard Mount, 111th Sanitary Train. (Dalton Hoffman.)

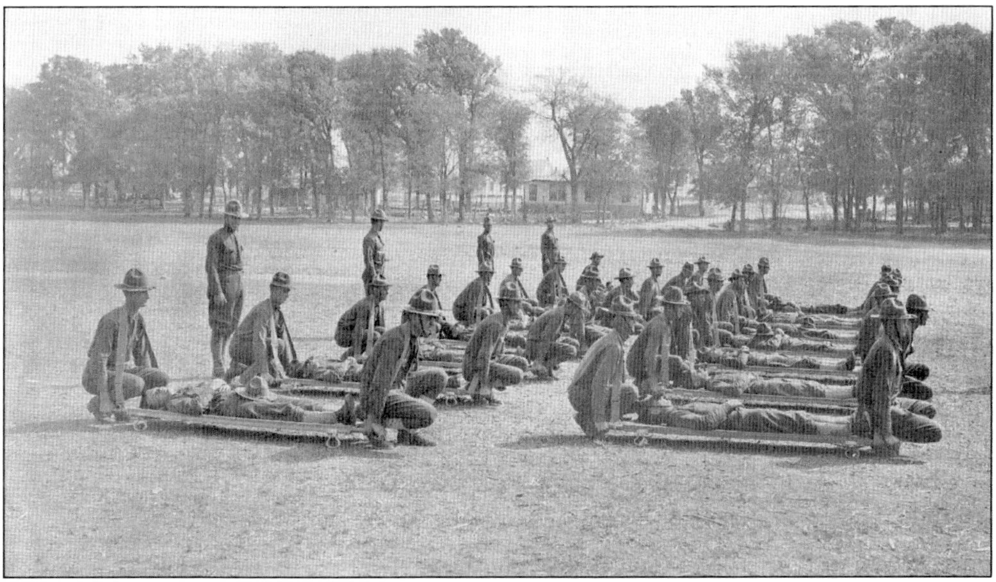

Proper training was essential for transporting injured men. Litter (stretcher) drill was performed to ready the soldiers for the horrific jobs they would conduct in war. Their training was put to the test when the units were shipped to France on July 18, 1918. After a short stay in Bordeaux and then in Bar-sur-Aube, the train was attached first to the Fifth French Army and then the Fourth. It participated in the Meuse-Argonne offensive from October 7 to 29 before rejoining the First American Army at Conde-en-Barrios. (Dalton Hoffman.)

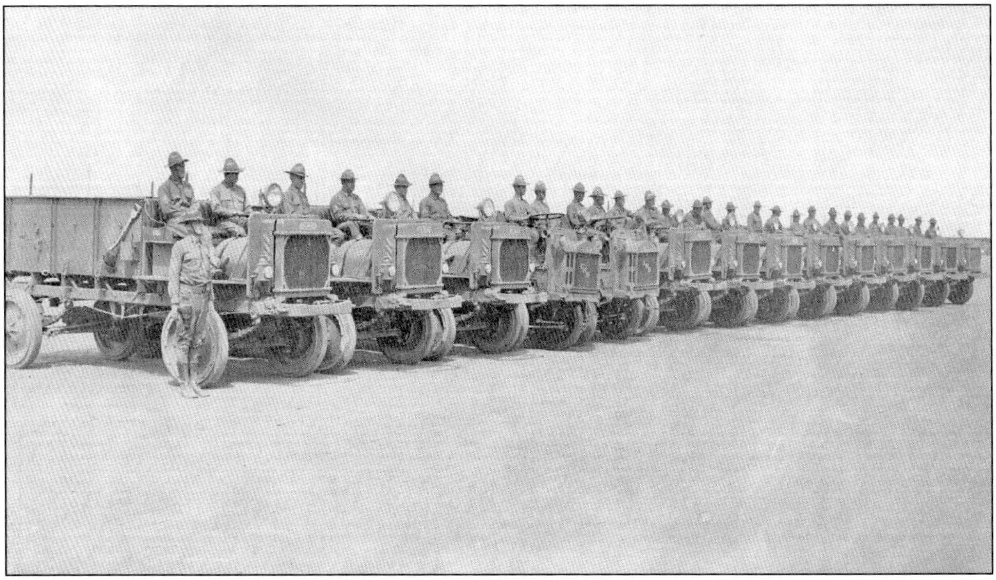

Men in the ammunition train were in charge of anything to do with explosives for rifles, side-arms, and artillery and used motorized as well as animal transportation. The supply train was commanded by Maj. J.H. Zachery and was formed from the transfer of men from the 36th Division. Supply trains handled items used for daily operations and subsistence from the rear to the front line, such as clothing, food, and fuel. Shown here is the motor section from the 111th Ammunition Train. (Dalton Hoffman.)

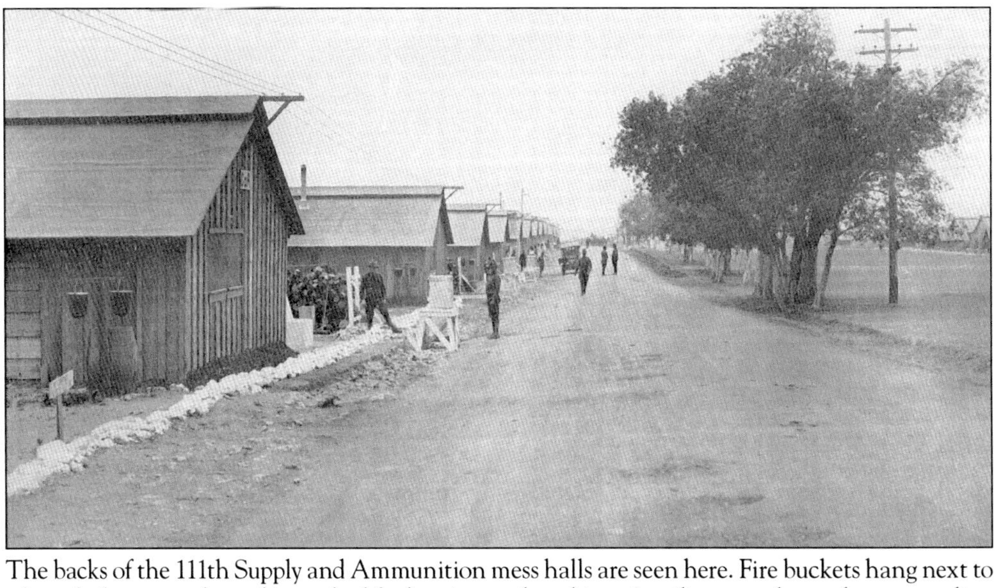

The backs of the 111th Supply and Ammunition mess halls are seen here. Fire buckets hang next to a barrel of water and wood is stacked for heating and cooking. A utility map shows that a waterline ran down Henderson Street, but it may not have been piped into the halls. Rocks on the side of Company A's hall have been white-washed, possibly for guidance in the absence of street lights. The boxes on the elevated platforms are trash cans, placed there for sanitation reasons and for ease of disposal when the collection truck drove through. (Dalton Hoffman.)

Auxiliary Remount Depot No. 328 was located on the south end of the current Will Rogers Complex property and extended all the way to Trinity Park. Before motorized vehicles, animals were used for the transportation of men and supplies during wartime. The Quartermaster Department began in 1775 and purchased, hired, and fed animals for military service. The Remount Service took over in 1908 and began training animals before assigning them to prospective units. (Ben Guttery.)

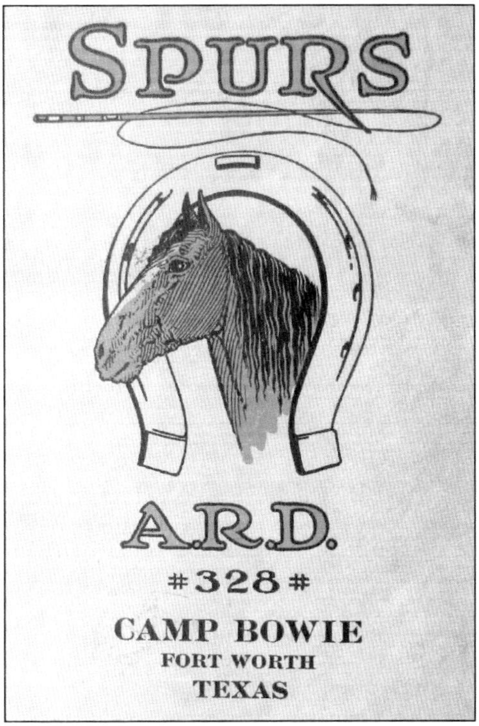

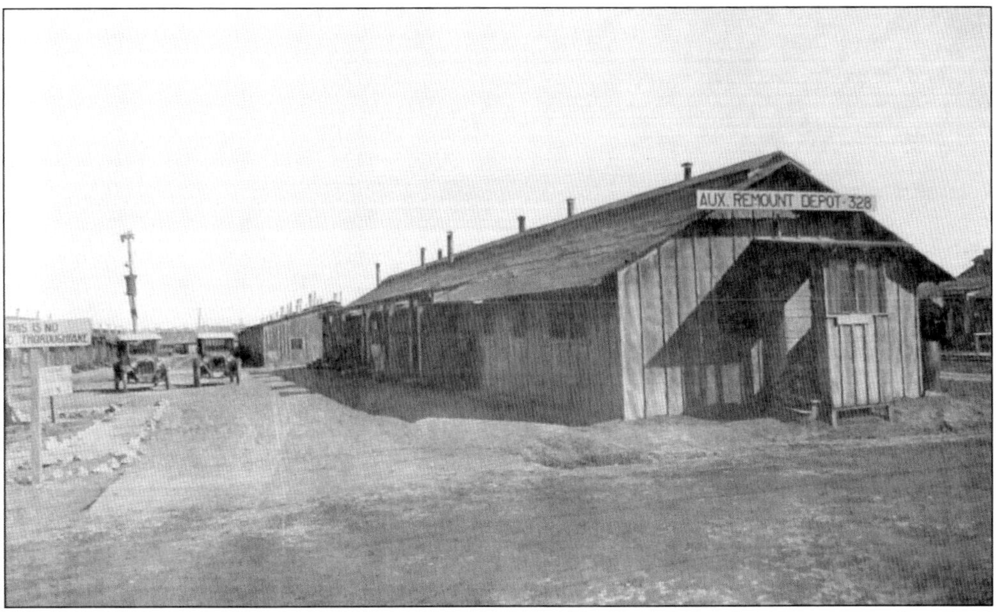

The Auxiliary Remount Depot was a separate entity in all matters other than sanitation, discipline, and general courts-martial. Men were trained in skills related to animal care such as farrier, saddler, stable sergeant, or wagon and pack transportation. War horses and mules hauled ammunition, heavy artillery, and food and water, and evacuated the wounded and transported soldiers. By World War II, motorized vehicles replaced most animals. Approximately 571,000 horses and mules were processed through the 39 remount stations during World War I, and more than 68,000 of them died in the line of duty. (Ben Guttery.)

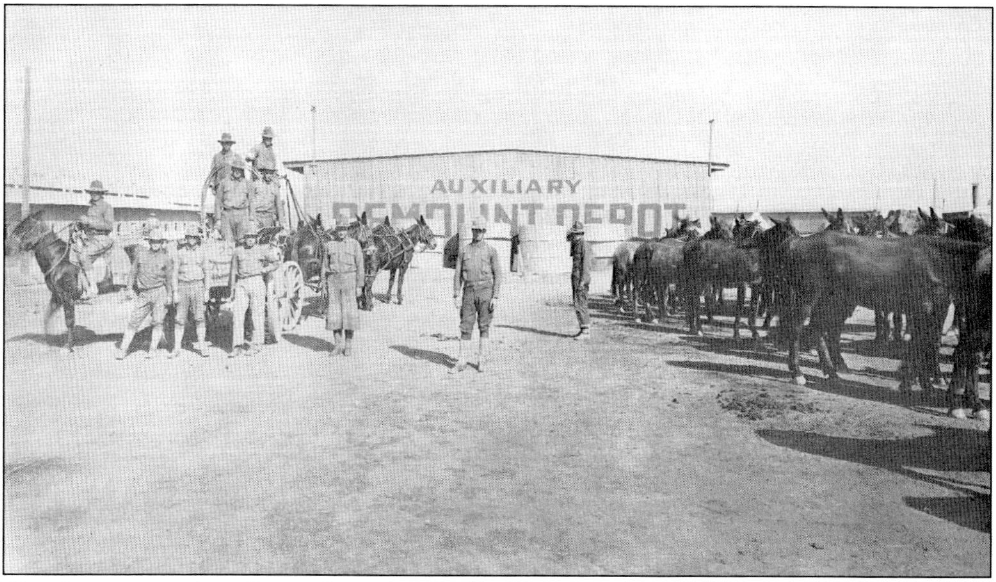

The depot opened on September 1, 1917, the first animals arrived seven days later, and by October, there were approximately 5,500 animals on the grounds. By the fall of 1918, there were 400 men at the depot who all arrived expecting to be trained and sent overseas to fight in the war. This did not happen, however, as the majority of the men stayed at the depot for the war. (Dalton Hoffman.)

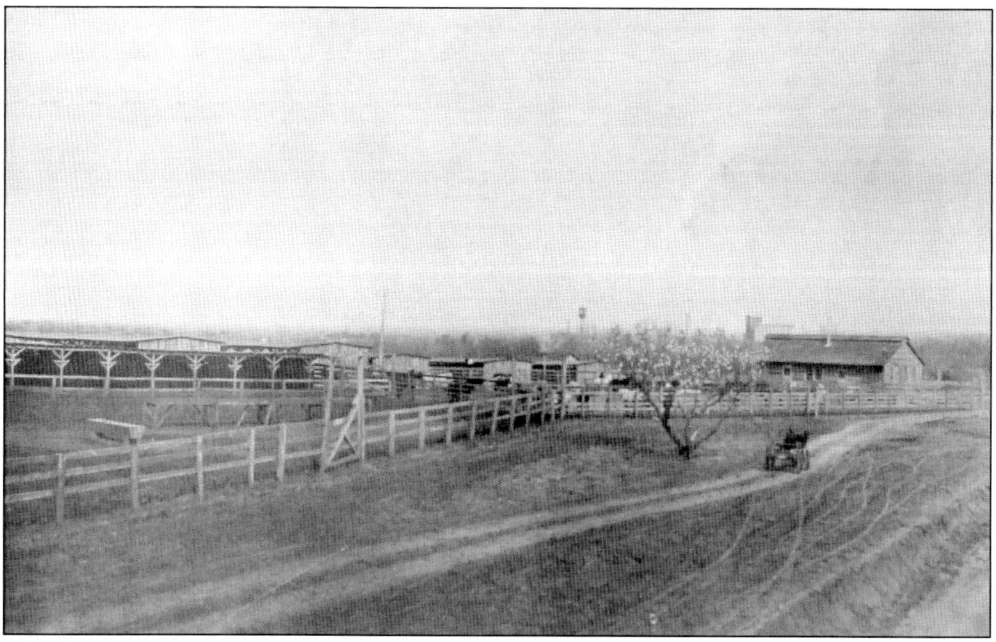

The depot was organized into four permanent detachments: the Depot Detachment, Wagon Company and Pack Train, Veterinary Corps Detachments, and Medical Detachment. There was also a temporary fifth detachment for horseshoeing. A total of 944 enlisted men served at the depot throughout its history, with many going on to officer's training schools. Shown here are the Wagon Company and Pack Train Corrals. The grain elevators on Main Street are seen in the distance on the left. (Ben Guttery.)

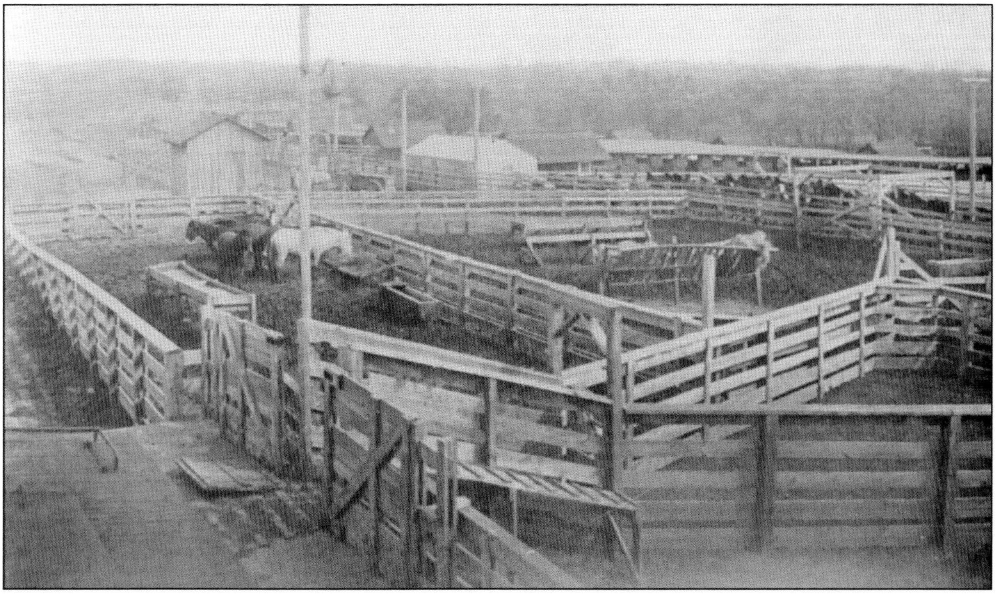

The depot handled 24,367 head while in operation. Most came from Fort Worth, but others came from around Texas and Oklahoma. The highest number of animals present at one time was 7,777. Except for the fall and winter of 1918–1919, when a few cases of glanders (a rare disease) resulted in the euthanizing of the infected, the animals' health was good. When the animals left for different destinations, these loading chutes were used to help with transportation. (Ben Guttery.)

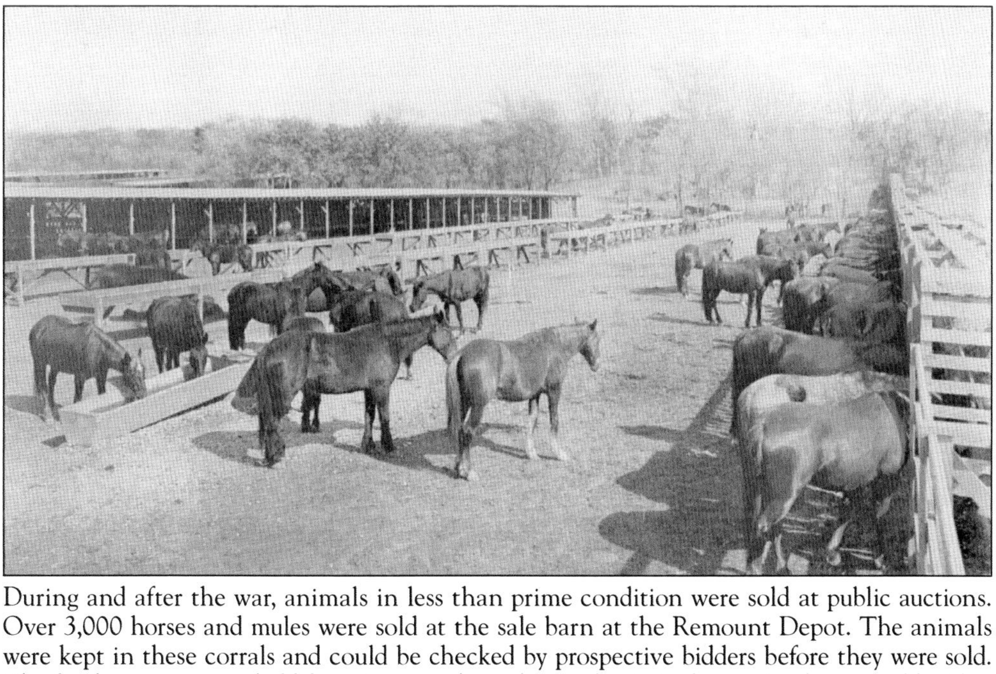

During and after the war, animals in less than prime condition were sold at public auctions. Over 3,000 horses and mules were sold at the sale barn at the Remount Depot. The animals were kept in these corrals and could be checked by prospective bidders before they were sold. The final auctions were held from January through March 1919, when animals were sold with a halter, shank strap, and a health certificate. Lunch was served at the grounds during the auctions. (Dalton Hoffman.)

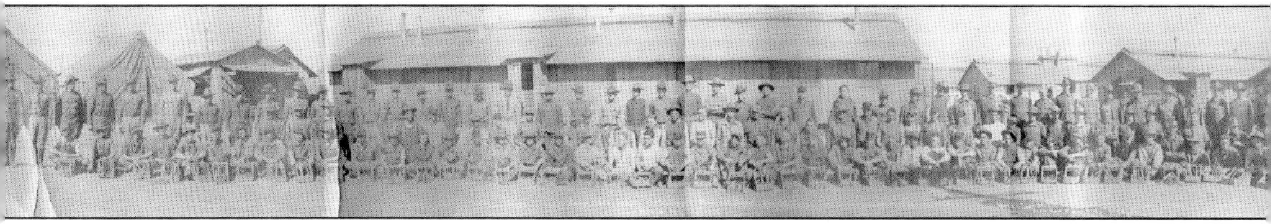

Four-month-long horseshoeing classes were taught by senior instructor Capt. Nicholas E. Dutro from January 9, 1918, through January 15, 1919. A total of 314 students graduated. The first class of 76 graduates went overseas and served with the Panther Division. Certified farriers were paid $35 per month. Many of these students had toolboxes that included all the necessary materials for shoeing the horses. (Dalton Hoffman.)

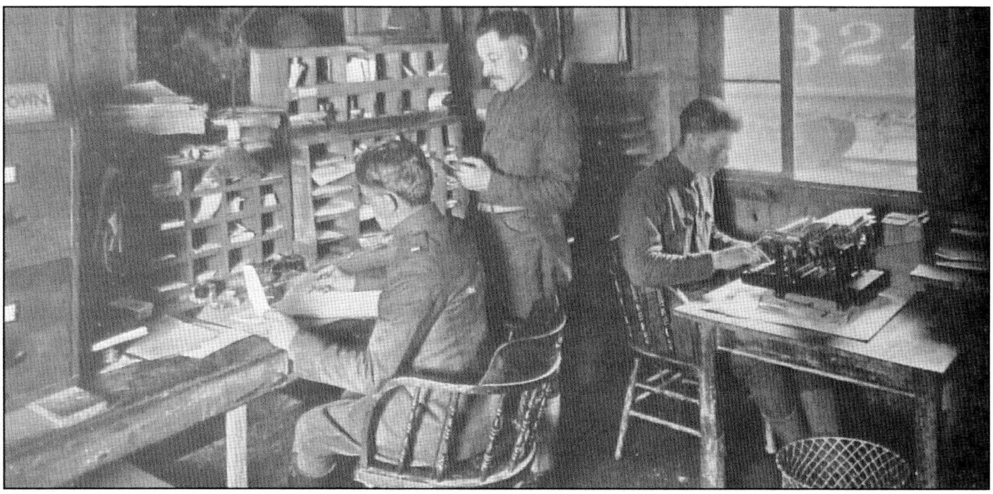

The Auxiliary Remount Depot's medical corps was stationed at the field hospital. Staff consisted of one medical officer, one dental surgeon, and five assisting enlisted men. Unlike the hospital at Camp Bowie, their workload was very light due to the excellent sanitary conditions at the camp. During the entire time the depot was used, the only reported death was Pvt. George Jackson, 23, who died in August 1918 from injuries acquired after being kicked in the head by a mule. (Ben Guttery.)

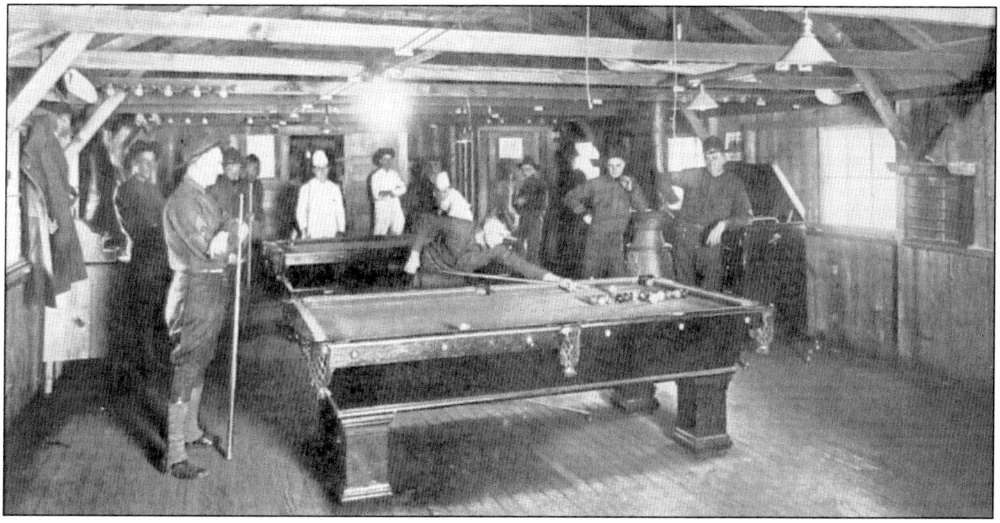

The depot exchange had a barber and tailor shop. Dividends earned at the exchange provided funds to build the recreation hall, which had two pool tables, a Victrola record player (right, by the window), and a collection of reading material. Heat was provided by wood stoves (next to the Victrola) in all of the buildings except for the hospital, which had steam heat. (Ben Guttery.)

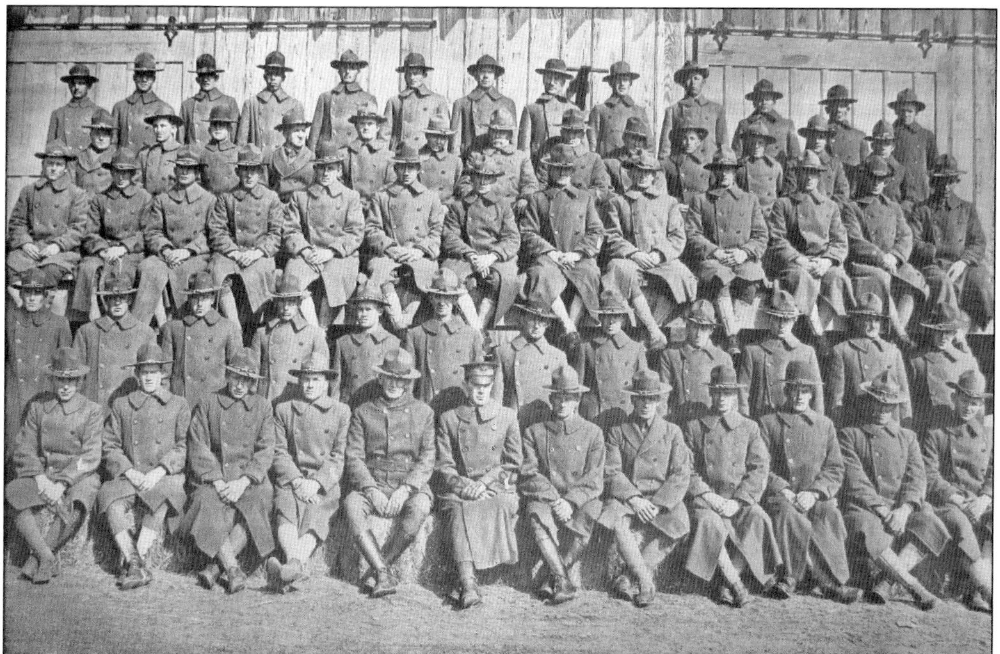

The Veterinary Corps tended to over 2,900 horses and 2,100 mules at the depot hospital. Organized in August 1917, it was headed by seven different commanding officers; the last was Capt. Edward J. O'Hara. In addition to the sick animals, there were newborns. On July 27, 1918, alone, 40 mules were born at the station. (Ben Guttery.)

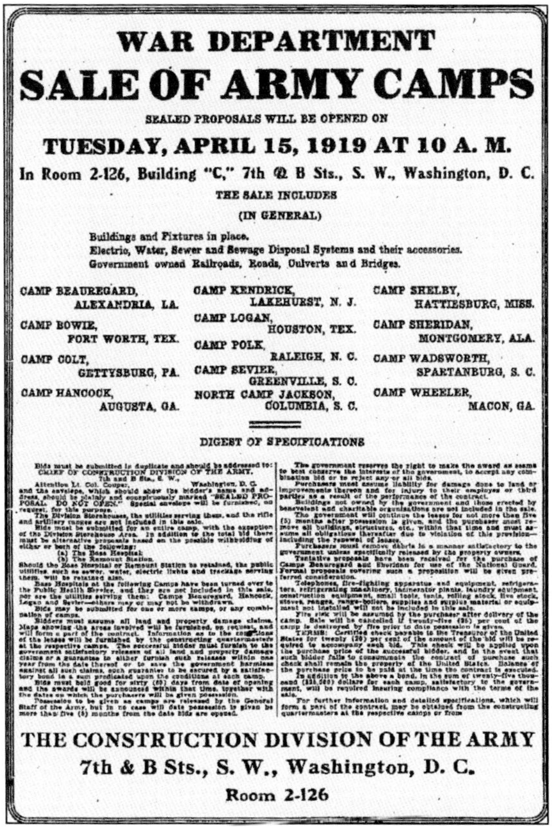

WAR DEPARTMENT

SALE OF ARMY CAMPS

SEALED PROPOSALS WILL BE OPENED ON

TUESDAY, APRIL 15, 1919 AT 10 A. M.

In Room 2-126, Building "C," 7th @ B Sts., S. W., Washington, D. C.

THE SALE INCLUDES

(IN GENERAL)

Buildings and Fixtures in place.
Electric, Water, Sewer and Sewage Disposal Systems and their accessories.
Government owned Railroads, Roads, Culverts and Bridges.

CAMP BEAUREGARD, ALEXANDRIA, LA.
CAMP BOWIE, FORT WORTH, TEX.
CAMP COLT, GETTYSBURG, PA.
CAMP HANCOCK, AUGUSTA, GA.
CAMP KENDRICK, LAKEHURST, N. J.
CAMP LOGAN, HOUSTON, TEX.
CAMP POLK, RALEIGH, N. C.
CAMP SEVIER, GREENVILLE, S. C.
NORTH CAMP JACKSON, COLUMBIA, S. C.
CAMP SHELBY, HATTIESBURG, MISS.
CAMP SHERIDAN, MONTGOMERY, ALA.
CAMP WADSWORTH, SPARTANBURG, S. C.
CAMP WHEELER, MACON, GA.

DIGEST OF SPECIFICATIONS

Bids must be submitted in duplicate and should be addressed to:
CHIEF OF CONSTRUCTION DIVISION OF THE ARMY,
7th and B Sts., S. W.,
Attention Lt. Col. Couper, Washington, D. C.
and the envelope, which should show the bidder's name and address, should be plainly and conspicuously marked "SEALED PROPOSAL. DO NOT OPEN." Special envelope will be furnished, on request, for this purpose.

The Division Storehouses, the utilities serving them, and the rifle and artillery ranges are not included in this sale.

Bids must be submitted for an entire camp, with the exception of the Division Storehouse Area. In addition to the total bid there must be alternative proposals based on the possible withholding of either or both of the following:
(a) The Base Hospital.
(b) The Remount Station.
Should the Base Hospital or Remount Station be retained, the public utilities, such as sewer, water, electric lights and trackage serving them, will be retained also.

Base Hospitals at the following Camps have been turned over to the Public Health Service, and they are not included in this sale, nor are the utilities serving them: Camps Beauregard, Hancock, Logan and Sevier—others may or may not be withdrawn.

Bids may be submitted for one or more camps, or any combination of camps.

Bidders must assume all land and property damage claims. Maps showing the areas involved will be furnished, on request, and will form a part of the contract. Information as to the conditions of the leases will be furnished by the constructing quartermasters at the respective camps. The successful bidder must furnish to the government satisfactory releases of all land and property damage claims or a guarantee to either furnish such releases within one year from the date thereof or to save the government harmless against all such claims, such guarantee to be secured by a satisfactory bond in a sum predicated upon the conditions at each camp.

Bids must hold good for sixty (60) days from date of opening and the awards will be announced within that time, together with the dates on which the purchasers will be given possession.

Possession to be given as camps are released by the General Staff of the Army, but in no case will date possession is given be more than five (5) months from the date bids are opened.

The government reserves the right to make the award as seems to best conserve the interests of the government, to accept any combination bid or to reject any or all bids.

Purchasers must assume liability for damage done to land or improvements thereon and for injury to their employes or third parties as a result of the performance of the contract.

Buildings not owned by the government and those erected by benevolent and charitable organizations are not included in the sale.

The government will continue the leases for not more than five (5) months after possession is given, and the purchaser must remove all buildings, structures, etc., within that time and must assume all obligations thereafter due to violation of this provision—including the renewal of leases.

Purchasers must remove débris in a manner satisfactory to the government unless specifically released by the property owners.

Tentative proposals have been received for the purchase of Camps Beauregard and Sheridan for use of the National Guard. Formal proposals covering such a proposition will be given preferred consideration.

Telephones, fire-fighting apparatus and equipment, refrigerators, refrigerating machinery, incinerator plants, laundry equipment, construction equipment, small tools, tents, rolling stock, live stock, stoves, ranges, range-boilers, supplies and surplus material or equipment not installed will not be included in this sale.

Fire risk will be assumed by the purchaser after delivery of the camp. Sale will be cancelled if twenty-five (25) per cent of the camp is destroyed by fire prior to date possession is given.

TERMS: Certified check payable to the Treasurer of the United States for twenty (20) per cent of the amount of the bid will be required to accompany each bid. This check will be applied upon the purchase price of the successful bidder, and in the event that such bidder fails to consummate the contract of purchase such check shall remain the property of the United States. Balance of the purchase price to be paid at the time the contract is executed.

In addition to the above a bond, in the sum of twenty-five thousand ($25,000) dollars for each camp, satisfactory to the government, will be required insuring compliance with the terms of the sale.

For further information and detailed specifications, which will form a part of the contract, may be obtained from the constructing quartermasters at the respective camps or from

THE CONSTRUCTION DIVISION OF THE ARMY
7th & B Sts., S. W., Washington, D. C.
Room 2-126

Shortly after the armistice on November 11, 1918, Camp Bowie served as a demobilization center. After 31,584 men were discharged there, it was closed on August 15, 1919. The War Department put all Army camps up for sale en bloc and announced that it would open sealed bids on Tuesday, April 15, 1919, at 10:00 a.m. There were several postings of the sale throughout the next few months, so it can be safely assumed that there were not many people who were interested in purchasing buildings from used war camps. After the buildings were sold, the land that had been occupied by the ammunition, sanitary, and supply trains and Auxiliary Remount Depot No. 328 remained vacant until 1936. (Left, Ben Guttery; below, FWPL.)

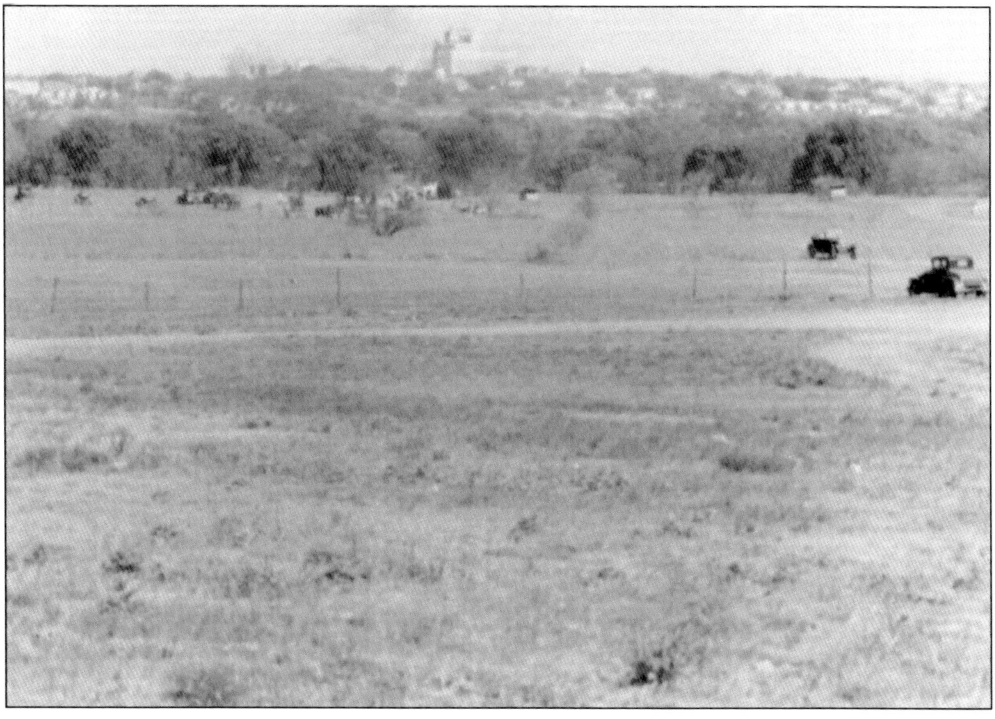

Two

Centennial Celebration, Fort Worth–Style

Planning an event to celebrate 100 years of independence from Mexico began at a meeting in Corsicana, Texas, on November 6, 1923. For the next 13 years, the event was promoted with two themes: commercialism and patriotism. Celebrations were planned throughout the state, while San Antonio, Houston, and Dallas competed for the main venue. Fort Worth decided not to compete in 1934, as it did not believe that a northern location would be selected, but, to its displeasure, Dallas won. A total of $500,000 was allocated for the advertising campaign alone, which included news releases, lectures, and countrywide advertising to promote the occasion outside of the state and to encourage people to come to Dallas to discover Texas. Business leaders in Fort Worth, namely Amon G. Carter, decided to use the opportunity to promote Fort Worth and formatted a plan to attract visitors from the Central Exposition. Dallas planned an educational event, so Fort Worth went the opposite direction, with a variety of shows, buildings, and characters straight out of the Western days of old. By the time it was over, Fort Worth successfully lured 986,128 people to its celebration from Dallas, where attendance was significantly under predicted totals. Touted by many as the "outstanding feature of the entire Texas Centennial," Fort Worth had successfully upstaged Dallas and established itself as the city "Where the West Begins."

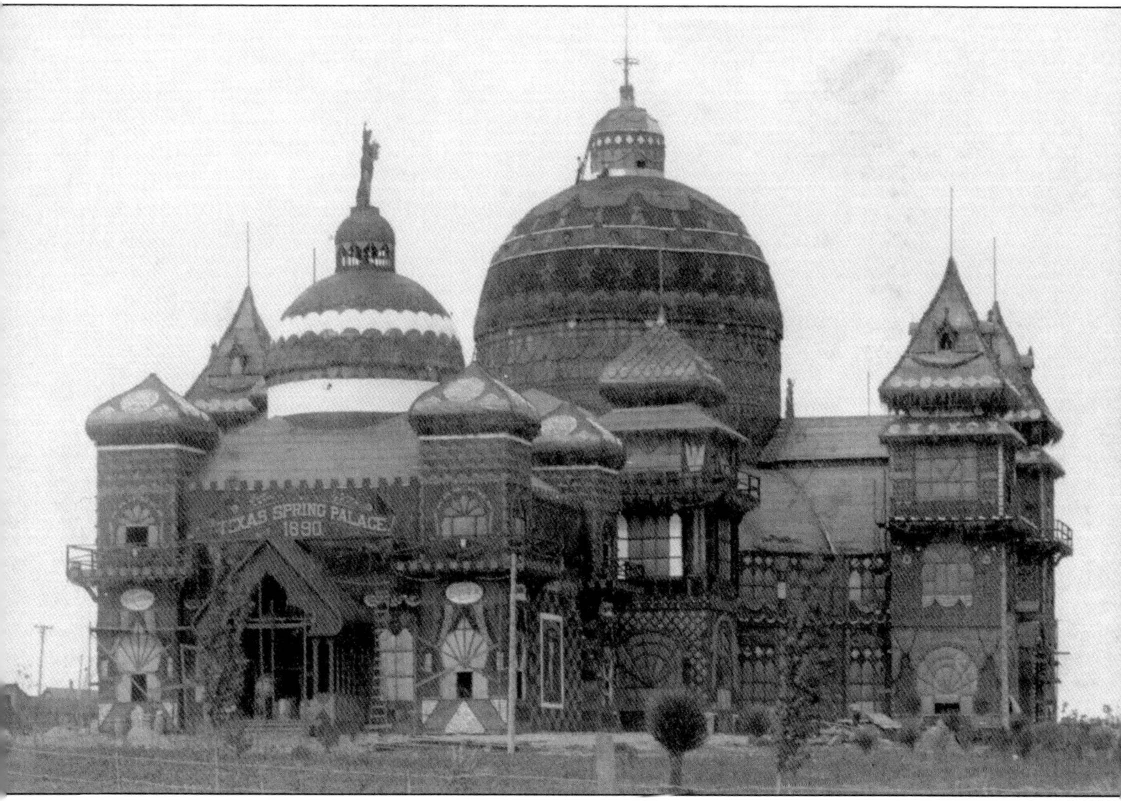

The idea of attracting people to Fort Worth through entertainment goes back to the Spring Palace. In 1889, B.B. Paddock, promoter and editor of the Fort Worth *Democrat*, and R.A. Cameron, railroad agent, created a venue to promote Texas and Fort Worth to outsiders. Built within five months, the Spring Palace showcased agricultural products of Texas. Fort Worthians promoted their city as a commercial metropolis, far removed from its "Wild West" image. On May 30, 1890, the Spring Palace burned to the ground. Within 50 years, the Centennial celebration occurred, but instead of Fort Worth promoting itself as a commercial metropolis, it took great pride in its past and as the city "Where the West Begins." (TCU.)

More than any one person, Amon Giles Carter Sr. was responsible for relentlessly promoting the city of Fort Worth all the way until his death on June 23, 1955. His civic spirit and drive to bring the world to Fort Worth is seen in many businesses, public works, and institutions that still exist long after his death. Never forgetting his humble roots as a blacksmith's son from Crafton in Wise County, Carter made it a point to make and keep friends with people from all walks of life, which served him, and the city of Fort Worth, well. (FWSS.)

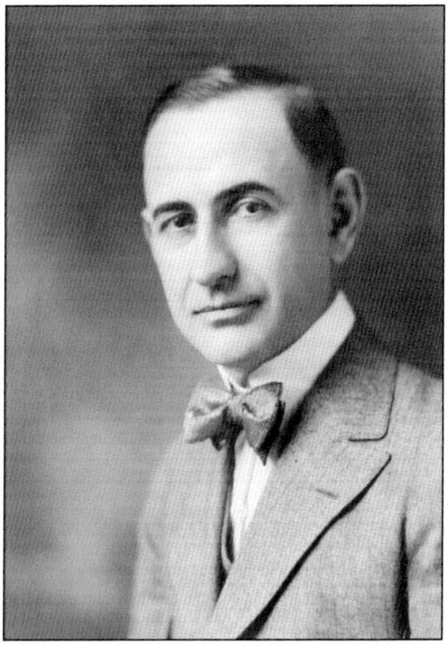

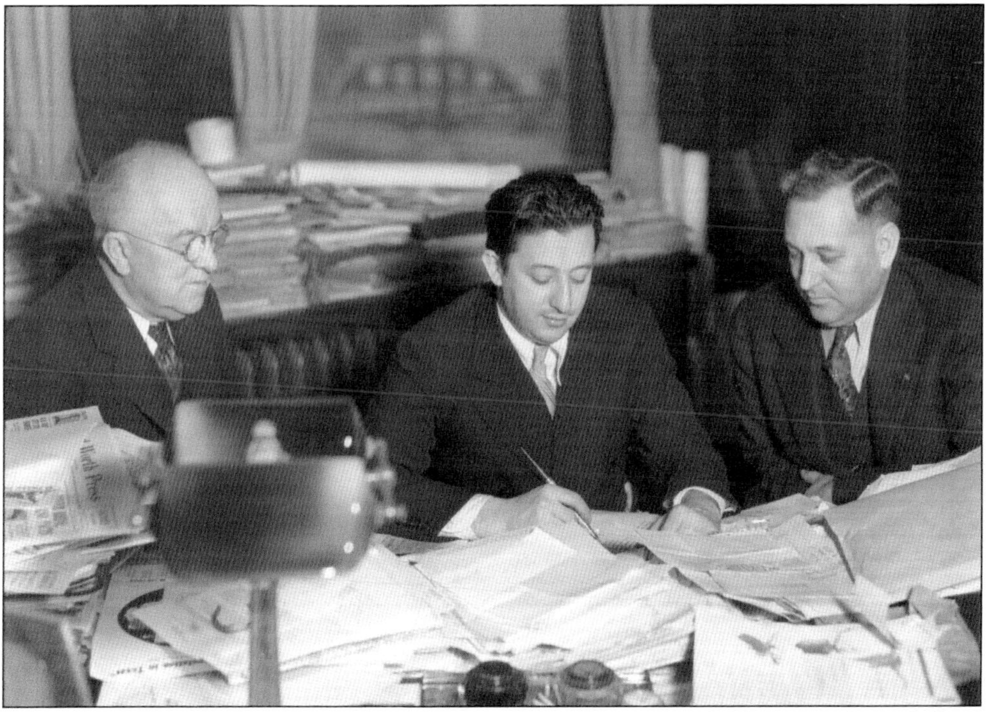

Initially, the women's division of the Texas Frontier Centennial, headed by Mrs. Edwin Phillips, was in charge of the entertainment program. Their celebration featured residents donning period clothing amid a mixture of Girl Scout shows, religious celebrations, and orchestra performances. Carter scoffed at that, took the reins, and contacted New York producer William Samuel Rosenberg—"Billy Rose." Carter and Rose (center) hashed out the details and entered a contract that paid $100,000, or $1,000 a day for 100 days. The signing took place in Carter's office at the Fort Worth *Star-Telegram* building on March 7, 1936, with councilman William Monnig (left) and John Davis (right), manager of the Southwestern Exposition and Stock Show. (TCU.)

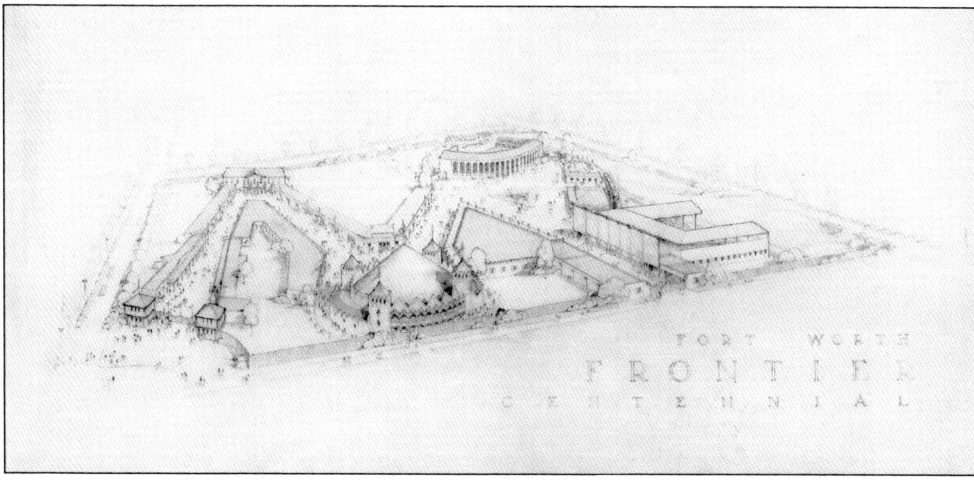

This sketch of the Frontier Centennial Grounds was the work of architect Joseph Roman Pelich. The main entrance (left) came off of newly extended Lancaster Avenue and led into the streets of the frontier buildings. The Sunset Trail included a blacksmith's shop, a newspaper office, a hotel, and a café before it turned back towards the Jumbo building. The next leg passed the Pioneer Dance Hall and Sally Rand's Dude Ranch and went to Casa Mañana. From this point, visitors walked past an Indian village, a replica of a railroad station, and finally up to the Frontier Stadium. (Special Collections, University of Texas–Arlington.)

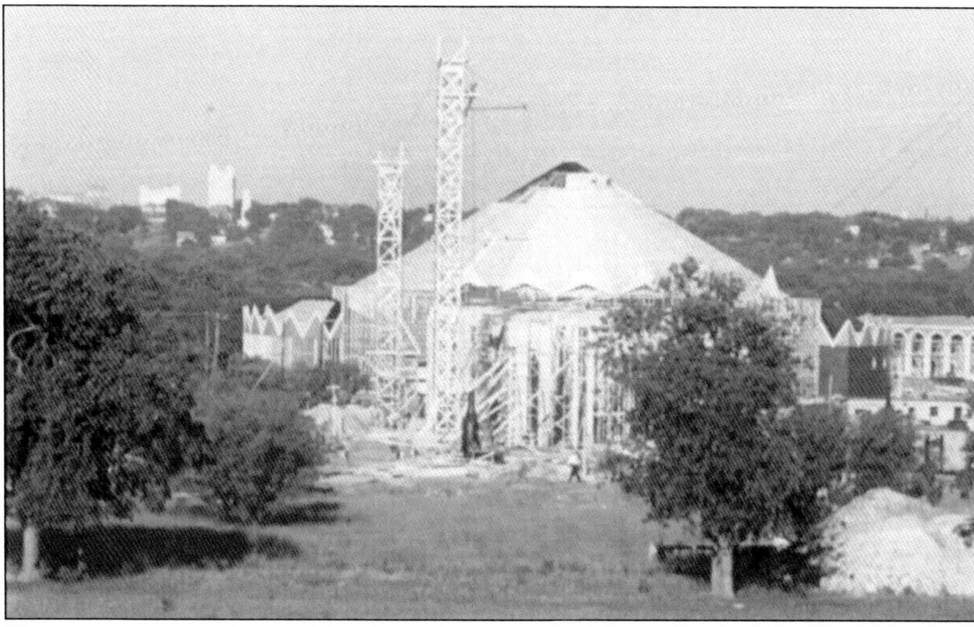

The event was paid for in part with federal funds. When the go-ahead was given on January 23, 1936, construction frantically began. According to reports, over 2,000 people were working by April, all trying to please Billy Rose, who barely slept and ran around the grounds drinking his newfound love, Dr. Pepper, bumming cigarettes, and shouting at everyone. Because construction was not finished, Fort Worth missed the June 6 opening date, which was when Dallas opened its show. As seen in this June photograph, construction of Jumbo was incomplete when a terrible summer storm swept through North Texas and not only smashed scenery at Casa Mañana but damaged the exhibit in Dallas. Repairs were made before opening day. (FWPL.)

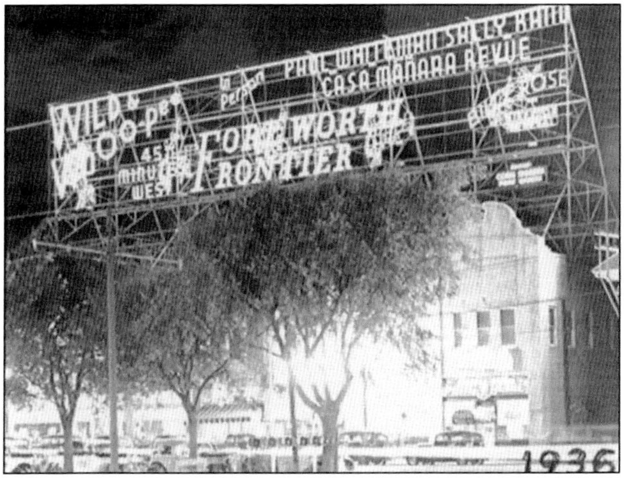

The crowning sign of achievement, and some might say gall, was the world's second-largest neon sign at the time, at 130 feet long and 60 feet high, which advertised the Fort Worth show. Placed strategically opposite the main entrance to the Dallas show, it was designed by Bill Jary from the Corn Sign Company. The green and red flashing lights advertised the fun the attendees were missing: "Wild & Whoo-pee, 45 minutes west Fort Worth Frontier." (Author's collection.)

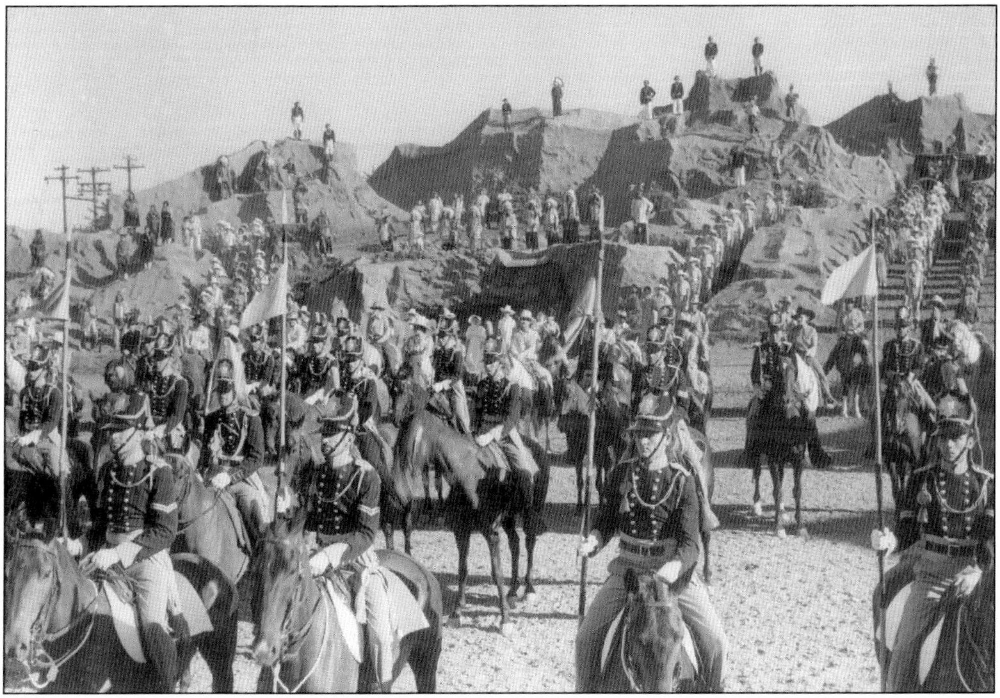

Dedication ceremonies in the Last Frontier Stadium began with a 100-year-old Wells Fargo wagon (top right) coming through the mountain pass and into the stadium with celebrity guests inside. Vern Elliot, codirector of the Wild West Show, sat beside Amon Carter, who was in frontier attire with a pistol in his belt. Next to Carter was Elliot Roosevelt, the son of the president, with a gun across his knees and a large white ten-gallon hat. At the rear of the coach sat Raymond Burk, leader of the Texas Young Democrats, and Cyrus Rowlett Smith, president of the recently formed American Airlines. Inside were Sen. Tom Connally, Gov. James V. Allred, Attorney General William McCraw, and H.J. Shannone, the general agent of the Railway Express Agency. Moments after it entered the stadium, it was attacked by outlaws amid a volley of gunshots. As everyone was herded from the coach, the cavalry charged in and rescued the men, who then climbed onto the platform and commenced their dedication speeches. (FWST.)

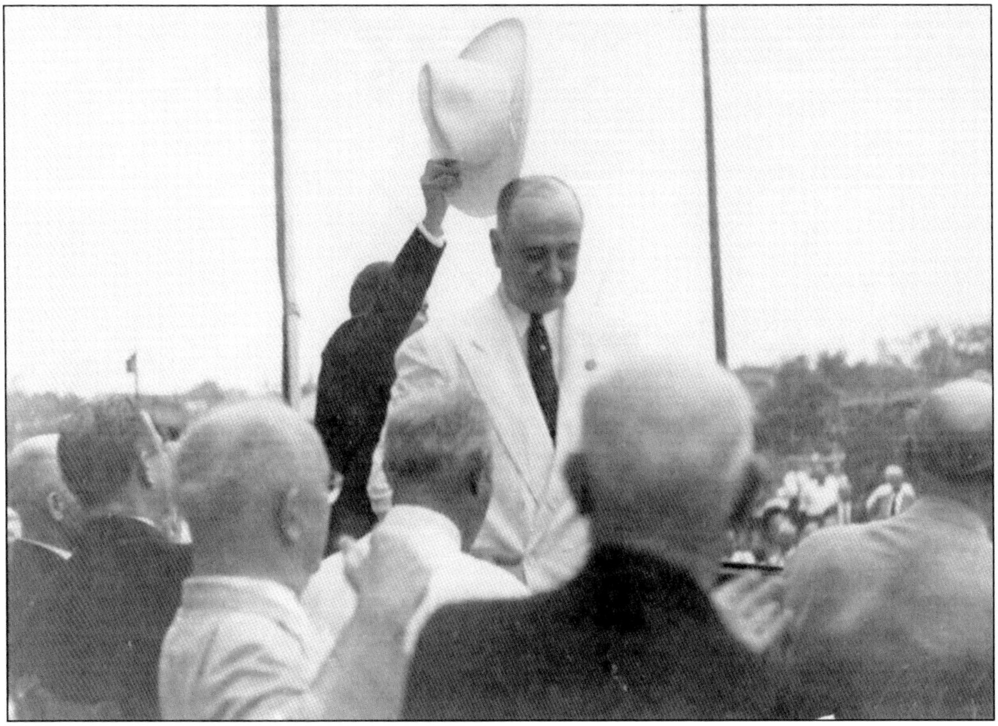

After the heroic rescue, the July 18, 1936, dedication speeches began. Amon G. Carter, along with Governor Allred and Senator Connally, spoke to the crowd, which included former governor Pat Neff, and to all who were listening to the National Broadcasting Company. They praised the brave men who fought for the independence of Texas, encouraged the crowd to remember the ideals of the pioneers, and stated that the Frontier Celebration was for the benefit of all Texans and their glorious past. (FWPL.)

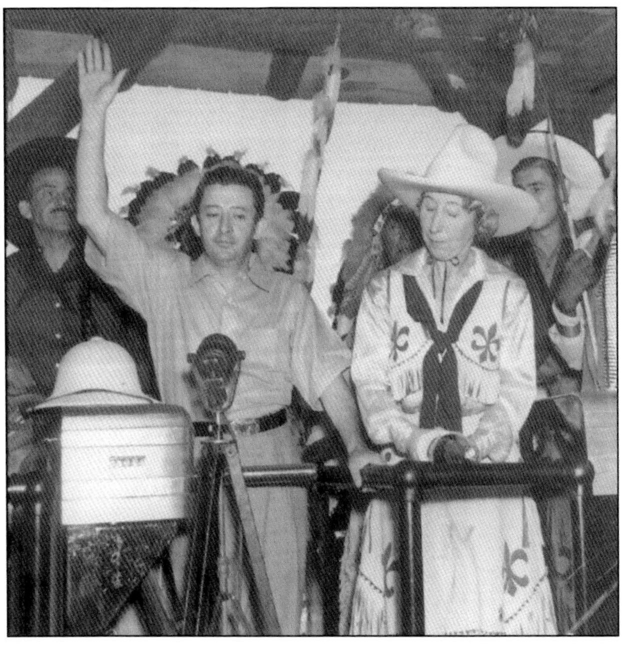

Billy Rose and Mrs. Verne Elliott—whose husband introduced Brahma bull riding to the Fort Worth Rodeo in 1933—welcomed the crowd of 25,000 people who they referred to as "Mr. and Mrs. America" at the opening on July 18, 1936. Pres. Franklin D. Roosevelt pressed a wireless key whilst onboard a US Navy cruiser off the coast of Maine to set the events in motion, and after Mrs. Elliott broke a bottle of champagne over the turnstile at the entrance, Rose declared the event open to the public. (FWST.)

As part of the promotional effort, a statewide beauty contest was held. Faye Cotton, a waitress from Borger, Texas, was crowned the winner. A tall, blond, shapely woman who enjoyed "dancing, shooting, and reading her Bible everyday"—the perfect Texan image—won the contest. Her likeness appeared on advertising material, which helped the celebration as well as Cotton, who signed a movie contract and moved to Hollywood the following year. (FWPL.)

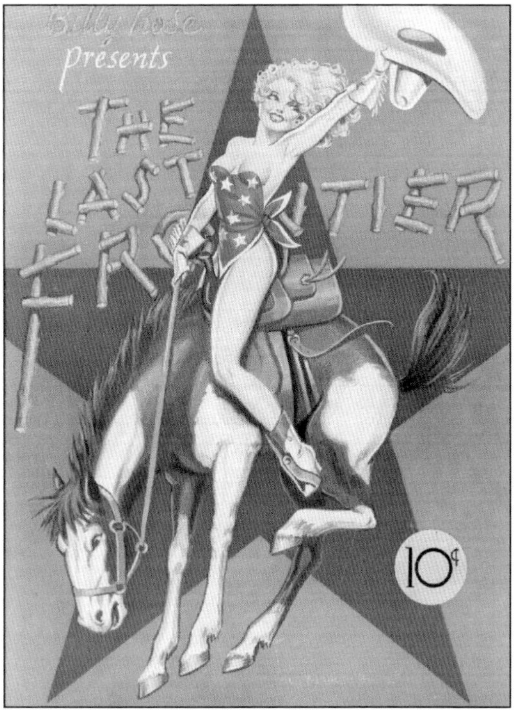

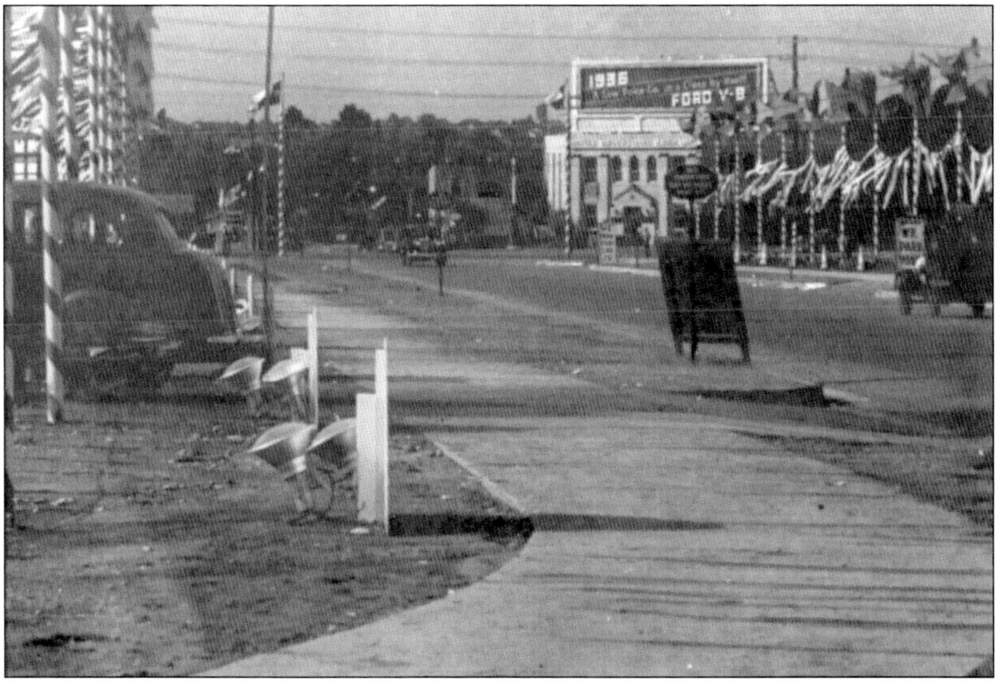

As guests arrived at the Frontier Celebration, they walked or drove through the Street of Pinwheels, which led off Camp Bowie and ended in circular plaza in front of the blockhouse entrance gates. Shown here is the concourse looking towards West Seventh Street with the pinwheels on both sides. At the entrance to the celebration area was a banner that spanned the street stating, "Howdy Stranger—Frontier Fiesta." (FWPL.)

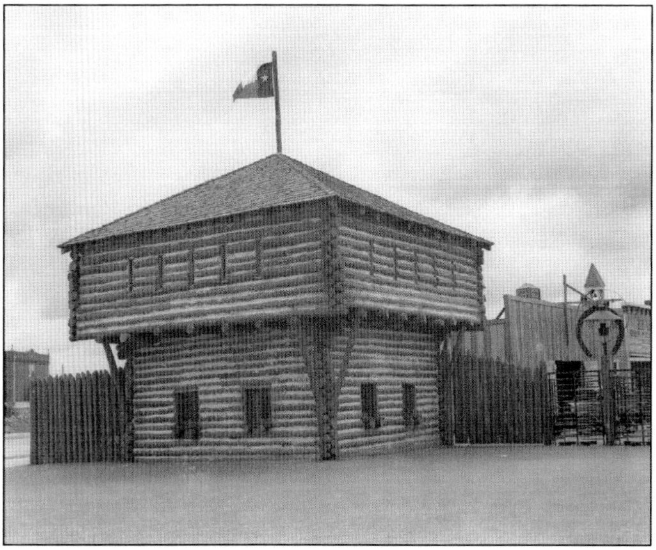

Two blockhouses marked the entrance to the Frontier grounds modeled after those used as protection from the Indians in the old days. The blockhouses and most of the buildings on the Sunset Strip were built using new wood that was roughed-up to look old. Turnstiles were located between the blockhouses under the saying "Where the West Begins," Amon Carter's trademark reference to Fort Worth. (FWSS.)

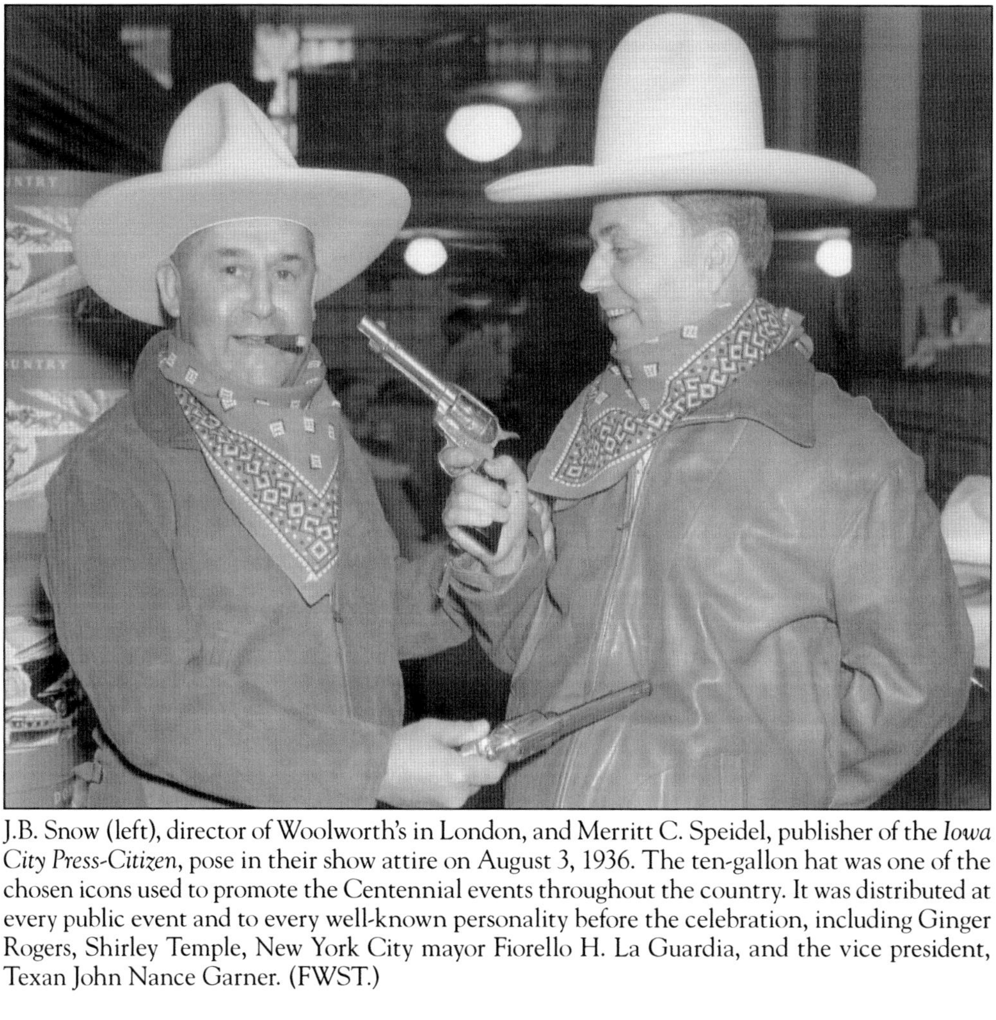

J.B. Snow (left), director of Woolworth's in London, and Merritt C. Speidel, publisher of the *Iowa City Press-Citizen*, pose in their show attire on August 3, 1936. The ten-gallon hat was one of the chosen icons used to promote the Centennial events throughout the country. It was distributed at every public event and to every well-known personality before the celebration, including Ginger Rogers, Shirley Temple, New York City mayor Fiorello H. La Guardia, and the vice president, Texan John Nance Garner. (FWST.)

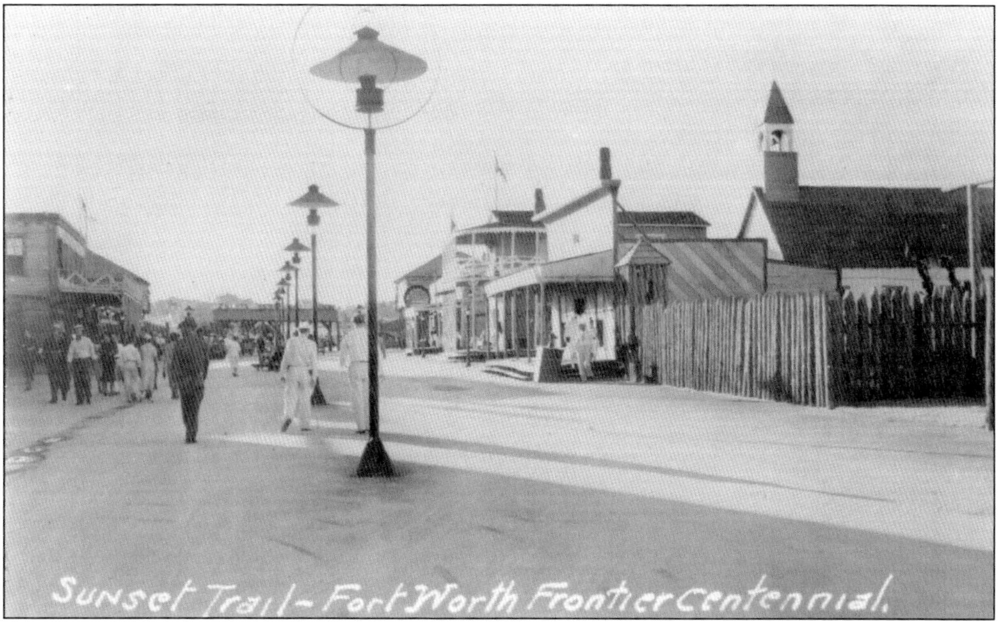

To help provide a more Western atmosphere, Billy Rose advertised in Carter's newspaper, the Fort Worth *Star-Telegram*, that he needed "whittlers, snuff-dippers, crackbox philosophers, old couples, ox-wagons and ox-drivers, town half-wits, the village drunk, etc." The Sunset Trail was the first area that guests walked into. The above view looks back to the entrance gates from near the Stockade Fort, the temporary home of the cavalrymen from the 2nd Dragoons, while the below view looks towards the brightly painted red Jumbo building from the same spot. On the right, wagons with half-wheels probably were not going anywhere soon. (Doug Harman.)

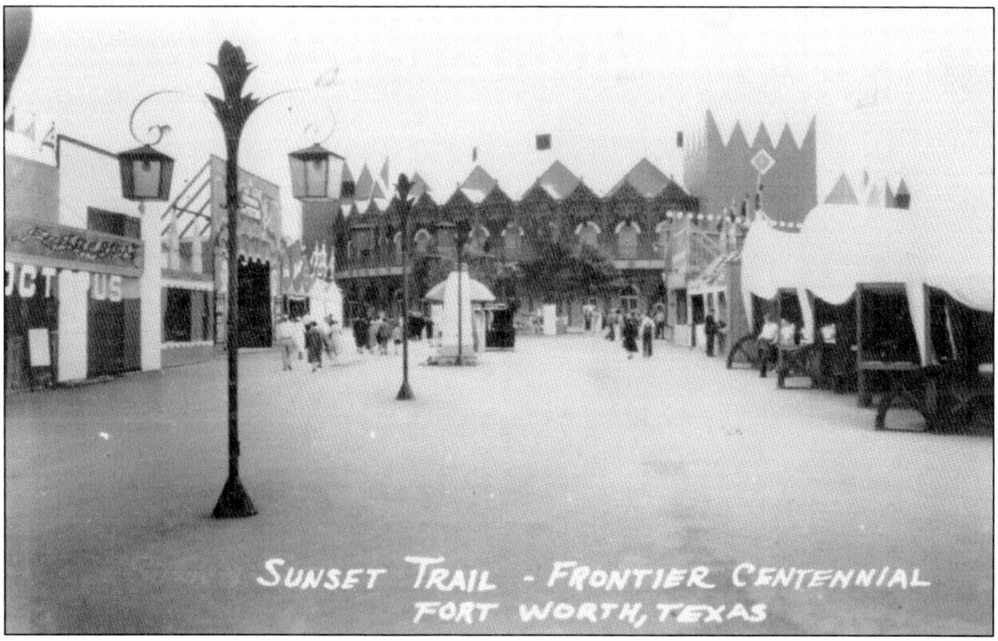

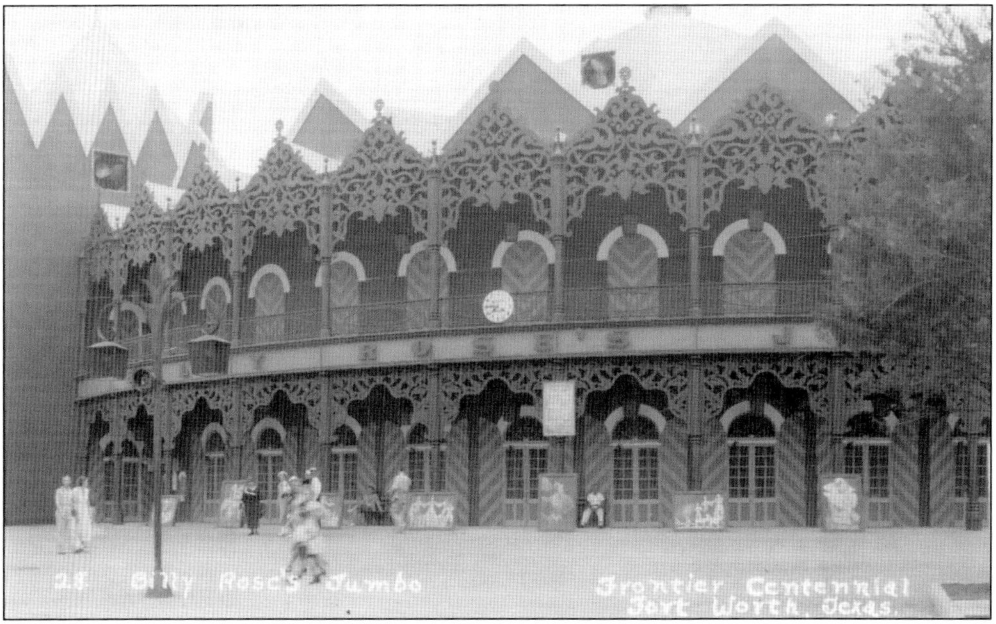

Billy Rose's Jumbo employed 986 people and it was reported that it took 20 double-length railroad baggage cars and Pullman sleepers to transport the personnel and their paraphernalia from New York City to Fort Worth. The circular theater had seats for 2,800 people and featured a variety of different acts from vaudeville to the circus. During August, the intense heat inside caused some performers to faint. (Doug Harman.)

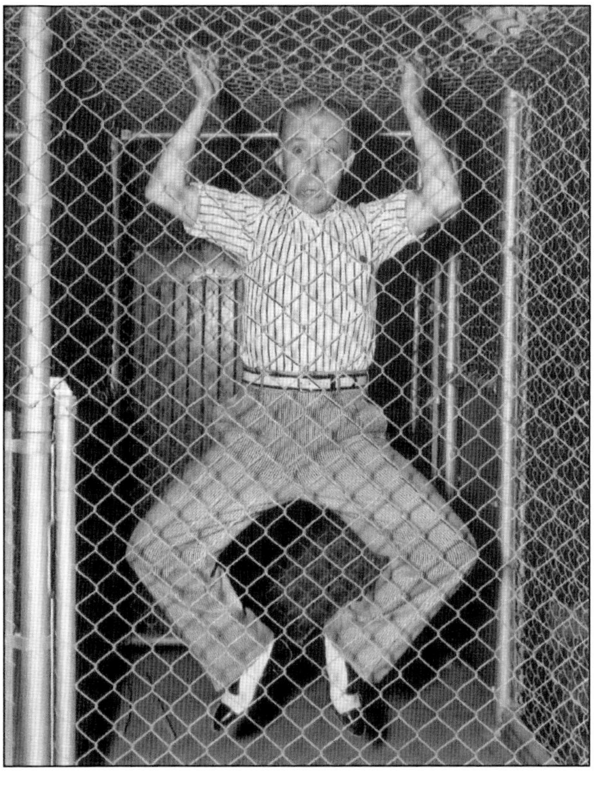

One of the many acts hired by Billy Rose was vaudeville entertainer Pat Rooney Jr. Here he is on June 25, 1937, doing his monkey act in the menagerie of the Jumbo building. One of the acts that Rose chose not to hire for his production was a young woman from nearby Weatherford, Mary (Martin) Hagman, and her backup performers, the Martinettes. Mary Martin went on to star in *Peter Pan* and dozens of other famous productions. (FWST.)

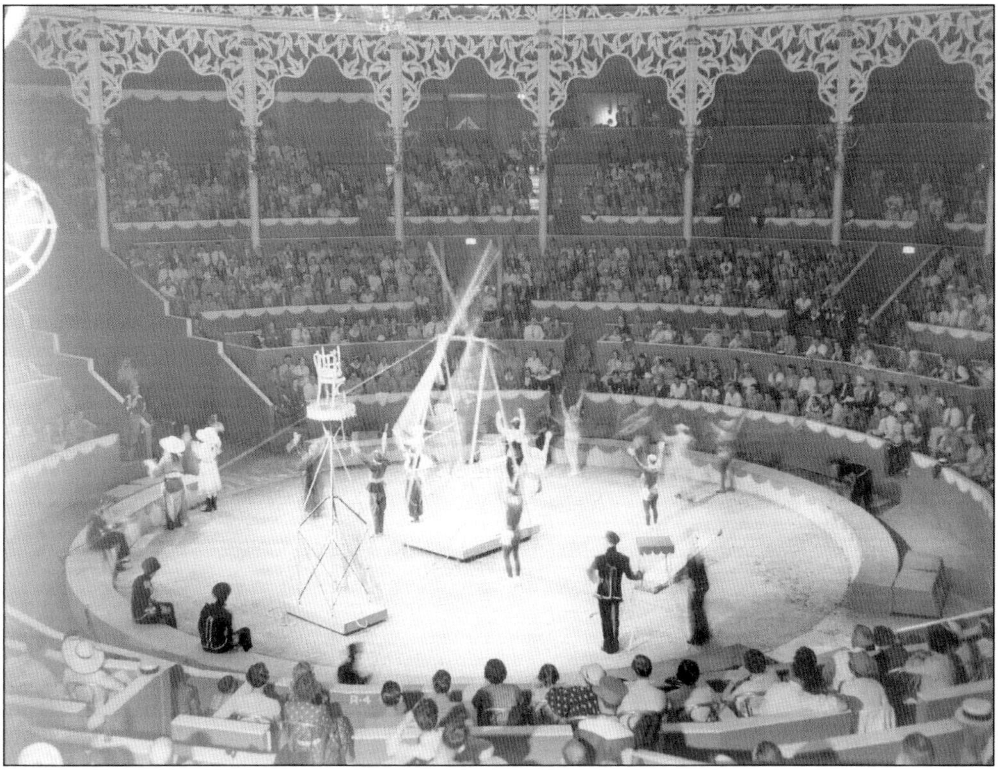

Jumbo was based on a Broadway production of the same name. The cast of 200 reportedly provided "emotional thrills that make the gooseflesh pop out, achieved through patterns of musical and romantic sentiment mixed with topnotch acts" for the cost $1 for adults and 50¢ per child. The opening show's cast included Poodles Hanneford, trick rider; the Kimires, aerial artists; Josie DeMott Robinson, a 76-year-old bareback rider; Camillas and her 100 cockatoos; France & Lepell, trapeze artists; Margaret Brooks, who was shot from a cannon; and an elephant named Big Rosie. There were two shows daily, at 6:30 and 10:00 p.m., with matinees on Sundays. Each show lasted two hours. (Above, FWST; below, FWPL.)

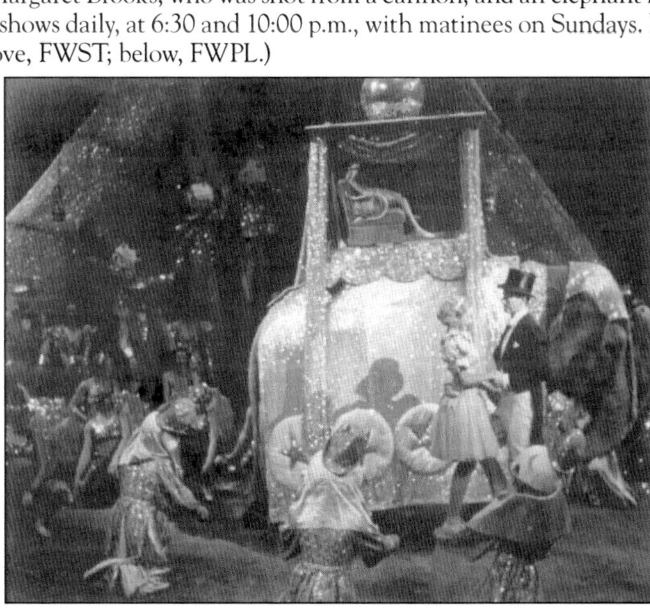

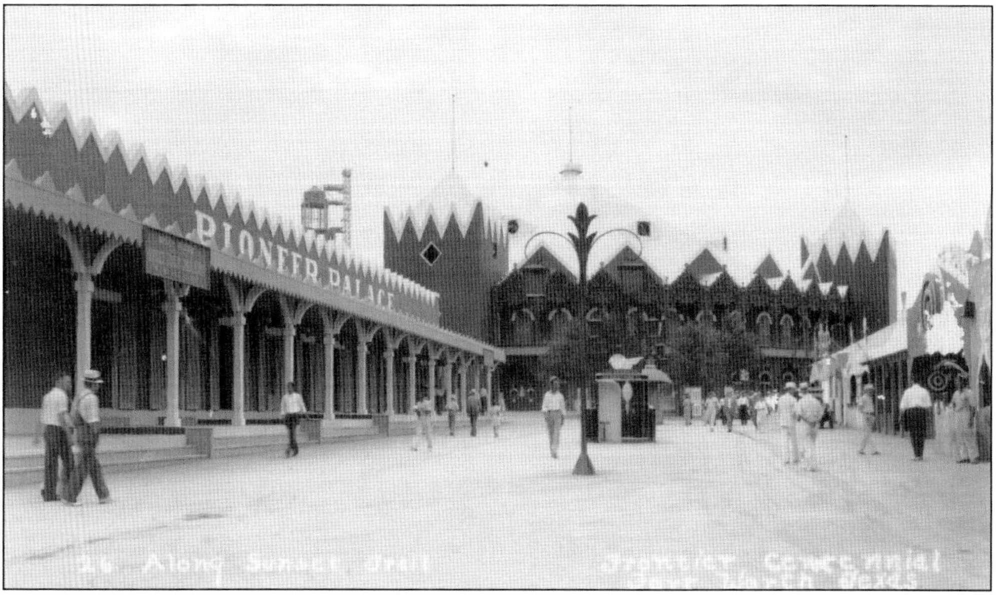

This side view of the Pioneer Palace and Billy Rose's Jumbo building at the Frontier Celebration taken on October 9, 1936, shows the very top of the Pioneer Tower under construction on the left. The sign hanging on the second post of the Palace advertises Billy Rose's Honky Tonk Parade at 7:00, 9:00, and 10:00 p.m. In the center, behind the lamppost, are two photograph booths. The Photomaton, a slot machine and self-developing photo-booth, was designed by Anatol Josepho, a Siberian immigrant who had become a successful photographer in Budapest, Hungary. First used on Broadway in New York in 1925, the booths took a strip of eight photographs for 25¢. (Doug Harman.)

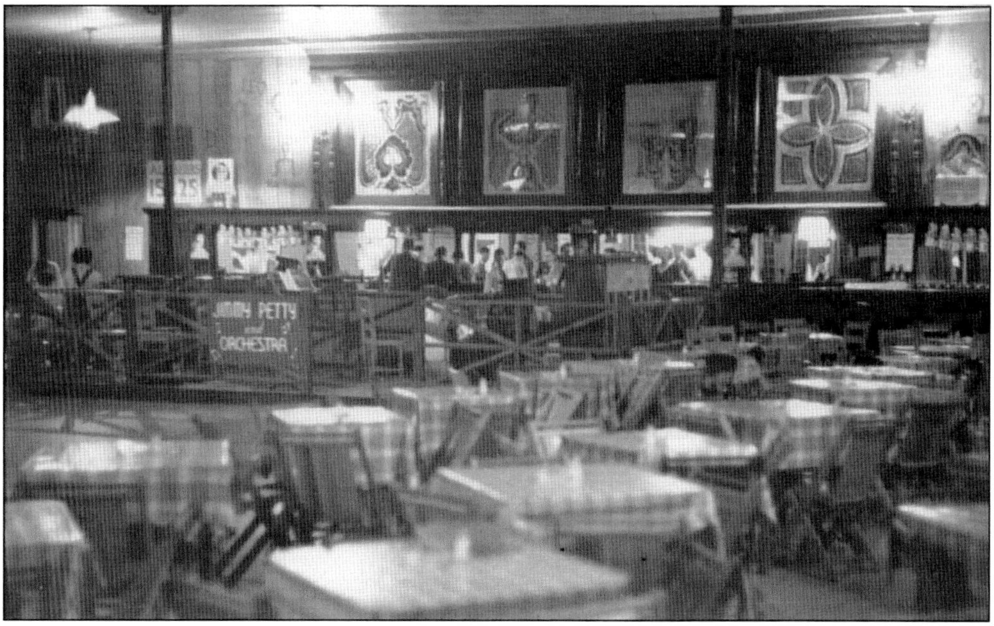

The Pioneer Palace was a huge eating facility and dance hall. Complete with a long bar and keno gambling hall, there was a stage where "honky-tonk" reviews and other acts showed at 4:00 p.m., 6:00 p.m., 8:00 p.m., 10:00 p.m., and midnight. (FWPL.)

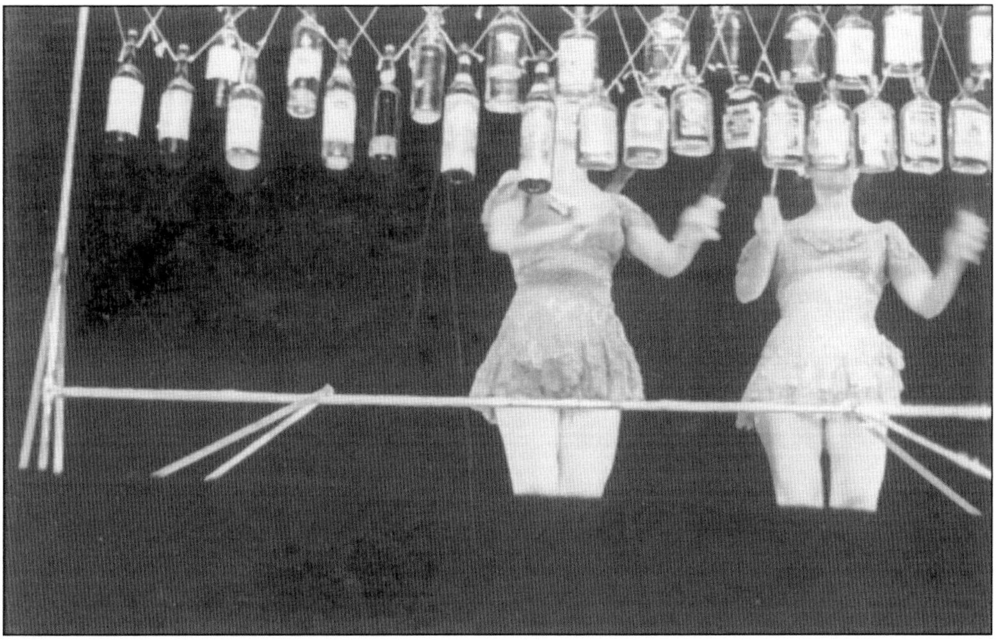

Among some of the early performers at the Pioneer were Six Tiny Rosebuds, a group of burlesque dancers all said to weigh over 200 pounds—who are not the ladies shown here playing tunes on liquor bottles. The decor in the Palace included collections of weapons and famous cattle brands. (FWPL.)

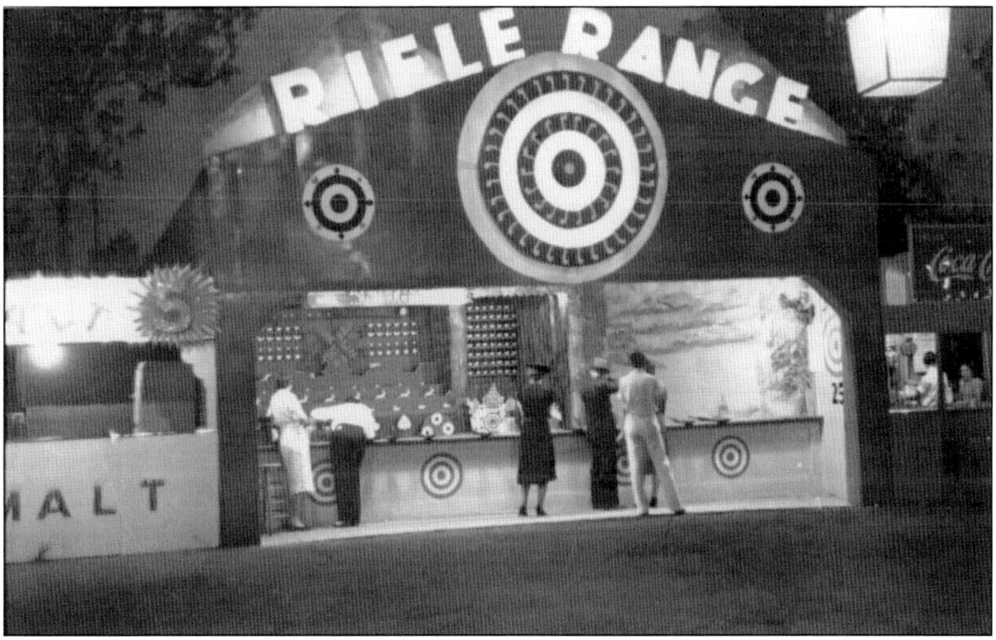

Before arriving at Sally Rand's Dude Ranch, which Reverend Schemack called the "contamination of the Centennial," there were other attractions. Located just across from the Pioneer Palace were several rifle ranges where a man could wow his woman with his marksmanship skills. (FWPL.)

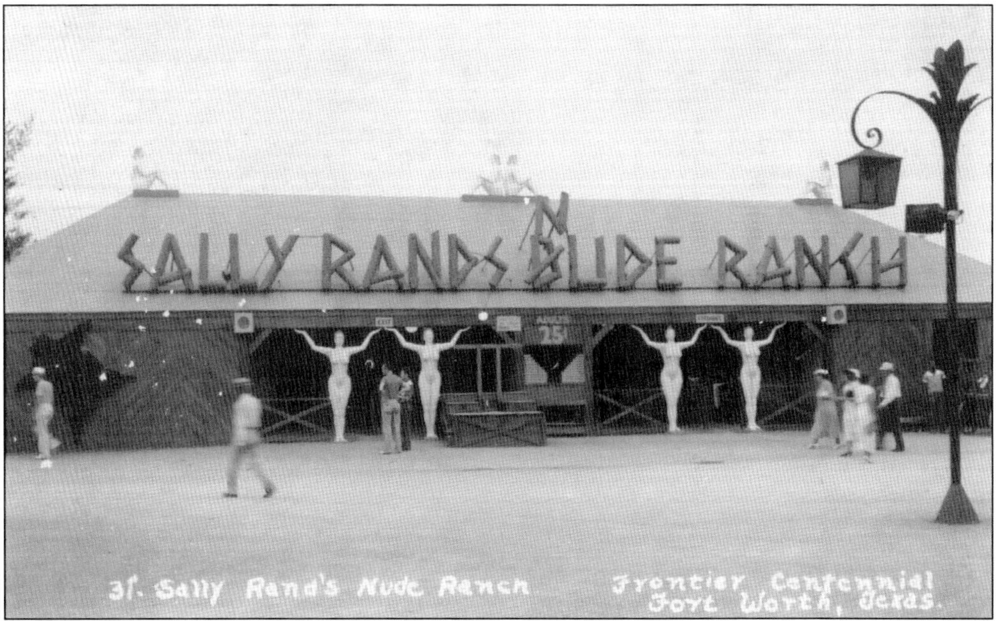

At Sally Rand's Dude (Nude) Ranch, young girls were very scantily dressed in hats and green bandanas, with gun-belts holding six-shooters on their hips. Sally herself did not perform at the ranch, since she worked at Casa Mañana. The indecency of the show was a constant source of conversation amongst local religious leaders and the city council, although city manager George D. Fairtrace pointed out that more nudity was seen at Forrest Park's swimming pool than at Sally's. As the temperatures rose over 100 degrees, the performers were certainly more comfortably dressed than the attendees and not nearly as hot under their collars as the protestors. (Doug Harman.)

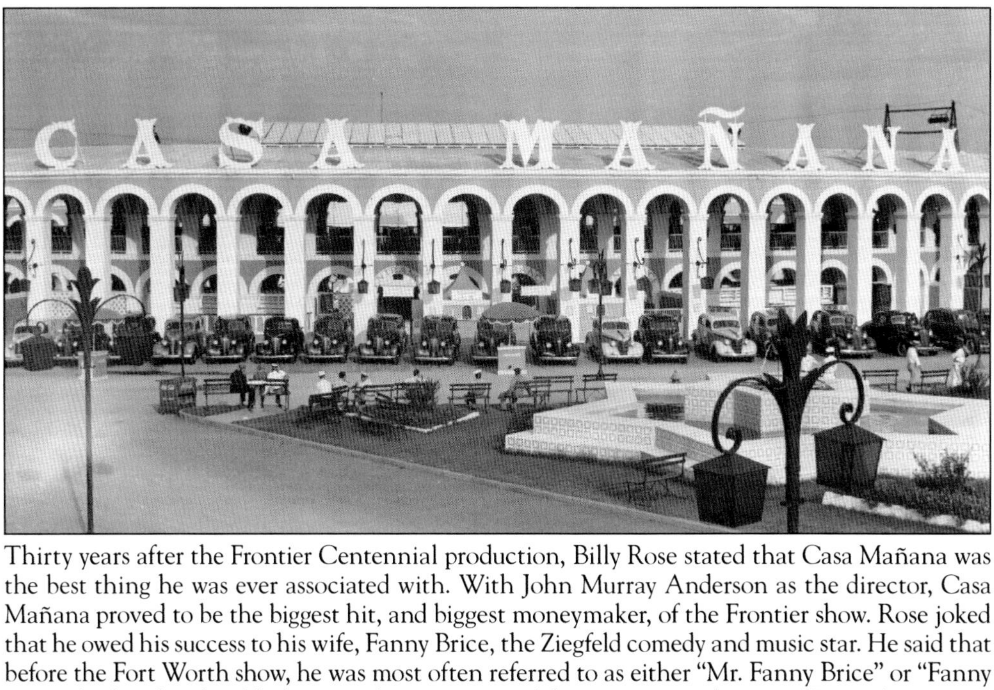

Thirty years after the Frontier Centennial production, Billy Rose stated that Casa Mañana was the best thing he was ever associated with. With John Murray Anderson as the director, Casa Mañana proved to be the biggest hit, and biggest moneymaker, of the Frontier show. Rose joked that he owed his success to his wife, Fanny Brice, the Ziegfeld comedy and music star. He said that before the Fort Worth show, he was most often referred to as either "Mr. Fanny Brice" or "Fanny Brice's husband." This fabulous car show was one of the events outside Casa. (FWST.)

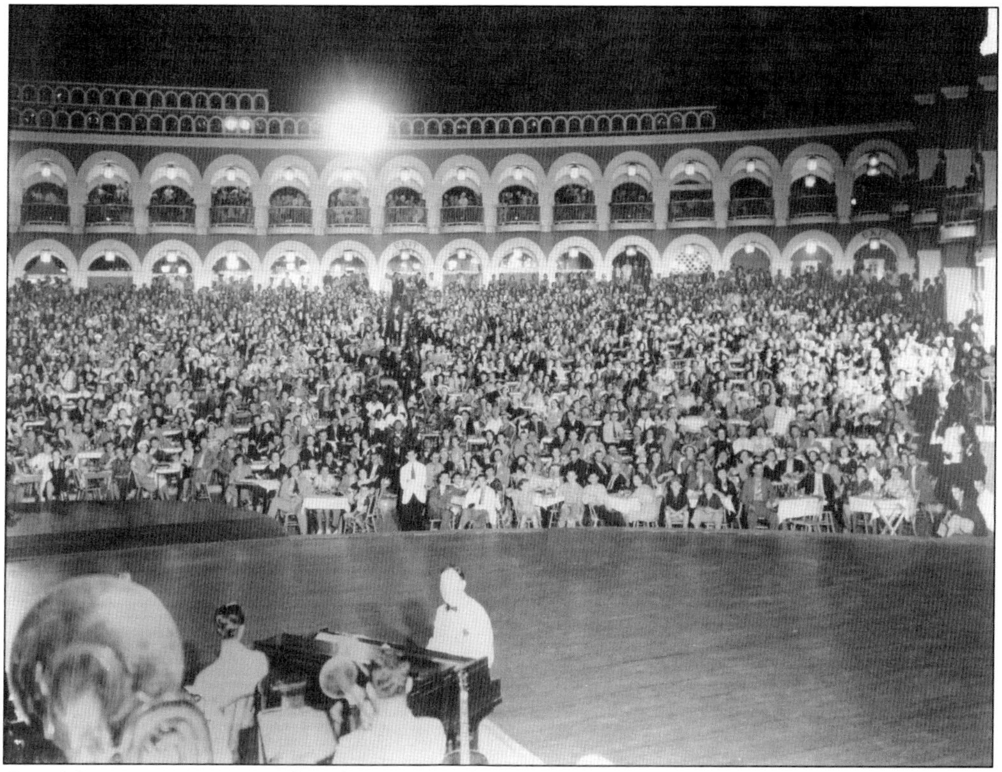

Casa Mañana was promoted as the "house of tomorrow," a decade ahead of its time, and as the largest theater stage constructed to date. Inside the blue and white arched structure, a gargantuan revolving and reciprocating stage, which was three-and-a-half times larger than the stage at Radio City Music Hall, had two 450-horsepower motors, required to operate the 4,264,000 pounds of dead weight plus the 250 beautiful performing women in a pool that contained 617,000 gallons of water. (FWSS.)

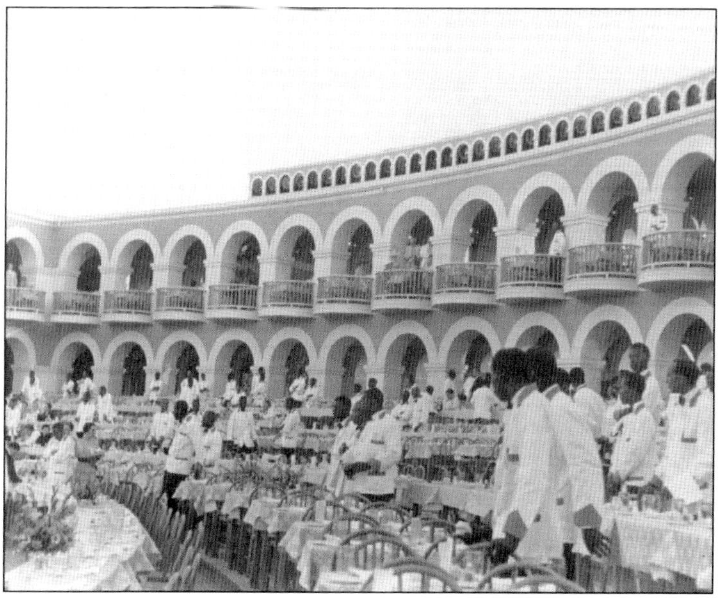

The wait staff prepares for the evening at dusk on opening night. Casa's outdoor dinner theater could seat 2,500 people for dinner and an additional 2,000 who could pay a dollar to just enjoy the show and maybe buy a 35¢ beer at the "world's longest" bar—50 feet long. The menu offered many items, including sirloin steak for $1.75, French jumbo frog legs with tartar sauce for $1.25, and filet mignon Bouquetier for $1.50. (FWPL.)

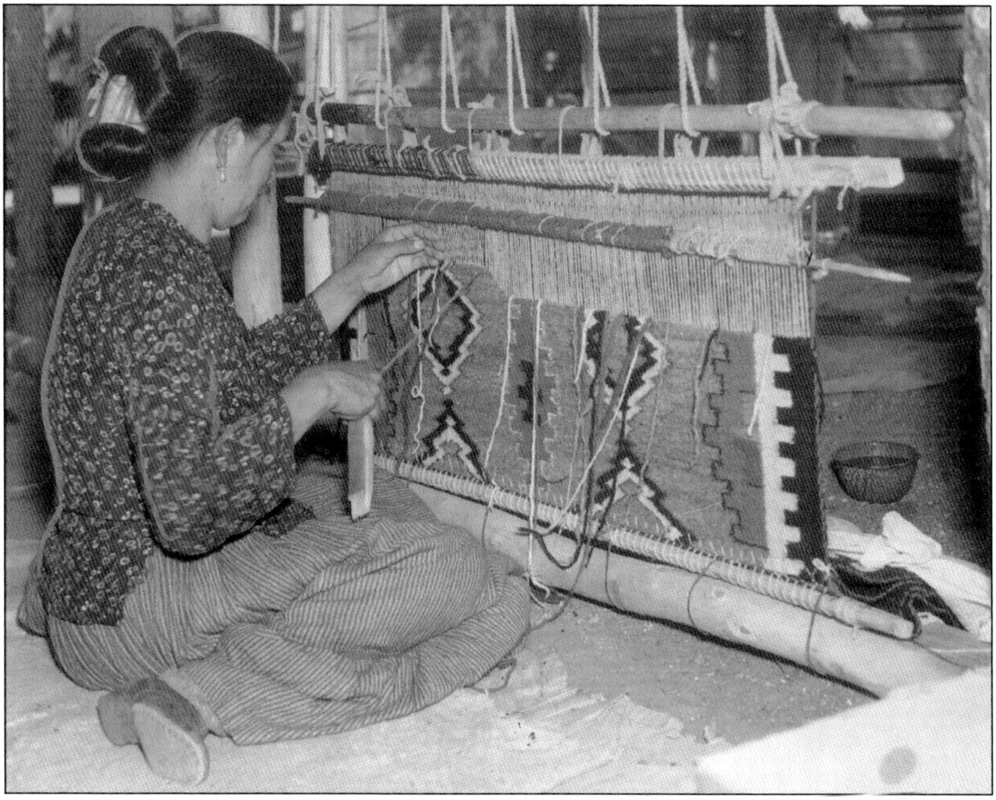

One of the exhibits featured Navajo women weaving rugs. As the woman shown here, known as "Crazy's Wife," wove the rugs, the wife of Hastin Acani, the snakebite doctor, spun the raw wool, which created a rug every 30 days. Members of four different tribes were present at the show. The *Fort Worth Press* wrote, "The funniest thing on the frontier centennial grounds is the way members of the four tribes of Indians look down their noses at each other. The Navajos are just dirt under the feet of the Sioux. The Hopis sniff the air when a Navajo or Sioux walks by. The Comanche ignores Sioux, Navajo and Hopi." (FWST.)

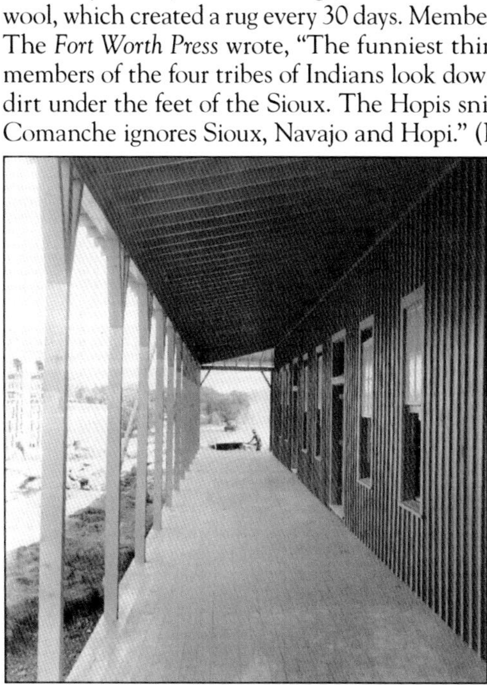

The West Texas Chamber of Commerce building was designed to represent a frontier railroad station. Reminiscent of the days of the Spring Palace, there was also an exhibition that displayed resources from 130 West Texas counties upon which Fort Worth was dependent. The regional chamber's manager, D.A. Bandeen, was in charge of the display, which also housed the Will Rogers room, one of the show's biggest attractions. Betty Rogers lent the show all of her late husband's souvenirs, trophies, and furniture from their Santa Monica, California living room, which was perfectly reproduced at the show. (FWST.)

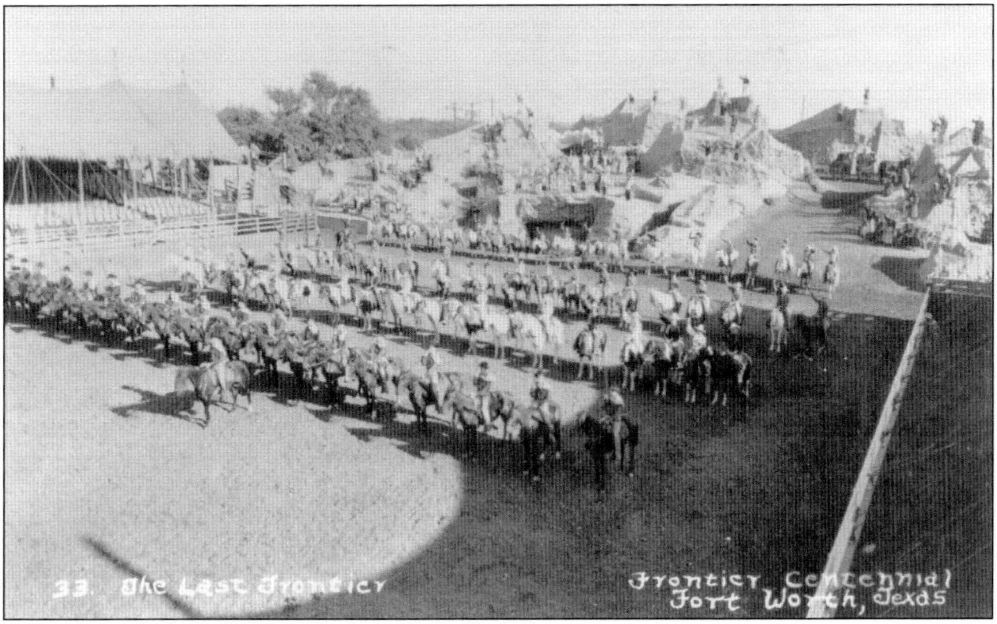

The mountaintop area, complete with arroyos, waterfall, and plateaus, was constructed behind the Last Frontier Stadium. Rose hired 100 square dancers, 75 cowboys and girls, 110 Indians from different reservations around the country, stagecoach drivers, 100 head of cattle, and 250 horses for the show. Cavalrymen from the 2nd Dragoons in Fort Riley, Kansas, were also present, compliments of the US War Department. The audience sat under the green and orange canopies to watch one of the twice-daily shows. Children such as Mitzi Riley, the nine-year-old daughter of trick rider Tad Lucas, were among the performers. (Doug Harman.)

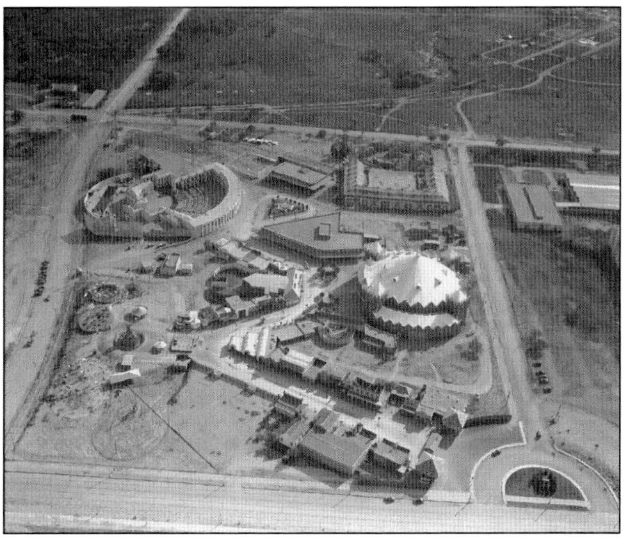

This view of the Frontier grounds from the Goodyear blimp *Resolute* is almost identical to Pelich's design. The buildings were designed by Albert Johnson, the 26-year-old art director for Radio City Music Hall. The east side of Will Rogers Coliseum (right) is barely visible. The newly extended Lancaster Avenue (bottom), named after J.L. Lancaster, president of the Texas & Pacific Railroad, led to the semicircle drive. The extension was urged by Amon Carter, who stated that he anticipated at least three million people at the event. (FWST.)

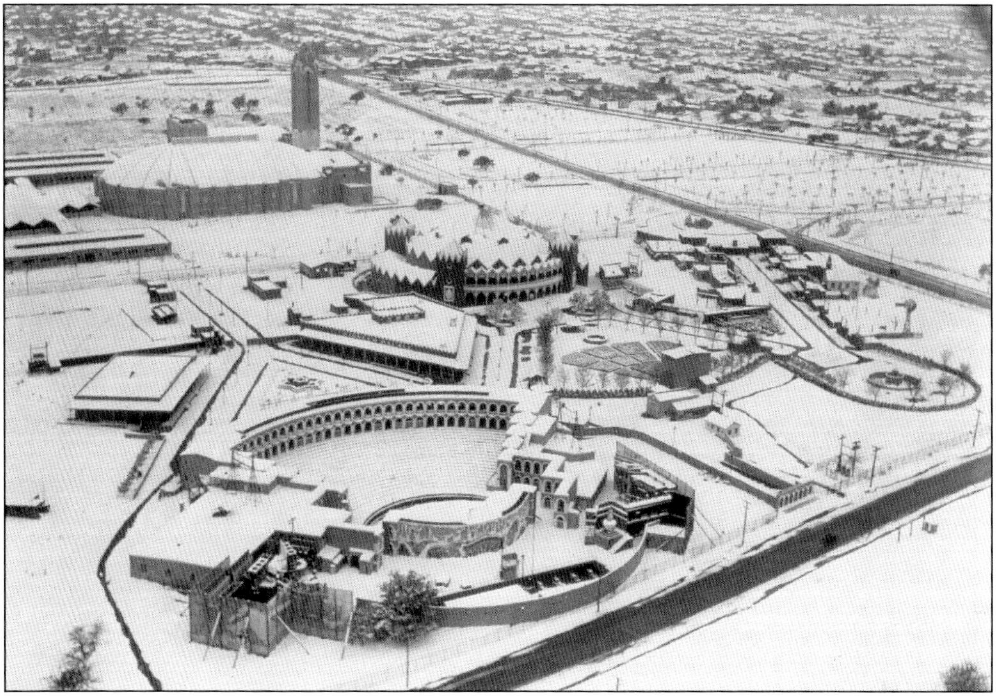

This picture, taken during the winter of 1936–1937, shows the enormous size of the Frontier grounds in comparison to the newly constructed Will Rogers Coliseum and Auditorium (top left). The Frontier celebration enjoyed a 1937 season and then, at a city council meeting in January 1938, it was recommended that many of the buildings be torn down. Casa Mañana and Pioneer Palace were left to enjoy other seasons. (FWST.)

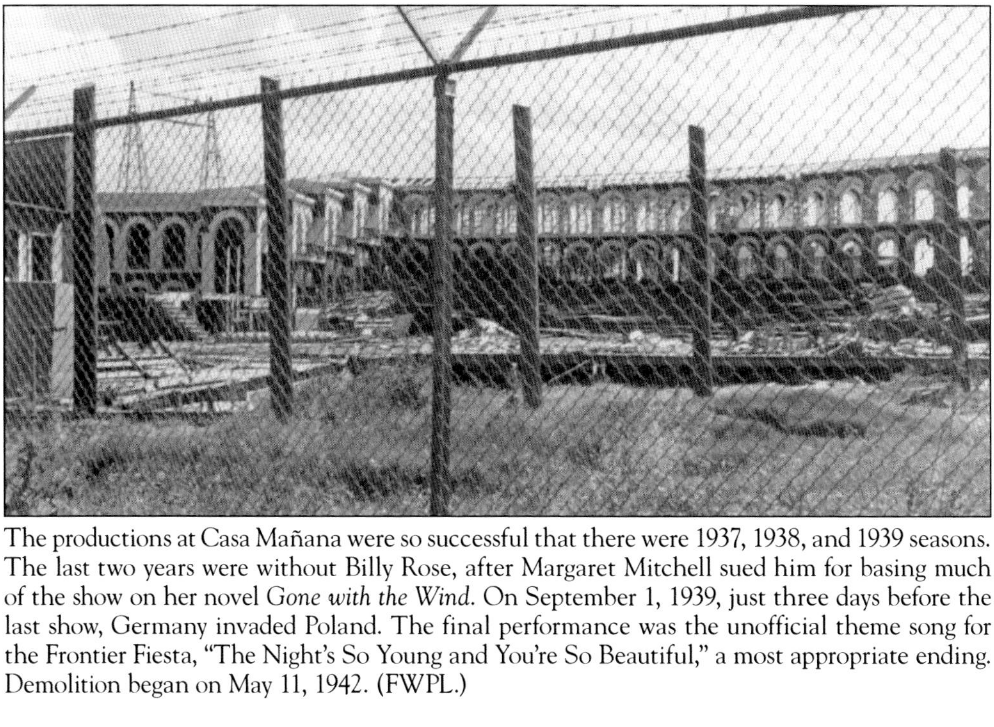

The productions at Casa Mañana were so successful that there were 1937, 1938, and 1939 seasons. The last two years were without Billy Rose, after Margaret Mitchell sued him for basing much of the show on her novel *Gone with the Wind*. On September 1, 1939, just three days before the last show, Germany invaded Poland. The final performance was the unofficial theme song for the Frontier Fiesta, "The Night's So Young and You're So Beautiful," a most appropriate ending. Demolition began on May 11, 1942. (FWPL.)

Three

AMON'S "COWSHED"

Along with a celebration of the historic Western past in the form of the Frontier celebration, there was a call to provide a new home for the Southwestern Exposition and Fat Stock Show, which had grown in popularity throughout the years and needed larger facilities. Knowing that a project this large could not be built without financial help during the Depression, and that combining it with the Centennial celebration would not hurt their chances of gaining pecuniary support, the unofficial celebration proposal included the structures now known as the Will Rogers Coliseum, Tower, and Auditorium. Within less than a year, PWA Project No. Tex 1342R became a reality. Because of the amazing collaborative vision of civic leaders and architects, the support of the community of Fort Worth, and the relentless work of the construction teams, the Will Rogers Memorial Complex is not only one of the most recognizable architectural features of Fort Worth's current skyline, it is the embodiment of the history of the city during the 20th century.

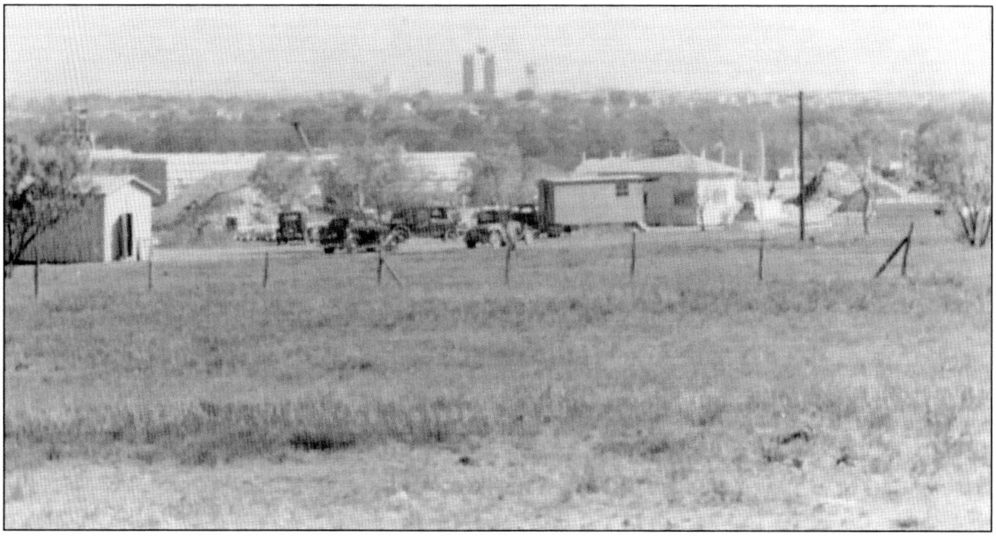

The land on which Will Rogers Coliseum and Auditorium was built is an 83.28-acre portion of the 320-acre Van Zandt tract. As can be expected during the Depression, many people wanted to sell the large quantity of land needed to build the facility. Ten locations were submitted for the site, some for much less than the $1,087.90 per acre—or a total of $150,000—that the city gave for the total of 137.88 acres, despite the fact that the Women's Club was not happy with the site. This view looks southward. On the horizon is the 12-story Forest Park Apartments, built in the 1920s. (FWPL.)

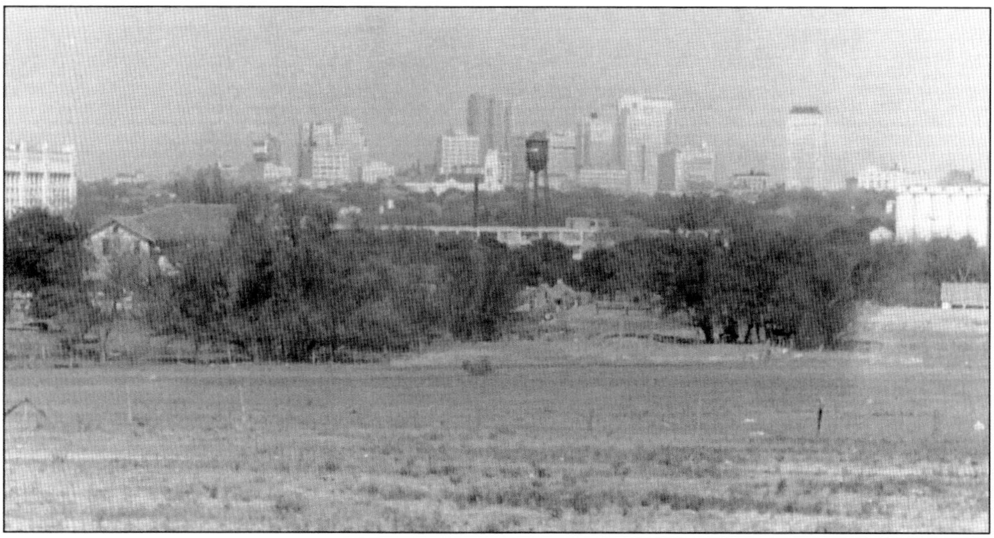

This westward view shows the skyline of Fort Worth. The tall building at right, with the black roof, was the Medical Arts Building, which was demolished in 1973. Left of the water tower are the white spires of the First Methodist Church, and in front of that is the old Chevrolet plant. Montgomery Ward is on the left. The foreground shows the gravel composition of the soil, which would prove to be a benefit during construction. (FWPL.)

On the southwestern horizon, past the trees from Trinity Park and the Botanic Rock Springs Rose Garden, is a view of the Grain Elevators Producers Corp., the Kimbell Corp.—Kay Kimbell's business, whose collection was the basis for the Kimbell Museum—and the Lone Star Elevator Company. These structures were located on Main Street next to the BSNF railroad tracks. In the center is a track probably used for exercising horses. (FWPL.)

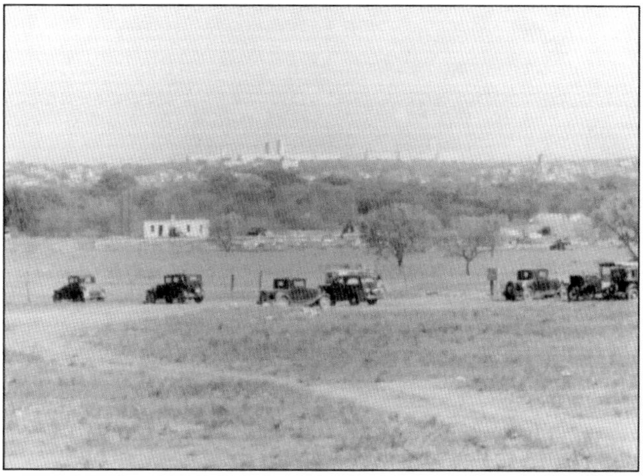

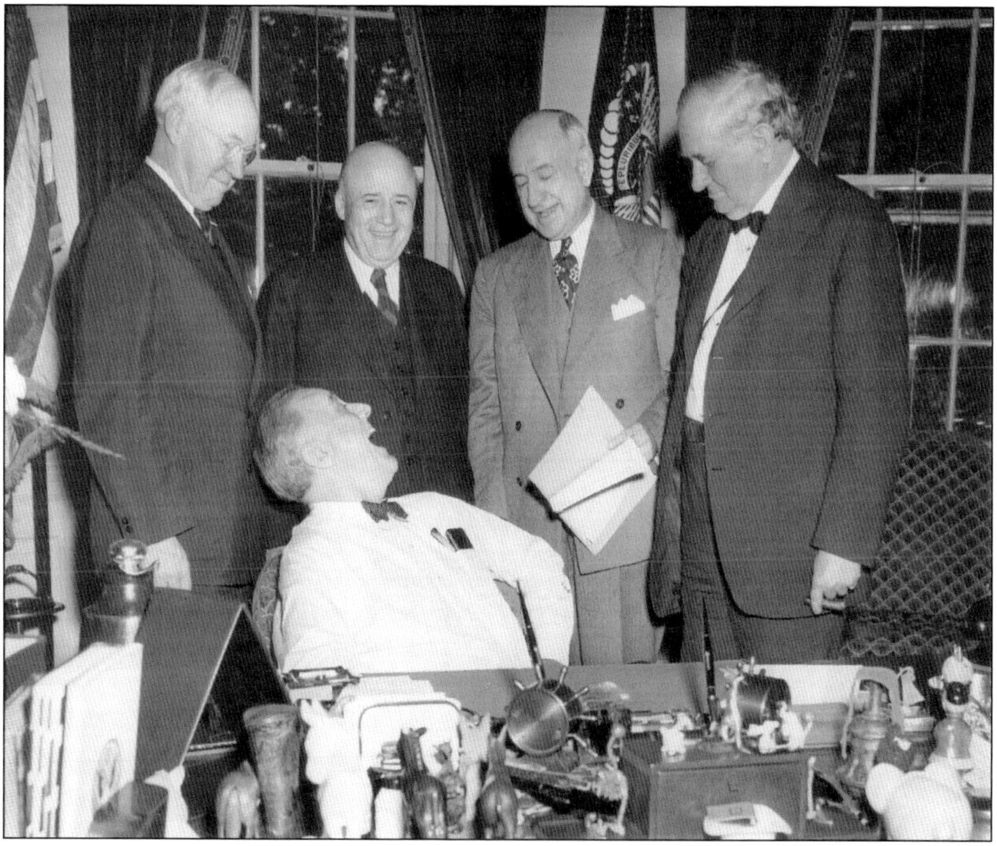

Amon G. Carter's friendship with those in Washington, and many other places, was important to Fort Worth's growth. His relationship with Pres. Franklin D. Roosevelt was instrumental in obtaining the Public Works Administration (PWA) funds needed to build Will Rogers Memorial Center. The president died less than a year after this photograph from June 6, 1944 (D-Day). Carter, then president of the Texas Big Bend National Park Association, is shown presenting the deed of Big Bend to FDR so that it could become a national park. From left to right behind the president are Rep. Ewing Thomason, chairman of the Texas delegation in the House; Speaker of the House Sam Rayburn; Amon G. Carter, and Sen. Tom Connally. (TCU.)

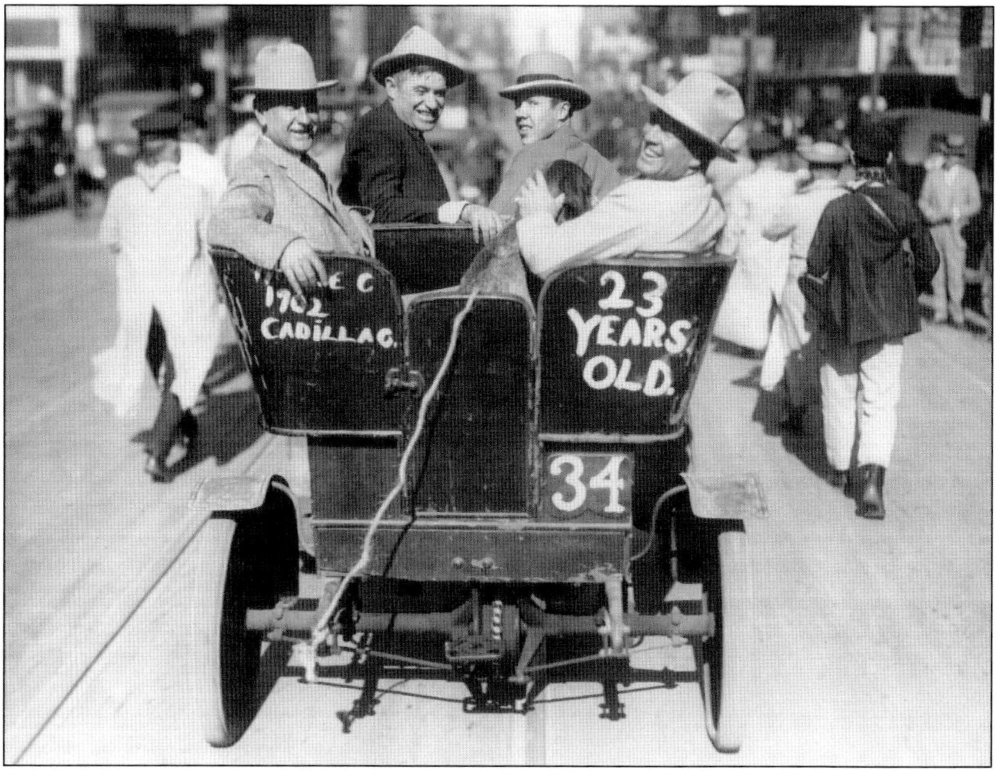

There are many photographs of Will Rogers and Amon G. Carter together. Their friendship was evident from the many correspondences and photographs that occurred not only while Rogers was alive but also in the letters and actions of Carter and Betty Rogers for years after Will died. These two different photographs show both men. The first was taken on November 12, 1925, in a parade to commemorate the seventh anniversary of Armistice Day. Rogers and Isham Taylor (driver) are in the front, and Carter and Tris Speaker are in the back with a coonhound. The second photograph shows Carter sitting at his desk at the Fort Worth *Star-Telegram* surrounded by images of his friend years after his death. (Above, TCU; below, FWST.)

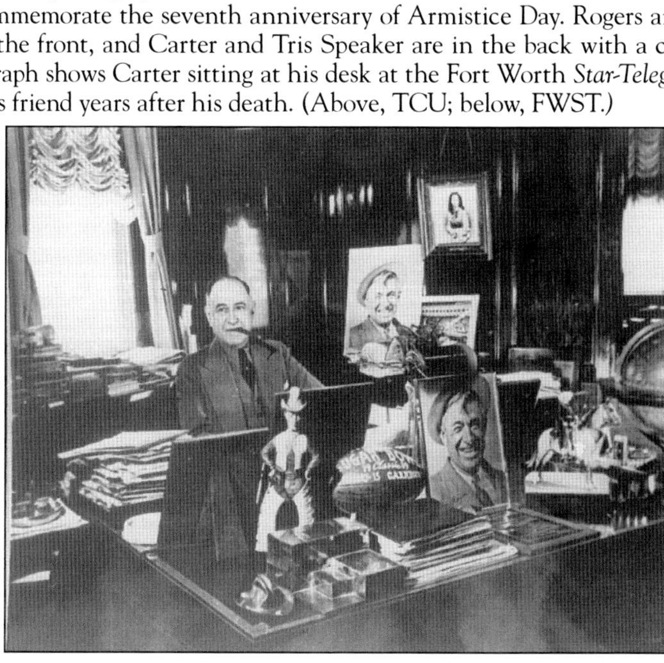

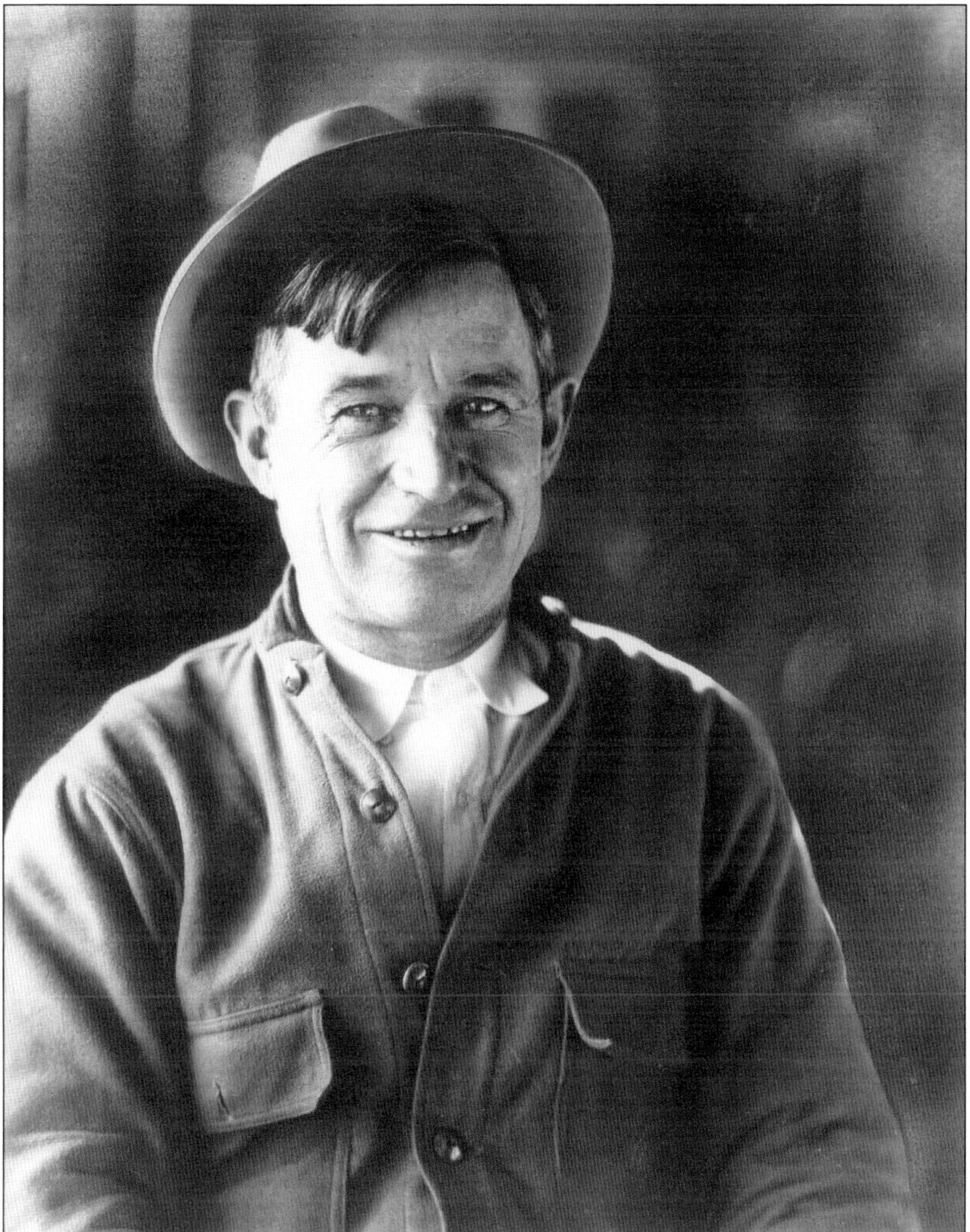

Will Rogers was undoubtedly the most popular man of his era. With over 70 movies on top of his newspaper columns, charity work, and adventurous character, his humor and philosophy captivated the country. Among the many people Rogers considered friends were Wiley Post and Amon G. Carter. On August 15, 1935, Post was piloting a monoplane with Rogers as his passenger near Point Barrow, Alaska, when the plane suffered engine problems and crashed, killing both Post and Rogers. The country instantly went into mourning, memorial funds were raised, and Amon Carter, among others, began a quest to make sure the world never forgot his friend. (Scott Barker.)

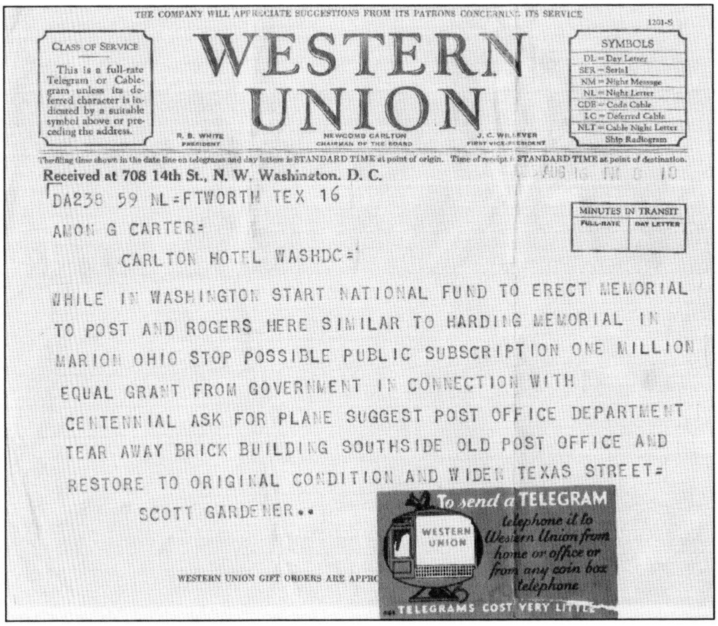

THE COMPANY WILL APPRECIATE SUGGESTIONS FROM ITS PATRONS CONCERNING ITS SERVICE

1201-S

CLASS OF SERVICE

This is a full-rate Telegram or Cablegram unless its deferred character is indicated by a suitable symbol above or preceding the address.

WESTERN UNION

R. B. WHITE, PRESIDENT — NEWCOMB CARLTON, CHAIRMAN OF THE BOARD — J. C. WILLEVER, FIRST VICE-PRESIDENT

SYMBOLS

DL = Day Letter
SER = Serial
NM = Night Message
NL = Night Letter
CDE = Code Cable
LC = Deferred Cable
NLT = Cable Night Letter
Ship Radiogram

The filing time shown in the date line on telegrams and day letters is STANDARD TIME at point of origin. Time of receipt is STANDARD TIME at point of destination.

Received at 708 14th St., N. W. Washington, D. C.

MINUTES IN TRANSIT — FULL-RATE — DAY LETTER

DA238 59 NL=FTWORTH TEX 16

AMON G CARTER=

CARLTON HOTEL WASHDC=

WHILE IN WASHINGTON START NATIONAL FUND TO ERECT MEMORIAL TO POST AND ROGERS HERE SIMILAR TO HARDING MEMORIAL IN MARION OHIO STOP POSSIBLE PUBLIC SUBSCRIPTION ONE MILLION EQUAL GRANT FROM GOVERNMENT IN CONNECTION WITH CENTENNIAL ASK FOR PLANE SUGGEST POST OFFICE DEPARTMENT TEAR AWAY BRICK BUILDING SOUTHSIDE OLD POST OFFICE AND RESTORE TO ORIGINAL CONDITION AND WIDEN TEXAS STREET=

SCOTT GARDENER..

To send a TELEGRAM telephone it to Western Union from home or office or from any coin box telephone

TELEGRAMS COST VERY LITTLE

WESTERN UNION GIFT ORDERS ARE APPR

After Rogers's untimely death, the country went into mourning but also collected funds to erect memorials and donate to needy people in Will Rogers's name. This Western Union telegram to Amon Cater from Scott Gardener on August 16, 1935, suggests the establishment of a fund, as well as the possibility of a $1-million grant for a memorial to Rogers connected with the Centennial celebration in Fort Worth. (TCU.)

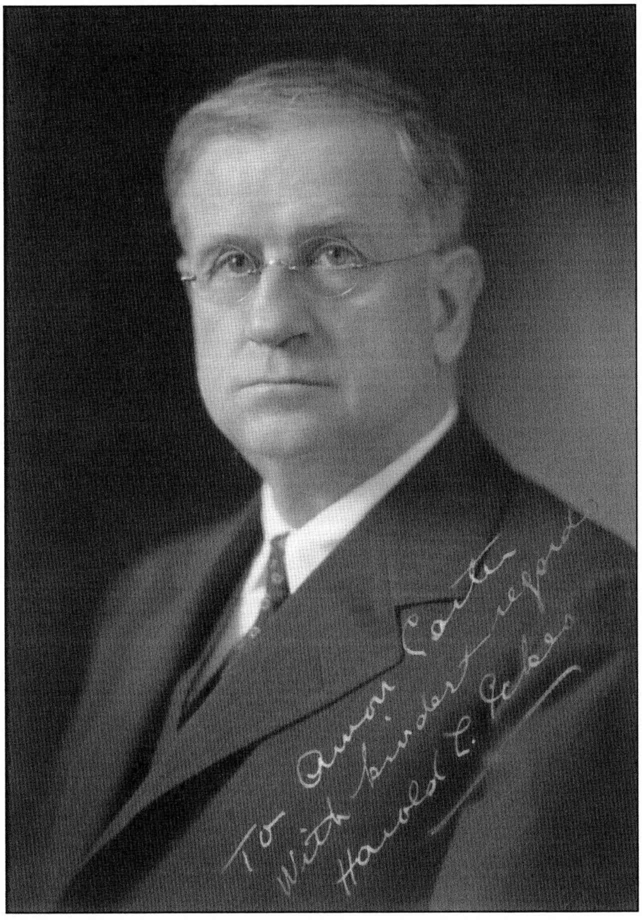

Because Carter hoped that the Coliseum would eventually become the home of the Fat Stock Show and Rodeo, it was dubbed "Amon's Cowshed" in Washington. Harold Ickes, director of the PWA, thought the idea of building a memorial to Will Rogers in Fort Worth ludicrous, so Carter contacted FDR directly. As Carter sat outside the president's office, the door was purposely left ajar, and Carter overheard Postmaster General James Farley say, "Amon wants to build a cowshed." The president's response made Carter go charging in shouting, only to find both men rolling with laughter. After a formal application was submitted by Fort Worth, Farley telegraphed Carter, "Your proposal received, was always in favor of large cowsheds." (TCU.)

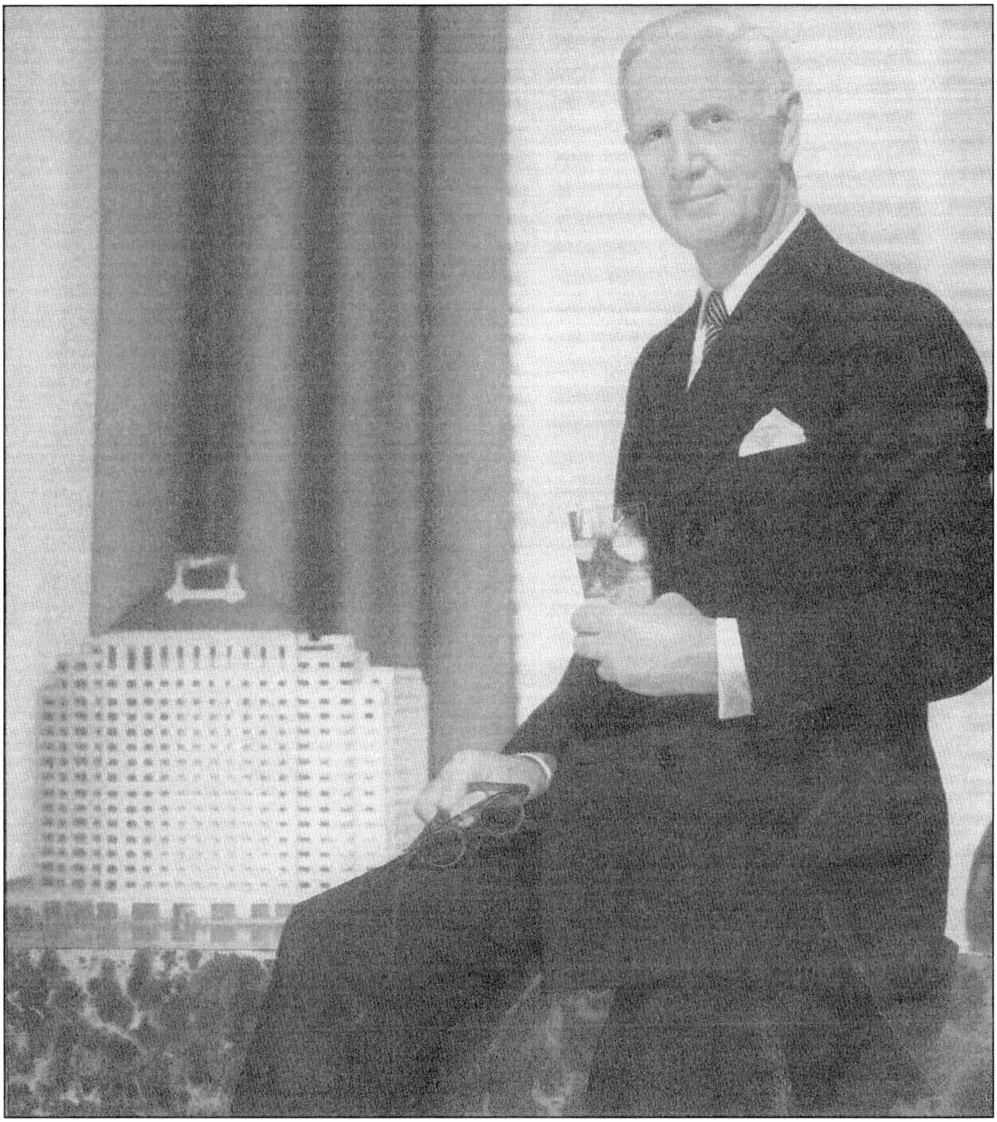

One of the architects hired for the job was Wyatt C. Hedrick, a transplanted Virginian who moved to Texas in 1913. In 1921, Hedrick went to work for Sanguinet & Staats, one of the most prestigious architectural firms in the southwest. By 1925, he was the sole owner of the firm and changed its name to Wyatt C. Hedrick: Architect and Engineer. Herman Koeppe was Hedrick's chief architect for the Coliseum, the Pioneer Tower, and the exterior of the Auditorium. His personal forte was the Moderne style, or Art Deco, and his distinguishing touches can be seen in the detail and style of the buildings. Hedrick and Koeppe were the perfect complement to each other and it is very possible that neither could have done as well without the other. (Ames Fender.)

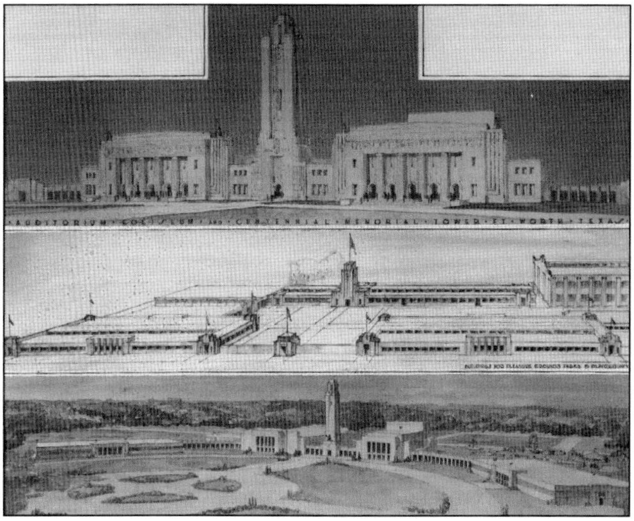

On October 30, Hedrick and Elmer Withers were hired as joint architects for the complex. Their responsibilities were for all architectural, engineering, and construction needs, including providing all surveys, plans, equipment, materials, and labor. In return, the city agreed to pay the architects five percent of the total cost, which amounted to $80,000. Their initial rendition, dated April 20, 1936, looked very different from the final product, not least because of the absence of a dome over the coliseum. (FWST.)

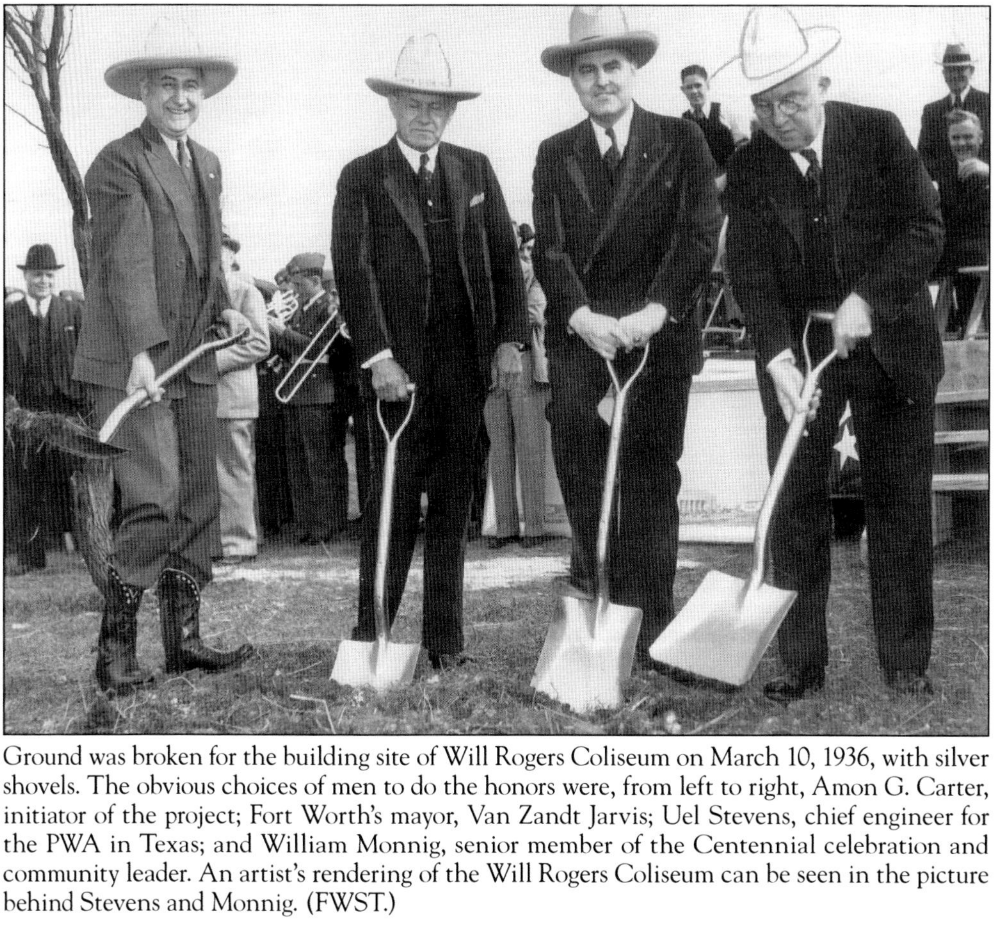

Ground was broken for the building site of Will Rogers Coliseum on March 10, 1936, with silver shovels. The obvious choices of men to do the honors were, from left to right, Amon G. Carter, initiator of the project; Fort Worth's mayor, Van Zandt Jarvis; Uel Stevens, chief engineer for the PWA in Texas; and William Monnig, senior member of the Centennial celebration and community leader. An artist's rendering of the Will Rogers Coliseum can be seen in the picture behind Stevens and Monnig. (FWST.)

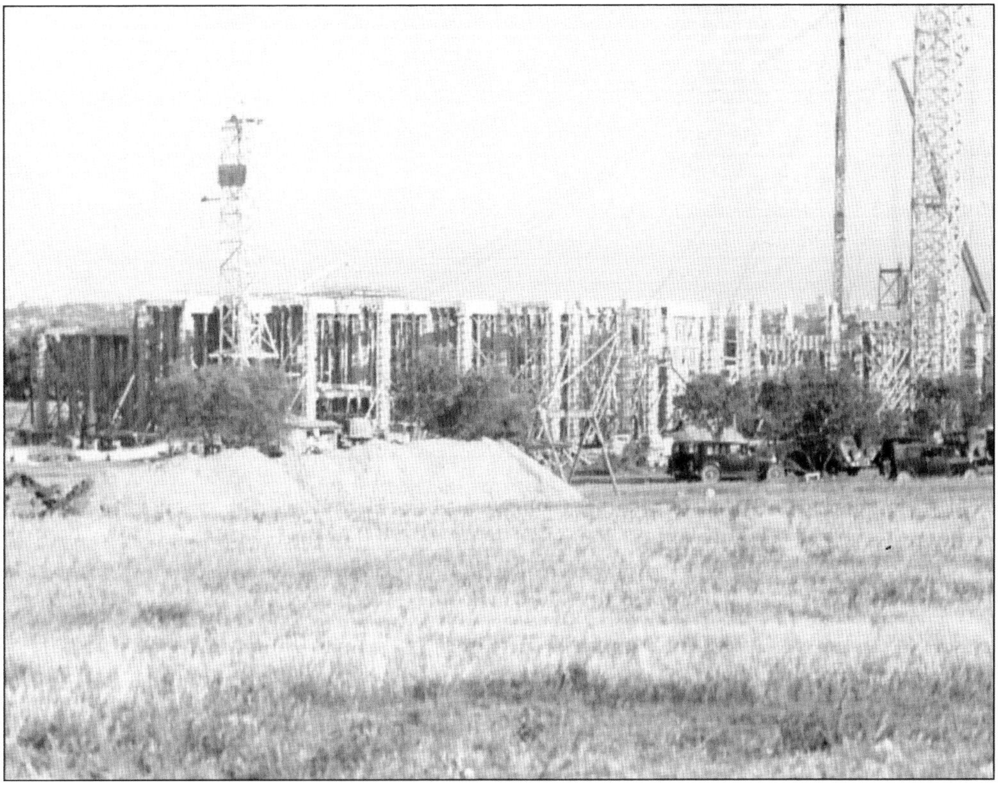

The skeleton of the back of the Auditorium is shown in this photograph taken from the west side of the building facing downtown Fort Worth, which is barely visible in the background. The mass of steel, fabricated in Memphis, was assembled under the direction of R.F. Ball Construction Company of Fort Worth. The tall structure is not the tower, but machinery that was used to lift the heavy steel girders into place. (FWPL.)

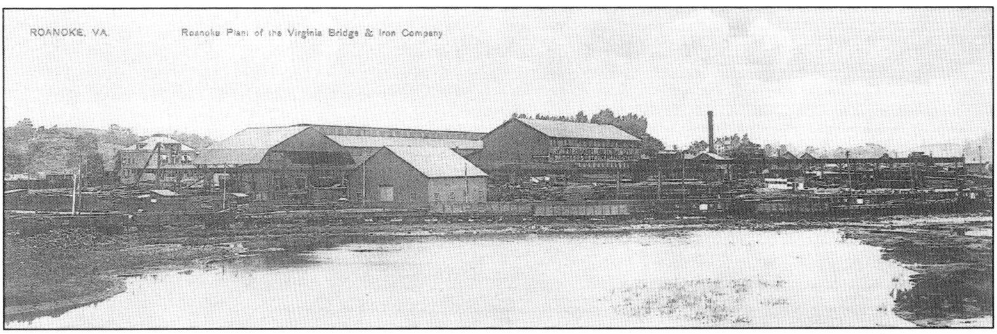

The Virginia Bridge & Iron Company of Roanoke, Virginia, was contracted to fabricate the structural beams for the Coliseum. Established in 1895, the company had an enormously successful track record of producing structural steel for bridges, skyscrapers, railroad bridges, and cars, not just in the United States but also in Mexico, Cuba, and Puerto Rico. During the production of the structural supports for the dome, engineer Herbert Hinckley Sr. went to Roanoke to work with B.L. Sneed, the general contracting manager, to make sure the fabrication was as requested. (Robert Stauffer.)

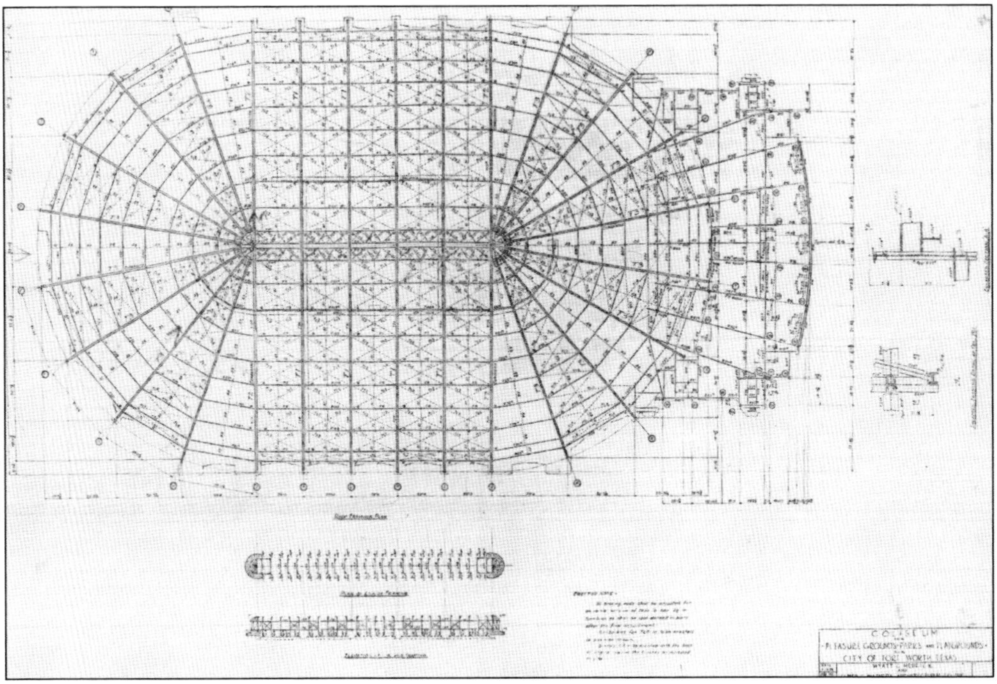

Herbert Hinckley Sr.'s plans called for circular steel framing that interlocked at the peak, allowing for expansion and contraction in hot and cold seasons. When put up for review, all the architects and engineers rejected his plans, including Hedrick, who worried that the structure would collapse. Hinckley prevailed, and the dome, with an approximate spread of 220 feet, was built—the very first of its kind. The middle section measured 125 feet and was joined at each end to a half-spherical section, making the total length approximately 345 feet. (FWSS.)

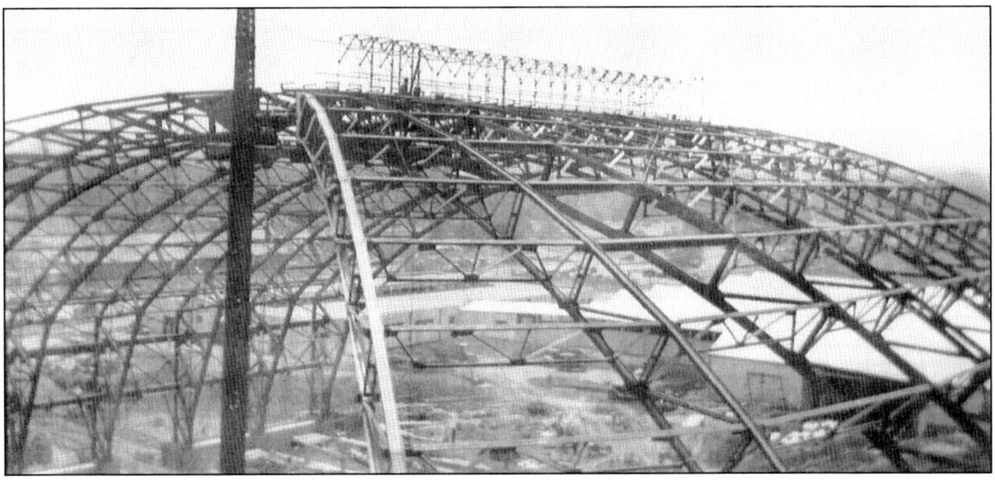

Hinckley went to work for Hedrick in 1935; they had met when Hinckley worked at Mosher Steel Company in Dallas as a youth. Hinckley's idea for a dome with no supporting columns most likely came from an experience of sitting in seats with an obstructed view at a boxing match. After the steel beams arrived at the Fort Worth train station, James T. Taylor, contractor of the coliseum, examined the steel and declared that it needed to be cut down. Hinckley had to convince Taylor that because of the heat, the steel had expanded, which had been accounted for in his plans. (Dalton Hoffman.)

As the framework for the dome was assembled, so was the entrance of the Coliseum. In this photograph, from the end of June or beginning of July 1936, a workman is walking across the framework that would become the balcony in the foyer. The reinforcement where the tile frieze was assembled is visible, as is Billy Rose's Jumbo, across the street at the Frontier Fiesta. (Dalton Hoffman.)

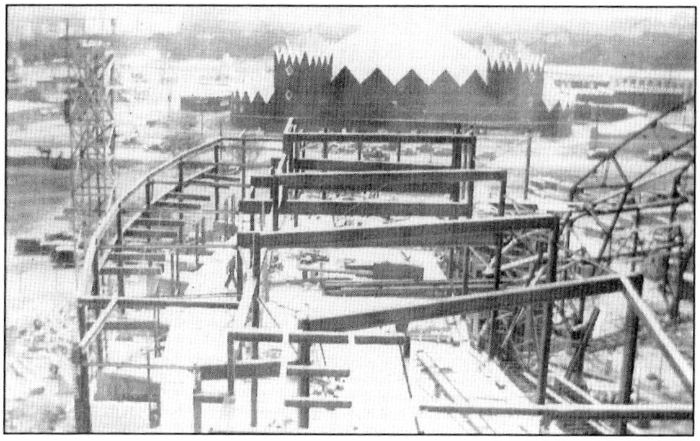

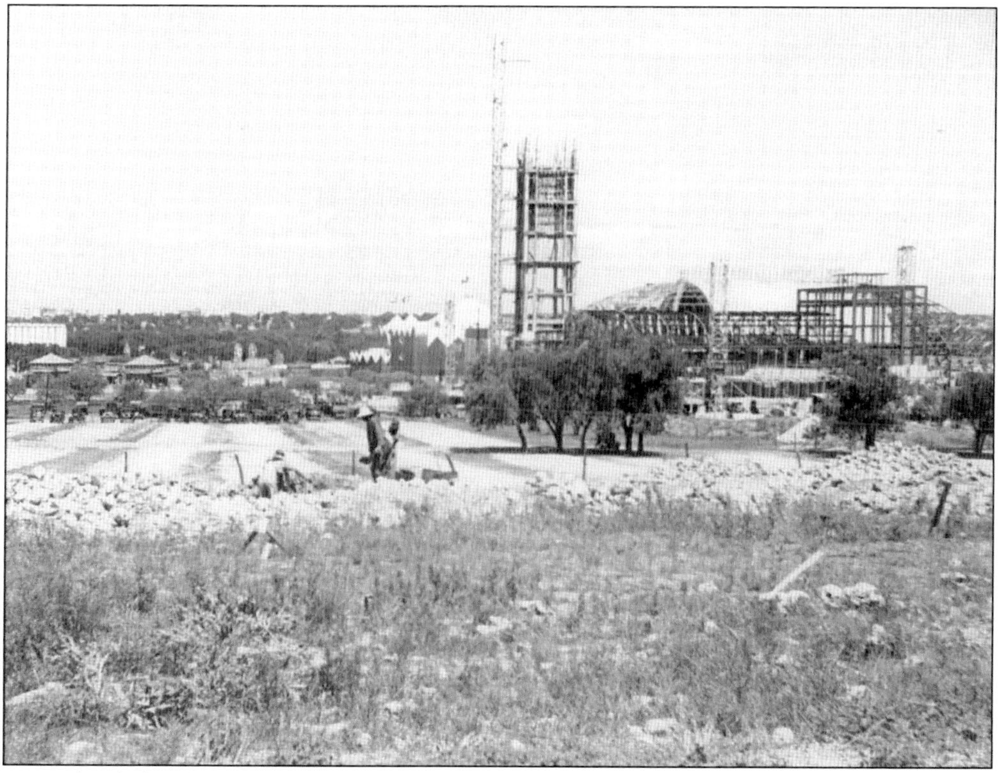

It was decided early in the project to give time preference to the Coliseum, because a horse show was going to be held there in October. That preferred status is obvious in this photograph. The roof of the dome is partially covered, while the basic structure of the tower and auditorium are in-situ. In the foreground, working men appear to be moving rocks. In front of the distant grain elevators (left) are the blockhouses that mark the entrance to the Frontier Fiesta. The large group of cars is parked in the designated parking area for the fair attendees. (FWPL.)

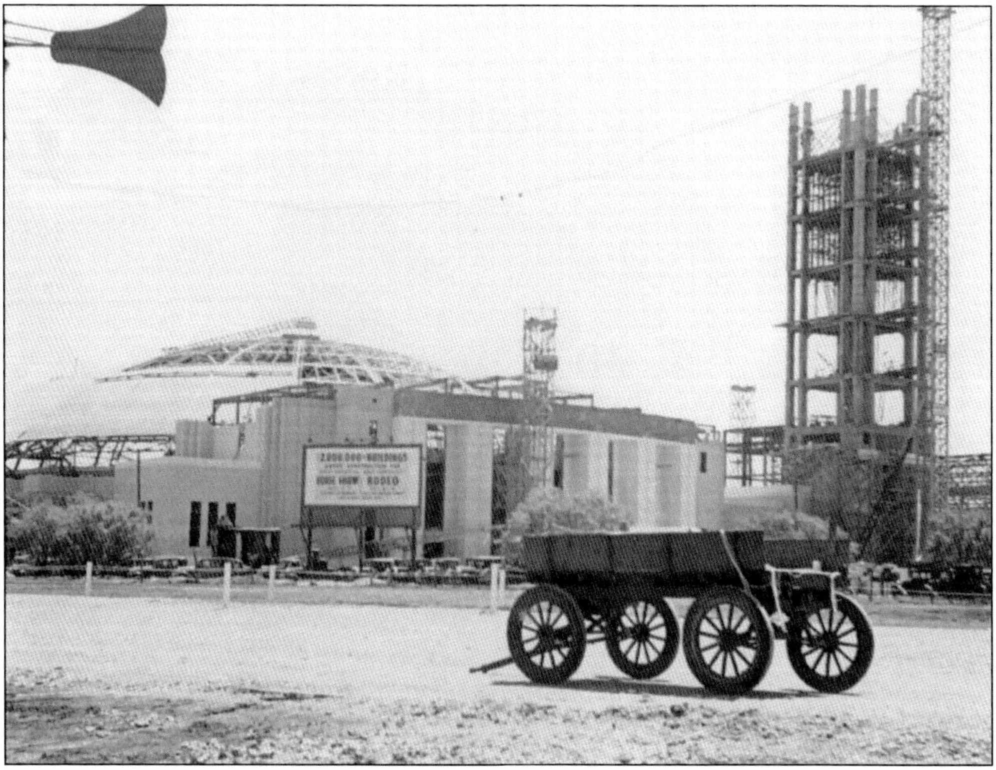

Progress was marked by August 1, 1936, when this photograph was taken. The sign in front of the building advertizes the upcoming horse show and rodeo. The Tower's frame was assembled and metal studs were in place on the fifth and sixth floor, having been passed up the temporary hoisting shaft. Wooden decking on the Coliseum crept closer to the casing for the ventilation system at the crest of the roof. The front columns of the Coliseum were encased with limestone from Texas quarries—used as a mandatory substitute for cast stone to cut costs—as was the base of the Tower. R.F. Ball of Fort Worth was the main contractor for the Tower. His original bid was $108,983, but after changes, which included omitting the terrazzo floor in the lobby and aluminum lanterns on the seventh level, the fee was reduced to $99,175; this allowed Ball to make a 15-percent profit. (Both, FWPL.)

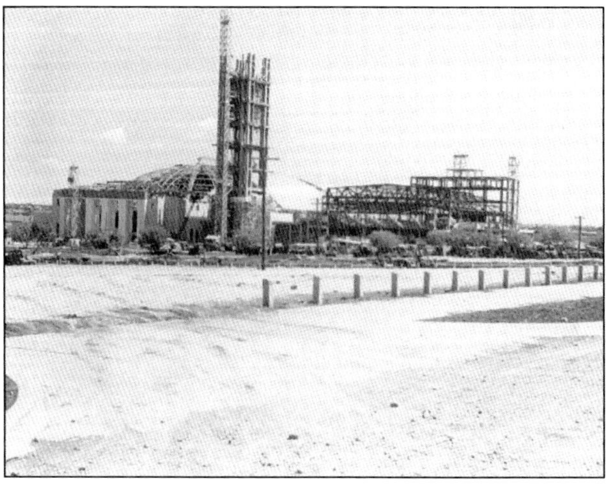

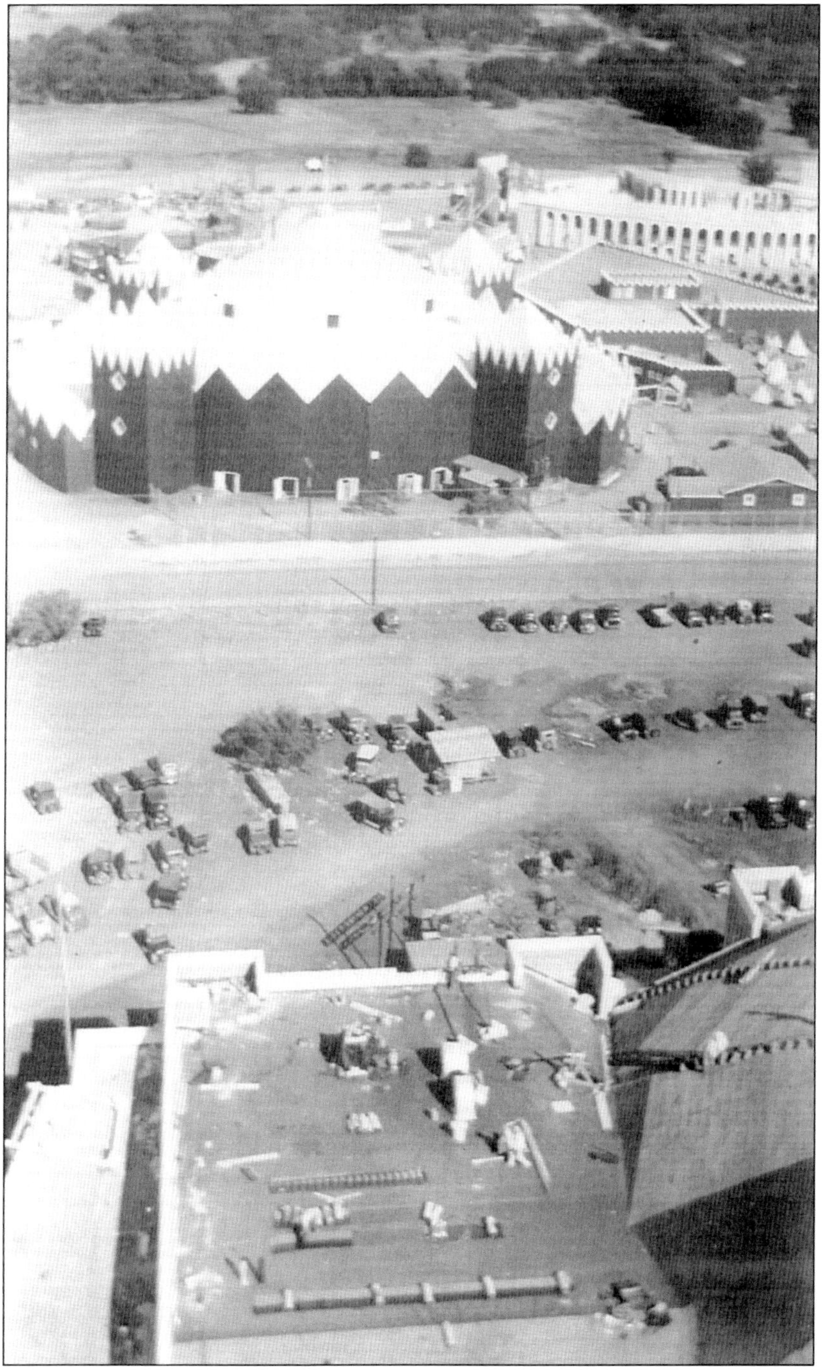

Pieces of wooden decking, rolled roofing, and perhaps the metal used to cover decorative rib work on the dome surrounded the workers. Below the top level of the foyer, men work in the shadows, probably finishing up the brick work before the frieze was installed. Across the street, which is now Rip Johnson Drive, were Jumbo, Pioneer Palace, and Casa Mañana at the Frontier Celebration. This image was probably shot in the early morning, as there are no visible guests at the Frontier grounds. (Dalton Hoffman.)

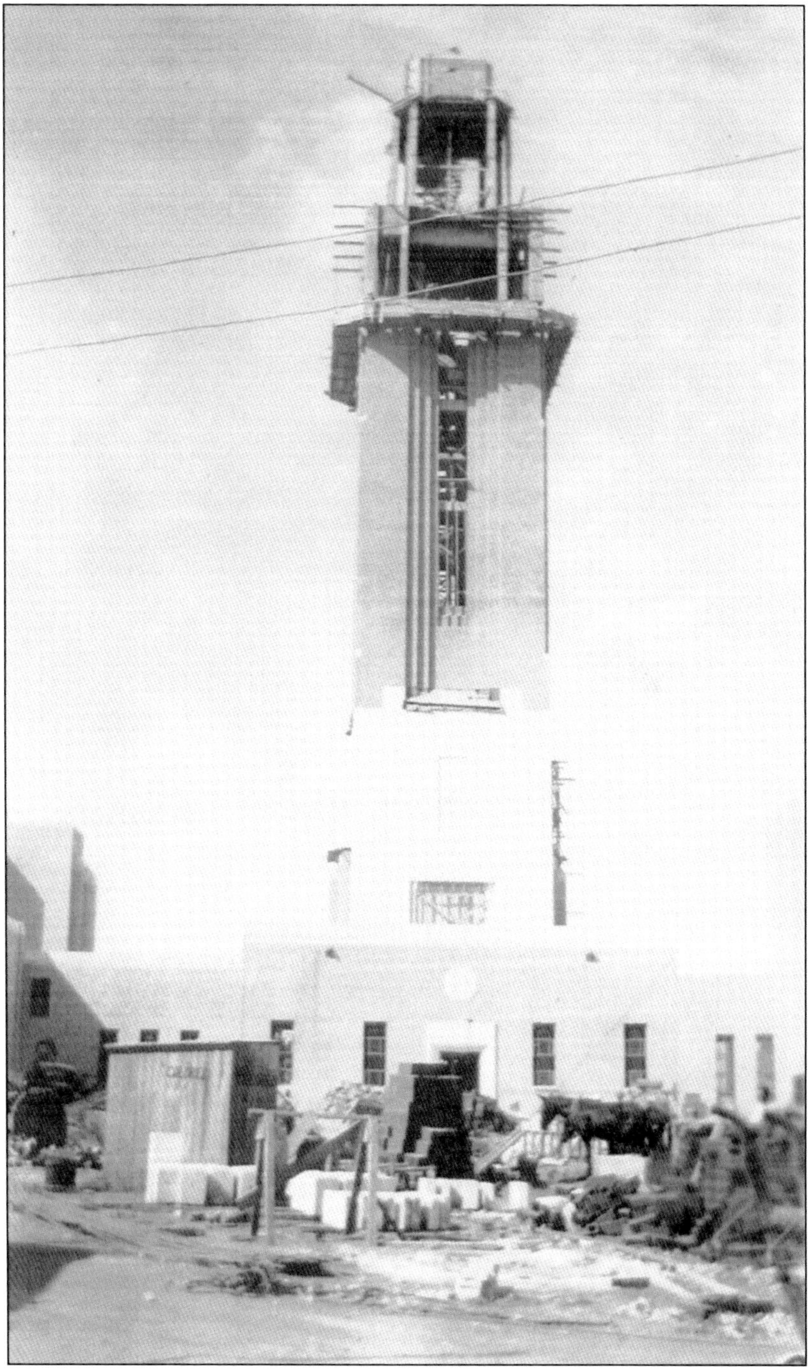

This image of the back of the Tower has multiple features of interest. The crown is partially installed, and the spiral staircase that goes to the top landing is visible. Through the glass block window slots in the center of the tower, the metal stairways of the fourth through seventh floors are barely visible. The times were also dated by a few details, including the mules (bottom right), which were often used for construction, and an outside toilet (bottom left) with the word "colored" on it. (Dalton Hoffman.)

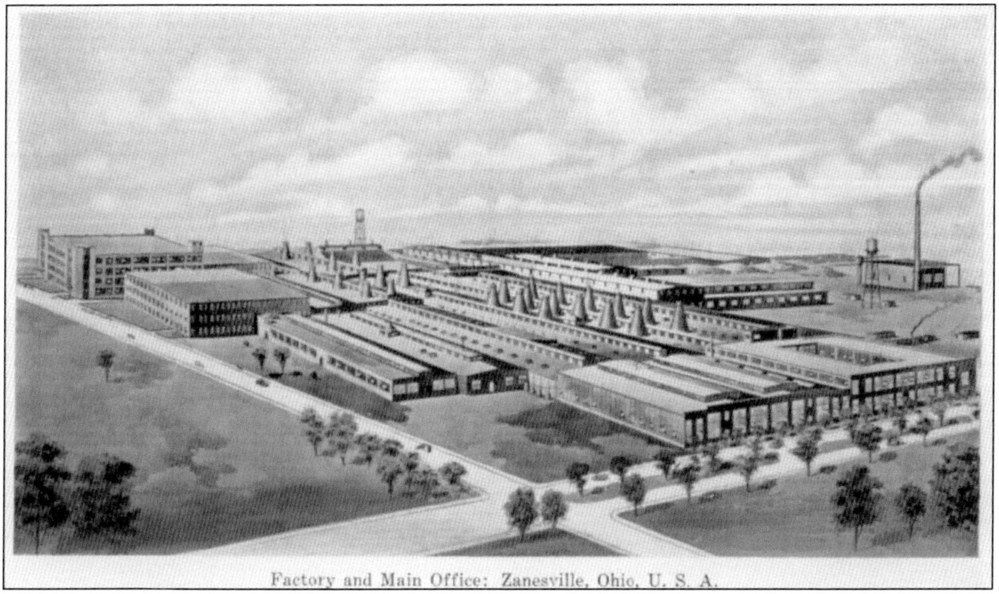

The Mosaic Tile Company of Zanesville, Ohio, constructed the tile for the friezes of the Coliseum and Auditorium. Begun in 1894 by Herman Mueller, the Mosaic Tile Company was one of many pottery and tile companies located in that area, which was rich in sand, clay, and iron deposits. Because of these attributes, Zanesville quickly became known as the "Pottery Capital of the World," as well as a center for glass and steel production. (Author's collection.)

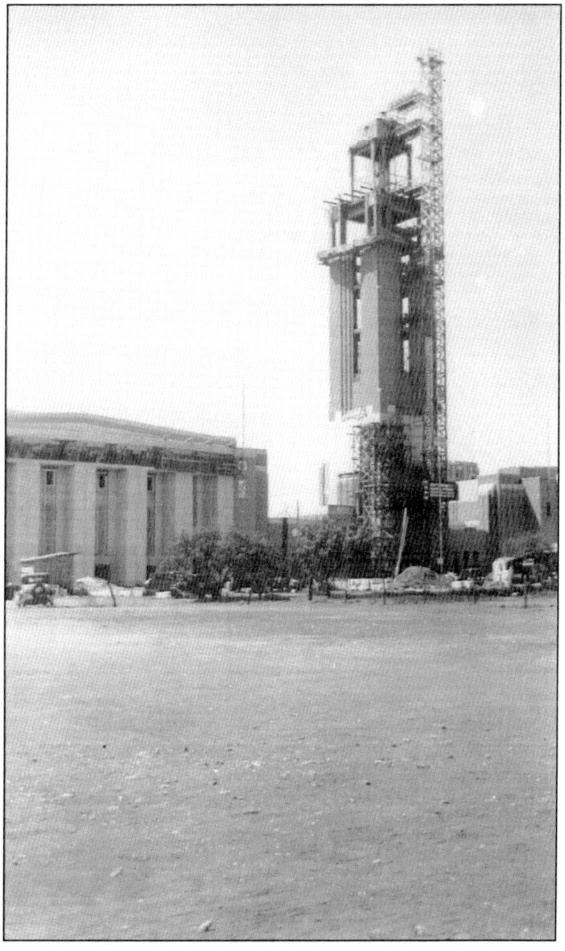

The Tower took as many contractors as the Coliseum and Auditorium. Excavation and foundation work was done by Butcher and Sweeney for $5,800; heating and ventilating was executed by Bush Brothers Plumbing and Heating for $1,856; Shotts Electric did the electrical work for $7,980; and Eugene Ashe Electric Company installed conduit and outlets for $484. At the right side of the frieze on the coliseum, there is scaffolding that holds men as they install the tile frieze. (Dalton Hoffman.)

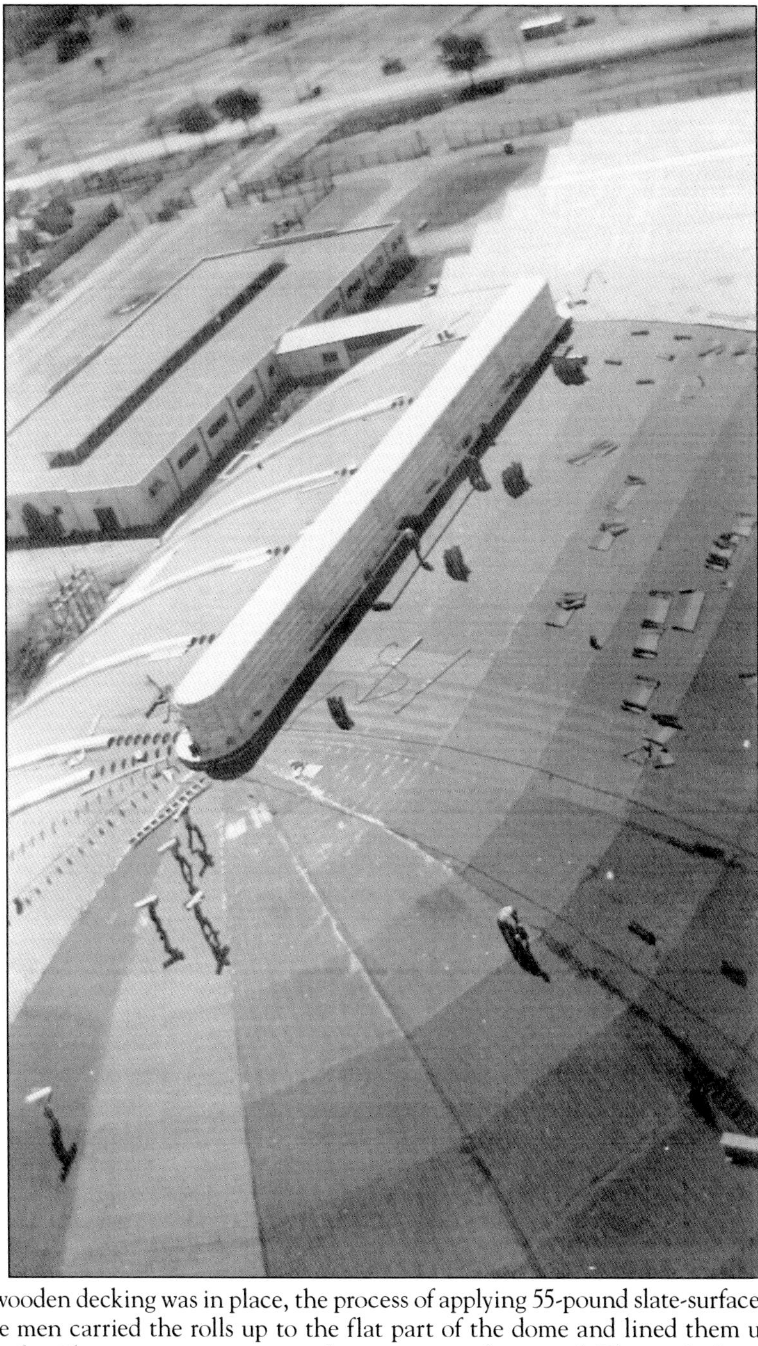

Once the wooden decking was in place, the process of applying 55-pound slate-surface roll roofing began. The men carried the rolls up to the flat part of the dome and lined them up for future use. On the far side, cosmetic separation ribs were encased in metal. This is the best view of the ventilation system and the louvered shutters. The exhaust system, which is still in use, requires a two-step process: first the vents are opened, and then the exhaust fans are turned on. This process removes the hot air from the top of the Coliseum and draws the cooler air upwards to maintain a comfortable temperature all the way up to the 13th seating level. As the Coliseum occupies 5.3 million cubic feet, this has proven to be a much more cost-effective method than air-conditioning alone. (Dalton Hoffman.)

The Cameron Roofing Company requested a wage change for it laborers on August 12, asking for a drop in pay for tar and gravel roofers to 75¢ per hour, their helpers to 50¢ per hour, and foremen to $1 per hour, instead of paying the higher WPA-approved wages. Considering that August was the hottest time of the year and the asphalt was required to have a meting point of 160 degrees, the workers could not have been pleased. These are the asphalt pits on the side of the Coliseum on October 2. (FWPL.)

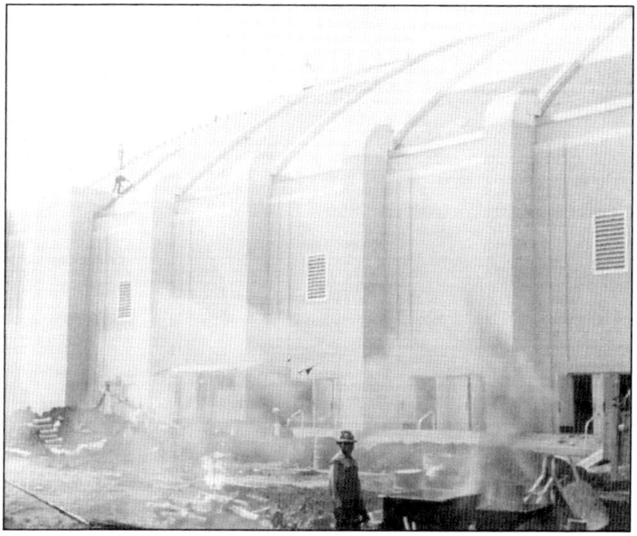

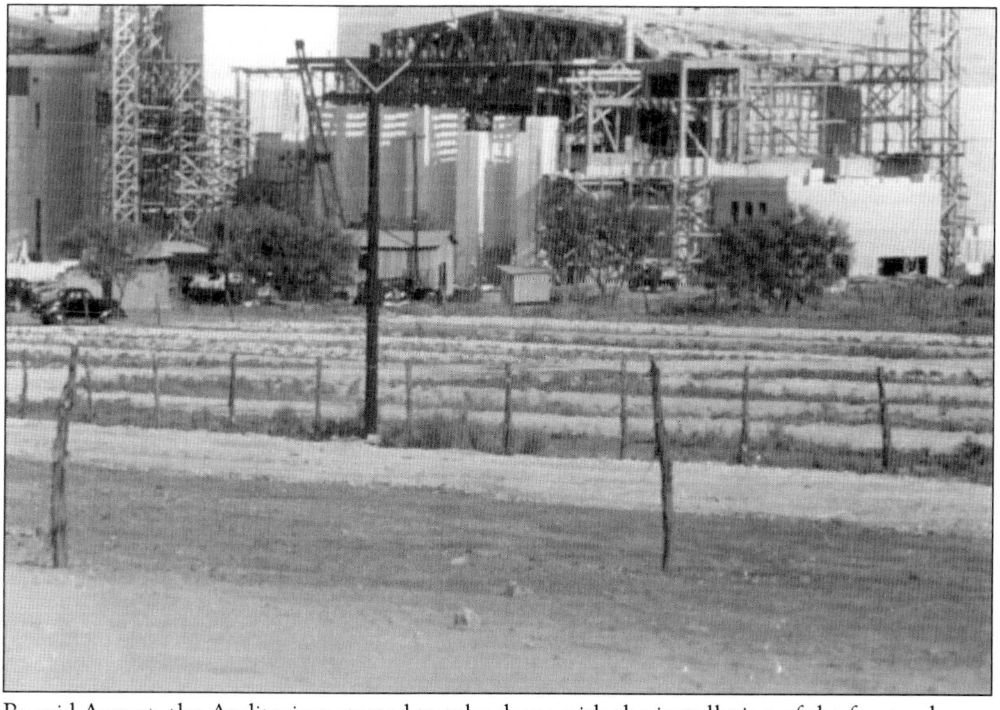

By mid-August, the Auditorium started to take shape with the installation of the front columns and brick. Will Rogers Day was Monday, August 24, 1936. In attendance were his wife, Betty, their two sons, Will Jr. and Jimmie, and old friends from around the country. The most popular attraction was the Will Rogers Memorabilia Room in the West Texas Chamber of Commerce building, but the main honor was the naming of the permanent exposition buildings, which would henceforth be known as the Will Rogers Memorial Center. (FWPL.)

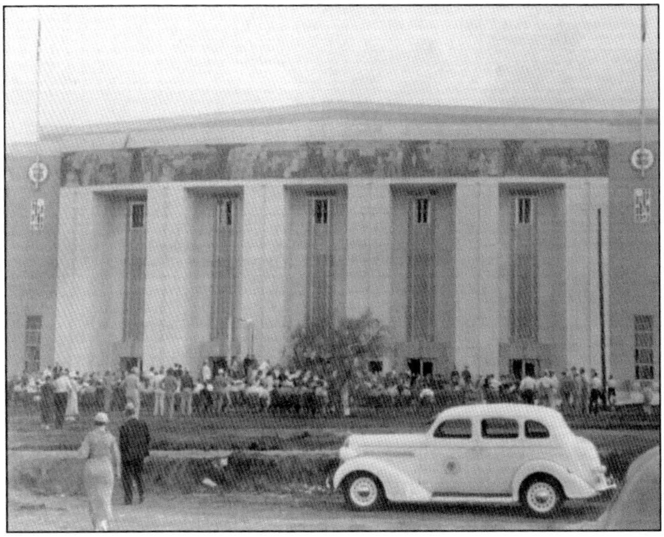

The Coliseum was dedicated on Monday, September 21, 1936, despite the fact that it was not 100 percent finished. Present for the grand occasion were Horatio B. Hackett, assistant PWA administrator from Washington, DC; Julian Montgomery, state PWA director; C.A. Johnson, assistant state director; Uel Stephens, chief engineer for the PWA; Walter Koons, chief counsel; Harlan Mayes, chief finance examiner; and, of course, Amon G. Carter. (FWPL.)

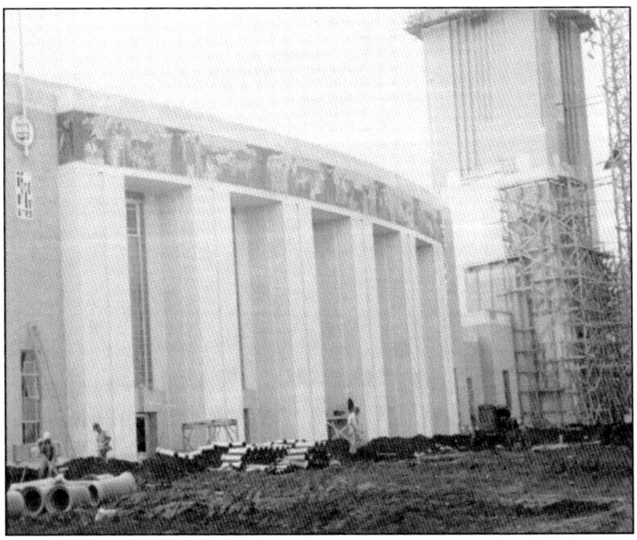

By October 1, 1936, the tile frieze was installed. At the time of installation, the friezes over the Coliseum and Auditorium were said to be the largest in the country. Keeping in theme with the Centennial, they depict scenes from the history of Texas and its economic products. Samuel Peters Ziegler, head of the art department at Texas Christian University, submitted drawings for the friezes but was rejected. But it is possible that Ziegler guided Kenneth Dale from the Mosaic Tile Company in Dale's version of the final design. (FWPL.)

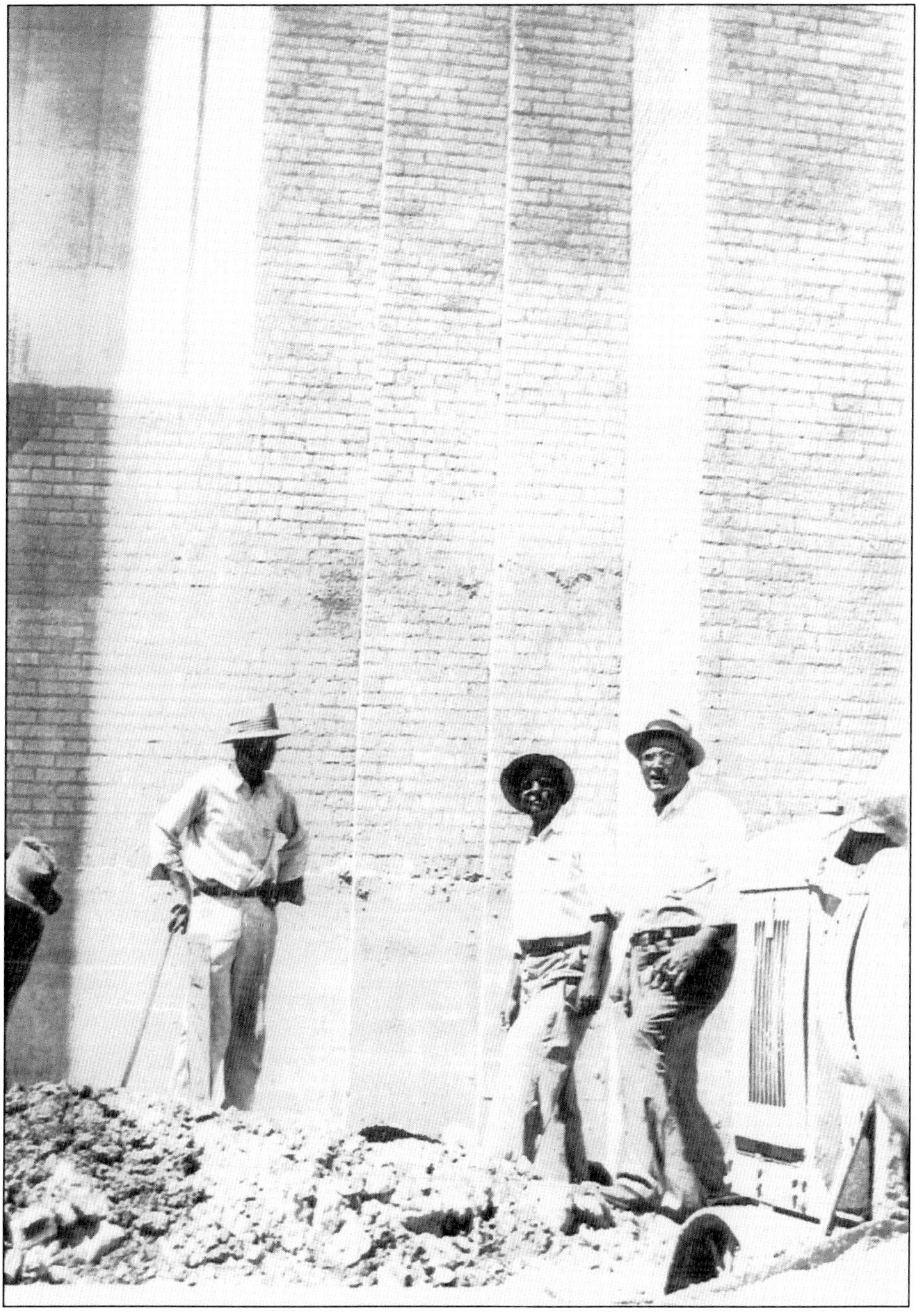

Laborers were in much shorter supply in Fort Worth than expected during the Depression because of the large number of PWA projects at the time. PWA rules stated that people could not work more than eight hours per day or 130 hours per month. Wages were also set by the PWA. Foremen, bricklayers, and metal-lathers earned the highest pay of $1.25 per hour, while first-year apprentices for all trades and two-wheel-loaders earned an hourly rate of 50¢. Skilled workers, such as carpenters, electricians, glaziers, and cement mixers, earned $1 per hour. Unskilled laborers, teamsters, and watchmen were paid 40¢. Water boys and messengers received $12 per week. (Dalton Hoffman.)

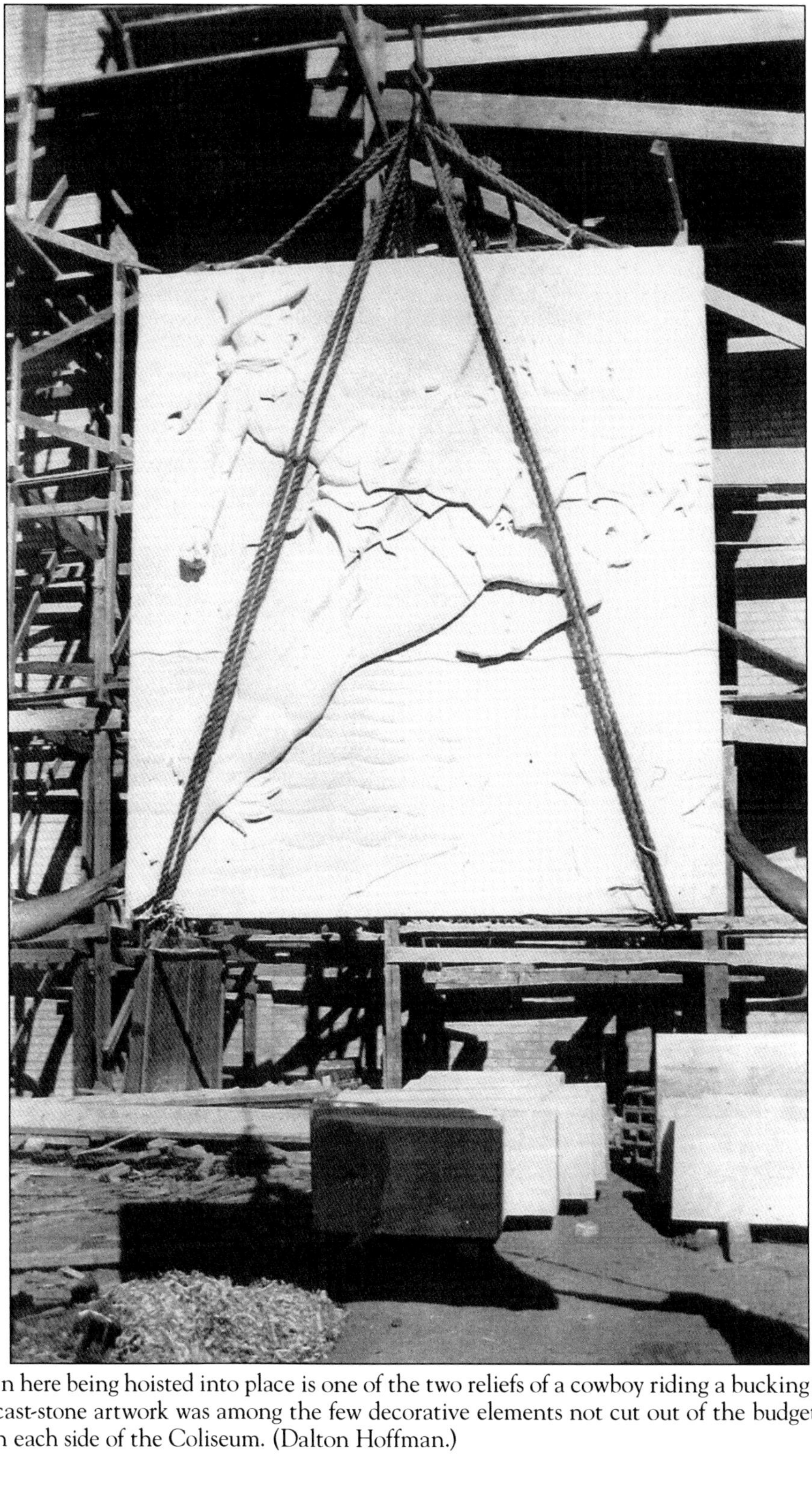

Shown here being hoisted into place is one of the two reliefs of a cowboy riding a bucking horse. The cast-stone artwork was among the few decorative elements not cut out of the budget; they are on each side of the Coliseum. (Dalton Hoffman.)

By October 1, the Tower had its limestone and brick veneer, was in the process of having the glass blocks installed in the window slots, and had a partially installed roof. Three electrical strips are visible in the window openings; they held strips of lightbulbs illuminating the glass blocks and making the Tower visible for miles at night. The highest level was still not enclosed, and the lights were not installed on the top four corners. The tile frieze was installed on the Coliseum but not on the Auditorium. Today, OSHA regulations would prohibit this type of scaffolding, especially the section with the handrail dangling off. (FWPL.)

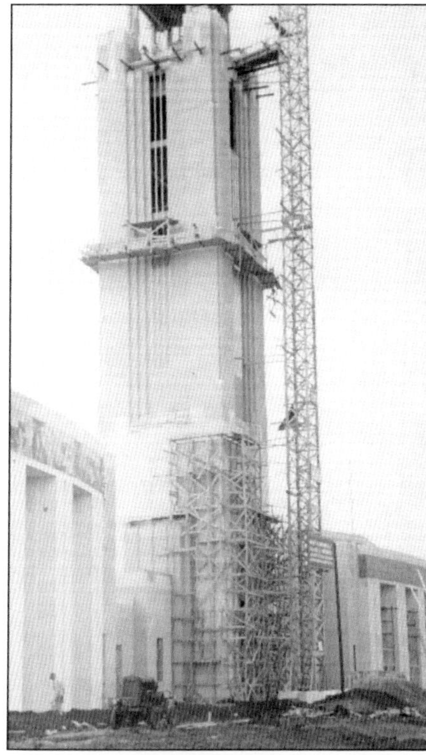

This interior view of the Coliseum shows the exposed steel framework of the dome, which all had to be painted. T.W. Carter Painting and Decorating estimated that it would take 100 days to spray 400 gallons of paint versus the 125 to brush 300 gallons. Seating for the Coliseum was provided by the American Desk and Manufacturing Company of Temple for $19,729.14. On the arena floor, a man uses two horses to pull him as he packs and levels the dirt mixture that pads the concrete floor. The gates covering the chutes at the back were not numbered. (FWPL.)

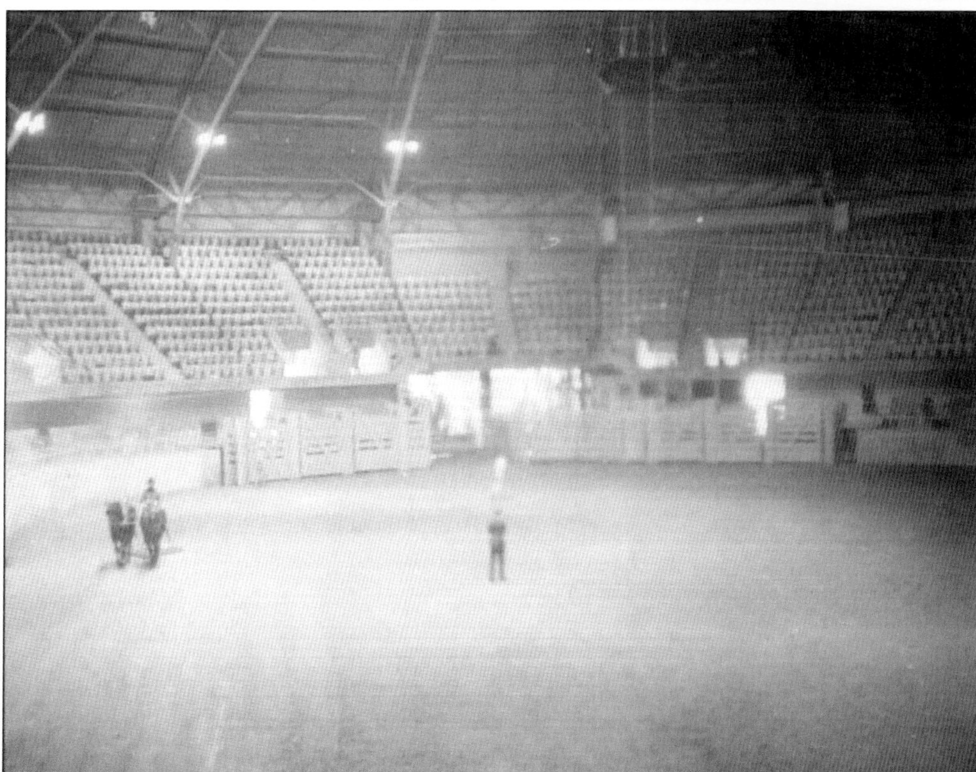

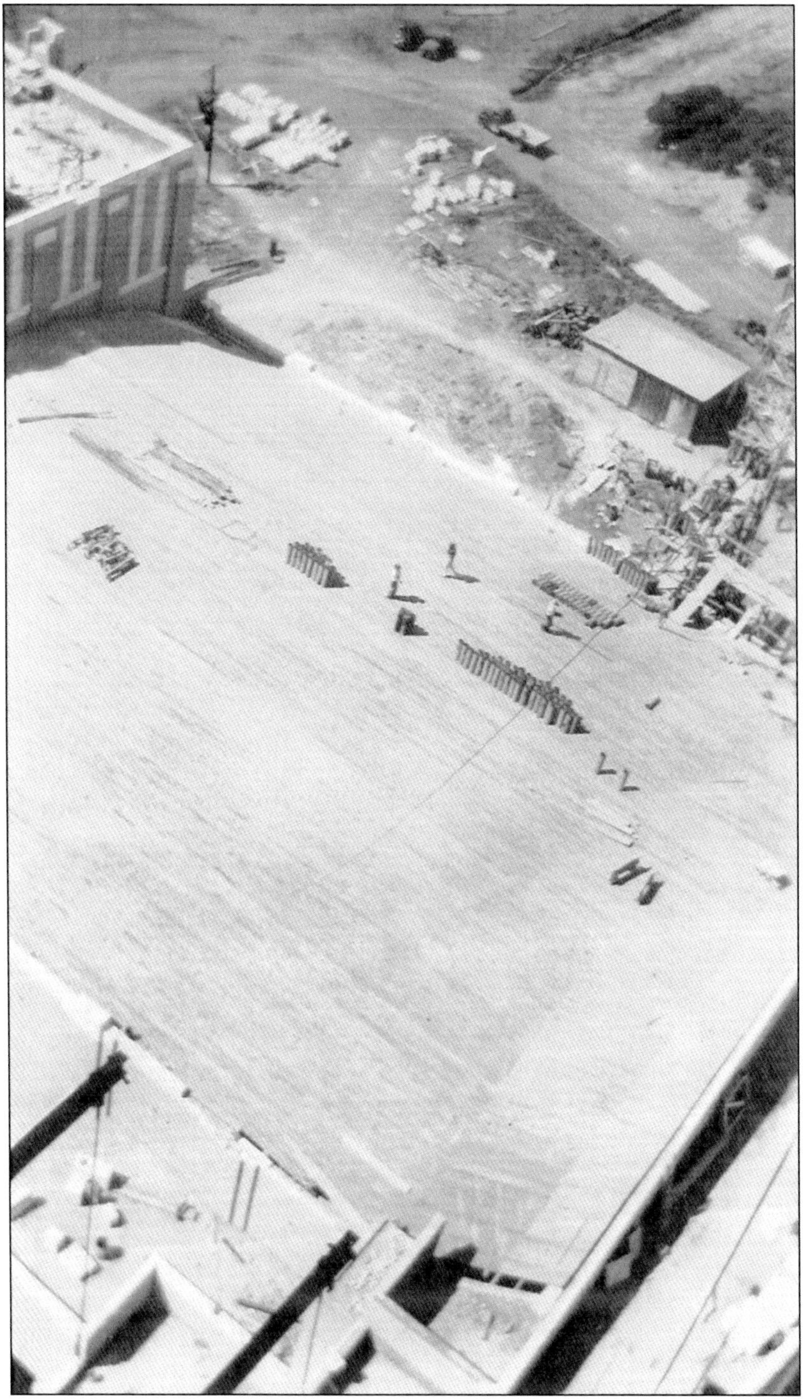

With the wooden decking almost complete on the roof of the Auditorium, the men undoubtedly appreciated the hoist elevators, seen at the bottom right of the roofline. Bundles of the rolled-slate roofing can be seen on the catwalk between the hoist and the roof and lined up on the roof, ready to be installed. The brickwork at the top level appears complete, but the front facade of the building still has scaffolding set up. (Dalton Hoffman.)

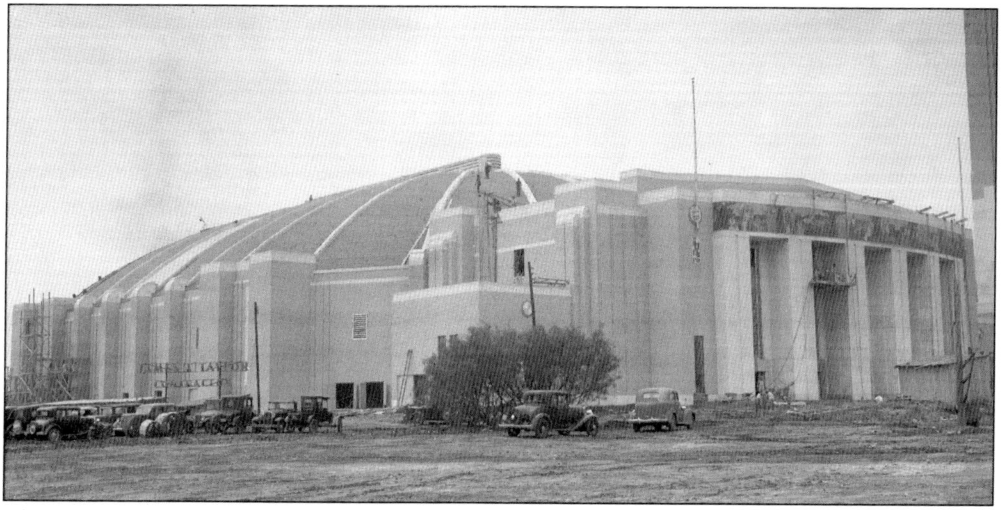

The sign to the left advertises James T. Taylor's construction company. Taylor, from Fort Worth, was the general contractor for the Coliseum, with the second lowest bid of $509,294—Bellows Construction Company from Oklahoma City was $714 less. Each bid submitted for consideration from the city council had to be accompanied with a certified check from a responsible Fort Worth bank or a bond for five percent of the bid, a financial statement from within the past three months, a list of experience, and a statement of equipment owned that would be used on the job. Due to these restrictions, it is possible that Bellows did not qualify. The photograph shows the men climbing up the roof without any form of safety harness and dangling from scaffolding in between the front columns. (FWST.)

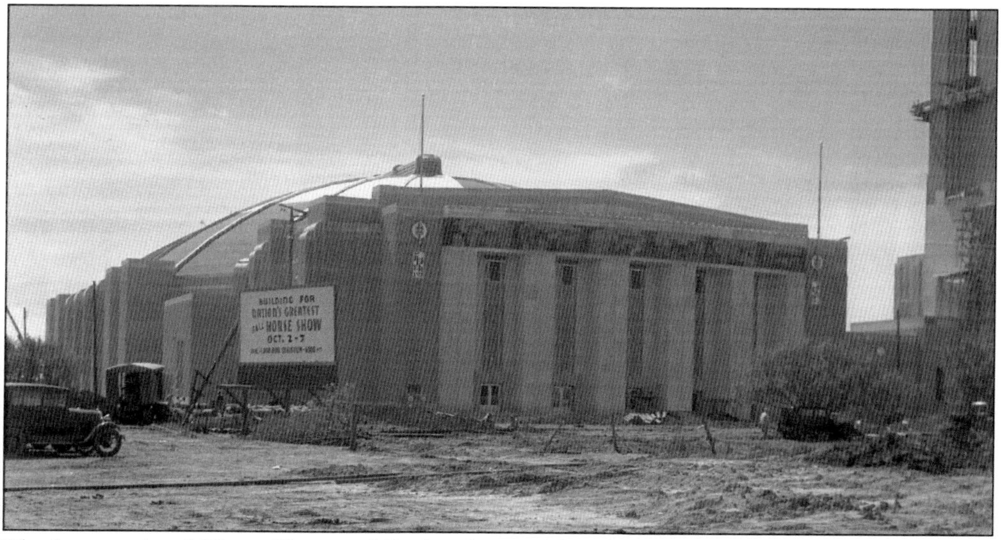

The International Horse Show and Rodeo dates of October 2–7, 1936, were picked when the contract to build was first signed, as the dates did not conflict with other shows around the country, freeing up competitors and vendors. The city began advertising immediately for the show. Along with all available laborers working primarily on this structure instead of the Tower and Auditorium, a request was submitted to the PWA to allow the laborers to work 40 hours per week instead of the maximum of 130 per month. Materials, such as the limestone from Texas quarries and the tile friezes from the Mosaic Tile Company, were also allocated to the Coliseum over the other two structures. (FWST.)

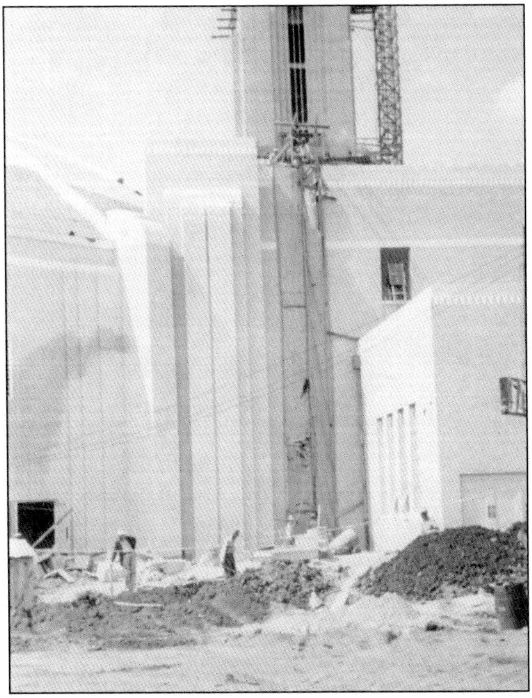

On October 4, 1936, during the horse show and rodeo, men worked over the foyer as they continued to install the Coliseum's roof. Money granted by the PWA came with restrictions, which included building standards for all phases of construction and a completion deadline of December 15, 1936, unless extensions were filed and approved. Knowing that there was little hope of completing the complex due to the shortage of skilled bricklayers, stone masons, plasterers, and cement finishers, and because Texas Quarries, Inc., the provider of the limestone used on all three buildings, could not cut and deliver all the needed stone in time, requests for an extension until January 10 were proposed on December 14. (FWPL.)

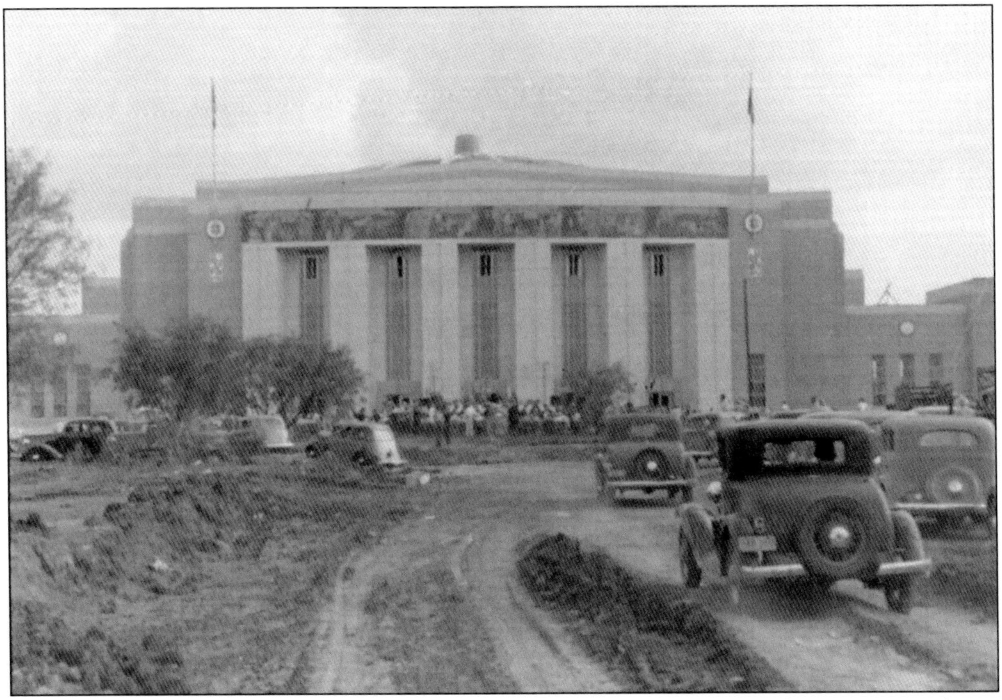

Newspapers reported that there was a "large gathering of Southwestern horse lovers" in attendance at the International Horse Show and Rodeo. Among the attendees were Betty Rogers and Amon G. Carter. The first rider to enter the new arena in the Coliseum was the very popular Paul Whiteman on his white horse, Popcorn. In the true spirit of the event, he rode over to his band and directed them from horseback. (FWSS.)

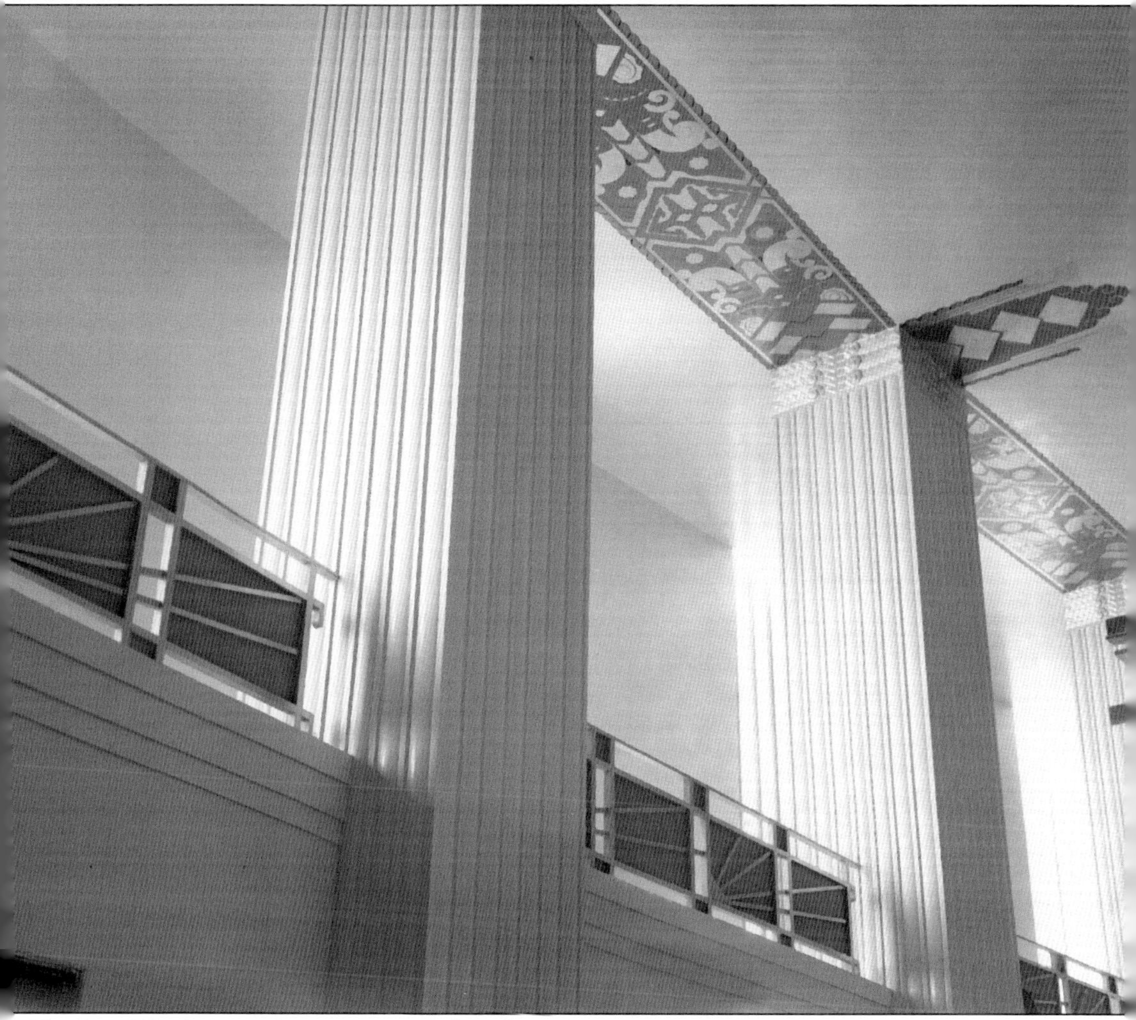

The Fort Worth *Star-Telegram* reported that the walls in the entrance of the Coliseum were "a shade of blue that electrifies without jarring the senses." With the crisp, classic lines of PWA Moderne, the design was simple and perfect at the same time. Aluminum grills, Monel panels, and stylized columns all worked together to create an atmosphere of timeless class. (FWST.)

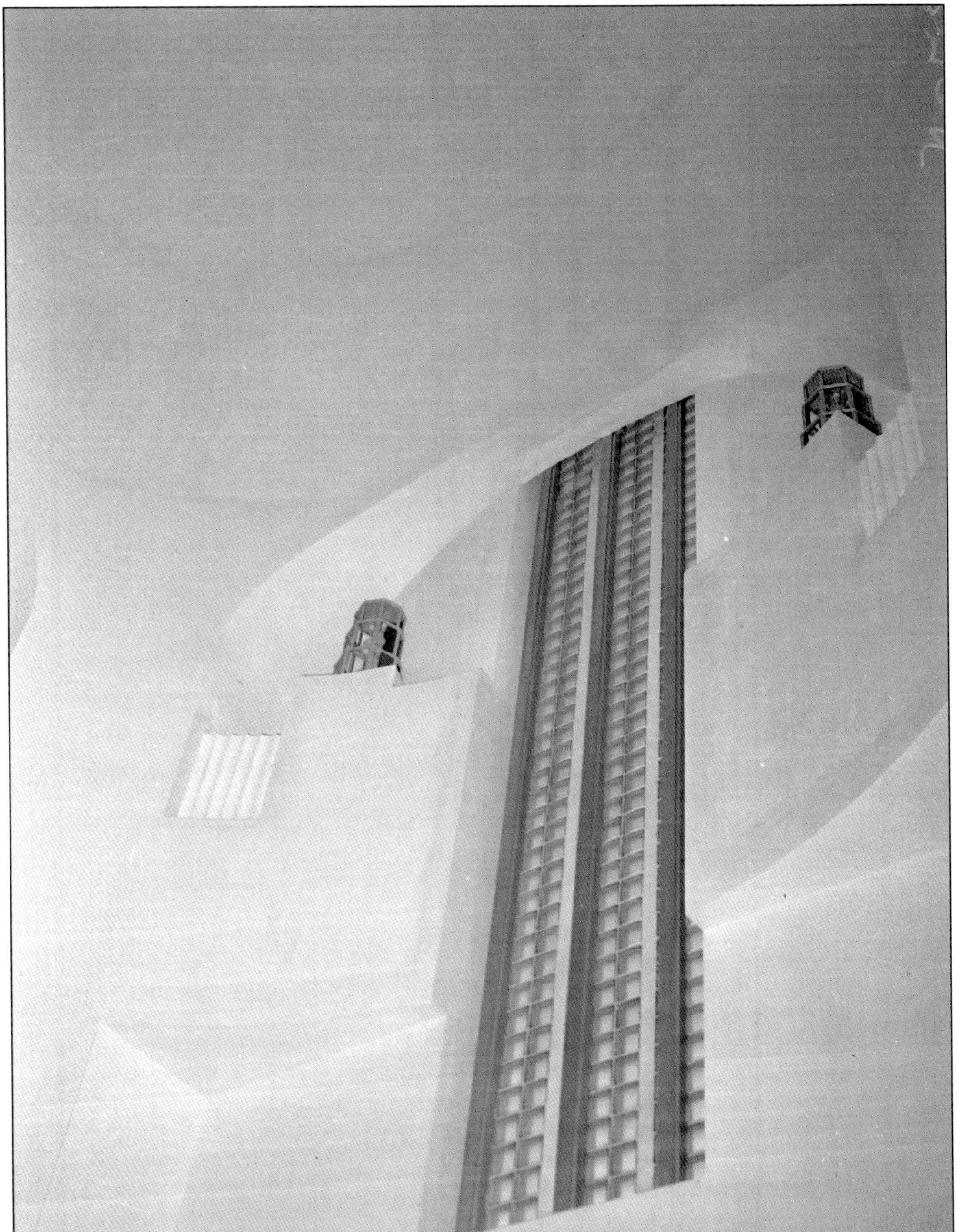

This interior photograph of the Tower from November 1936 shows it looking much the same as it does now, not counting the addition of the Will Rogers bust. Judith Cohen's description says it best: "Decorative elements within the rotunda include classical fluted columns, geometrically patterned air-conditioning vents, and four sets of pyramidal glass-and-aluminum light features. These lanterns, miniaturized replicas of the four gigantic tower lanterns, light the four recessed alcoves cut into the high, rounded walls of the foyer." Added to this are four plaques that quote Mirabeau B. Lamar on education, Lawrence S. Ross on economics, Britain R. Webb on the law, and the Texas Constitution on government. (FWST.)

Billy Rose tried to get a zeppelin from Germany to bring 50 "good-looking girls" from New York to Fort Worth for the grand opening. This never materialized, but on November 5, 1936, the Goodyear blimp *Resolute* circled 700 feet above the grounds. While people below were taking photographs of the blimp, a photographer in the blimp took photographs of the Centennial grounds and the almost complete Will Rogers Coliseum and Auditorium. (FWST.)

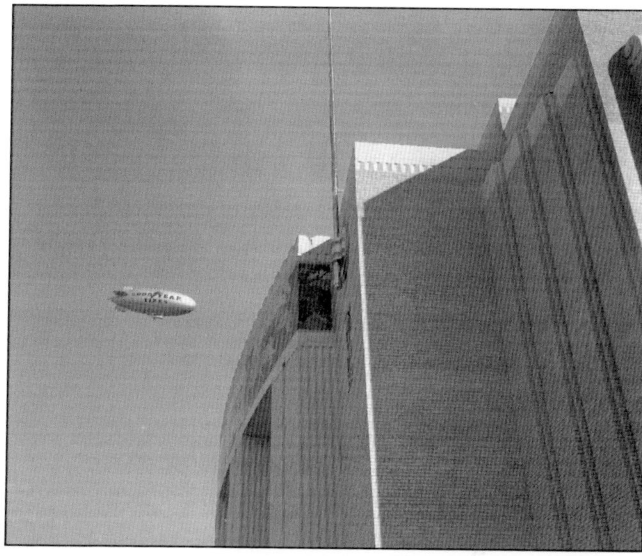

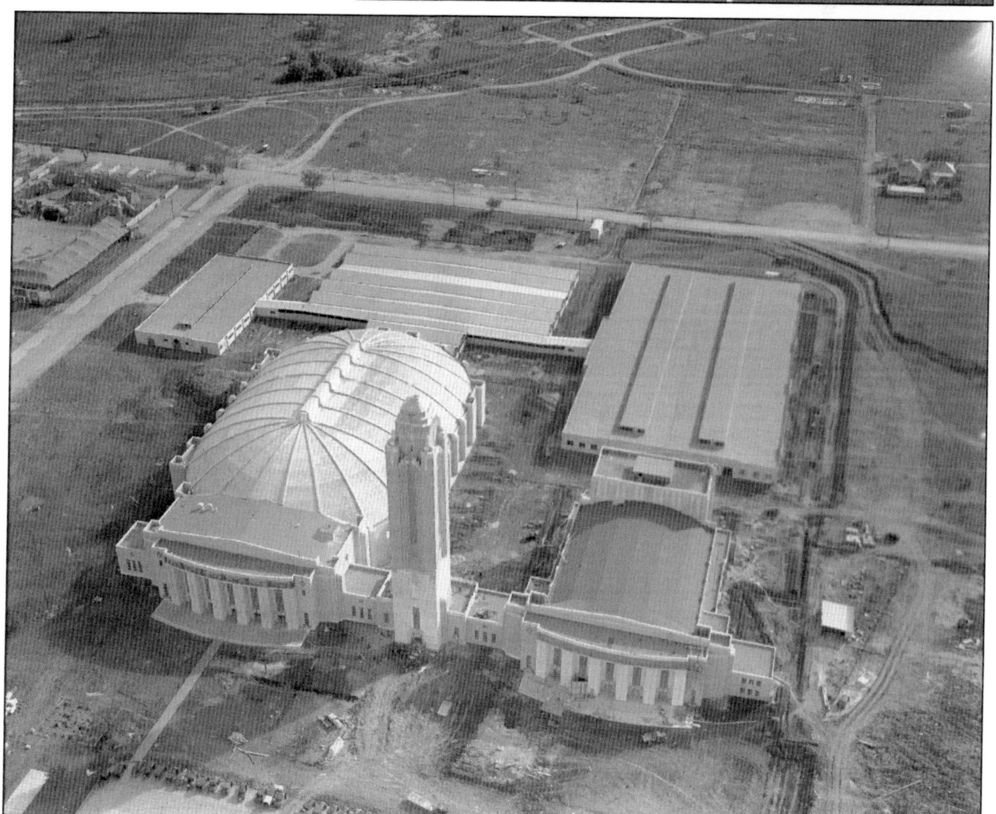

This is one of the photographs taken aboard the *Resolute*. Contractors were informed that they would be penalized $500 for every day the construction was not finished after August 1, 1936, although the date and amount were later changed and there is no evidence that the fines were imposed. Working with the city could not have been easy, as it was ultimately in charge of accepting and rejecting bids all the way through November 1936. The official dedication was held on December 23, 1936. (FWST.)

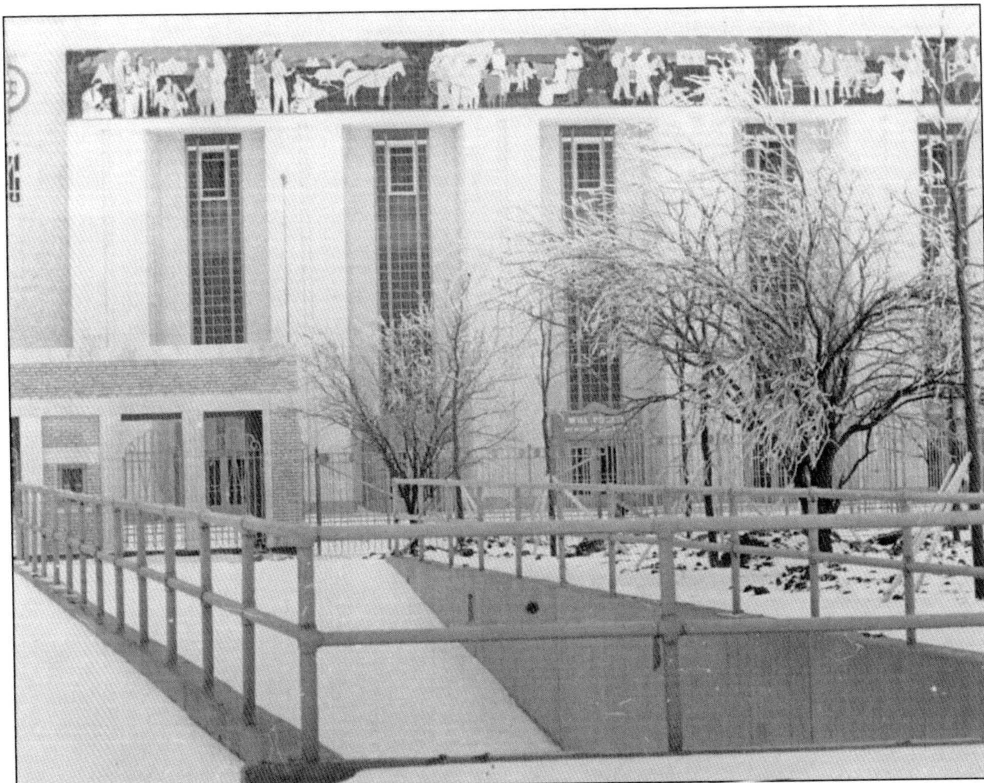

There were two underground walkways for pedestrians to go from the complex to the parking lot located under the newly expanded Lancaster Avenue. The parking lot, which was partly located on the grounds that later became the Amon G. Carter Museum of American Art, charged 25¢ for event parking. Pictured in January 1937, after the building was declared complete, the complex was dusted in a coat of snow, making the flattened PWA Moderne–styled columns and tile frieze sparkle in the sun. (Both, FWPL.)

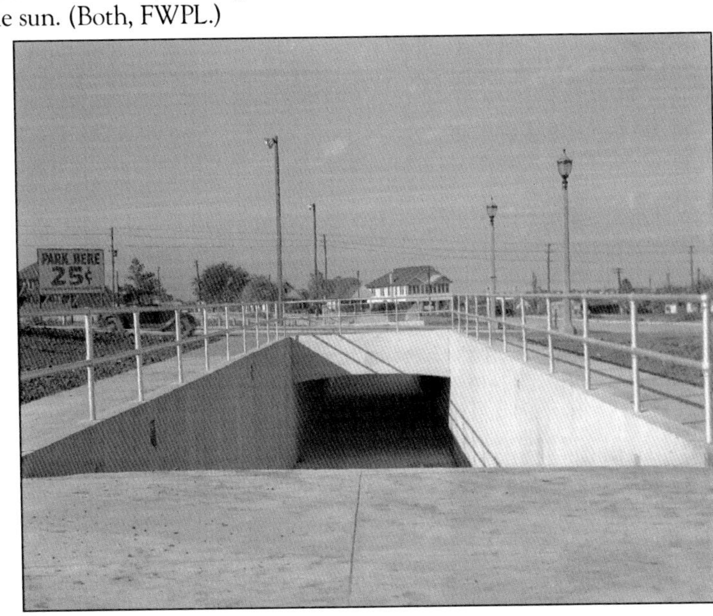

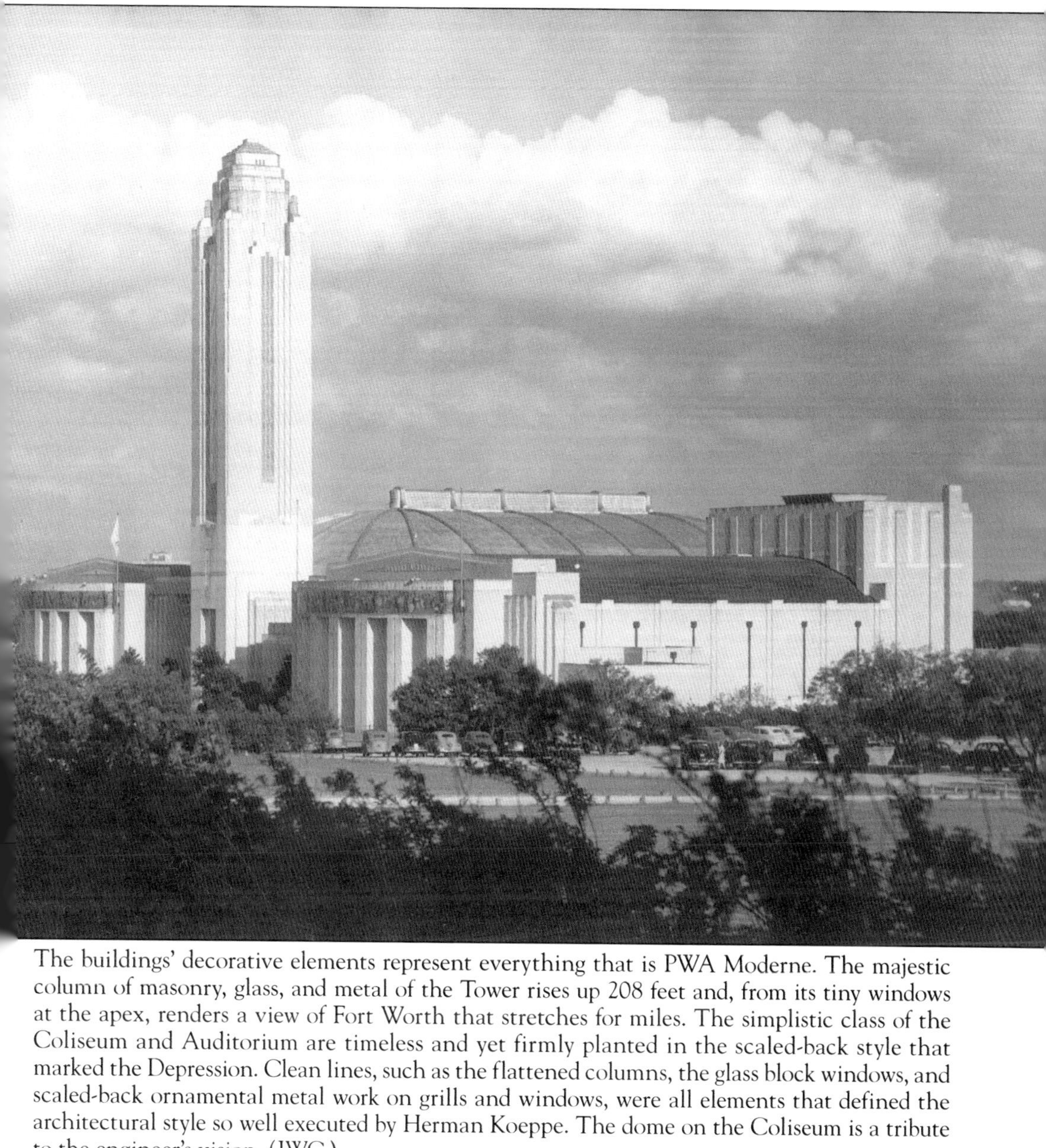

The buildings' decorative elements represent everything that is PWA Moderne. The majestic column of masonry, glass, and metal of the Tower rises up 208 feet and, from its tiny windows at the apex, renders a view of Fort Worth that stretches for miles. The simplistic class of the Coliseum and Auditorium are timeless and yet firmly planted in the scaled-back style that marked the Depression. Clean lines, such as the flattened columns, the glass block windows, and scaled-back ornamental metal work on grills and windows, were all elements that defined the architectural style so well executed by Herman Koeppe. The dome on the Coliseum is a tribute to the engineer's vision. (JWC.)

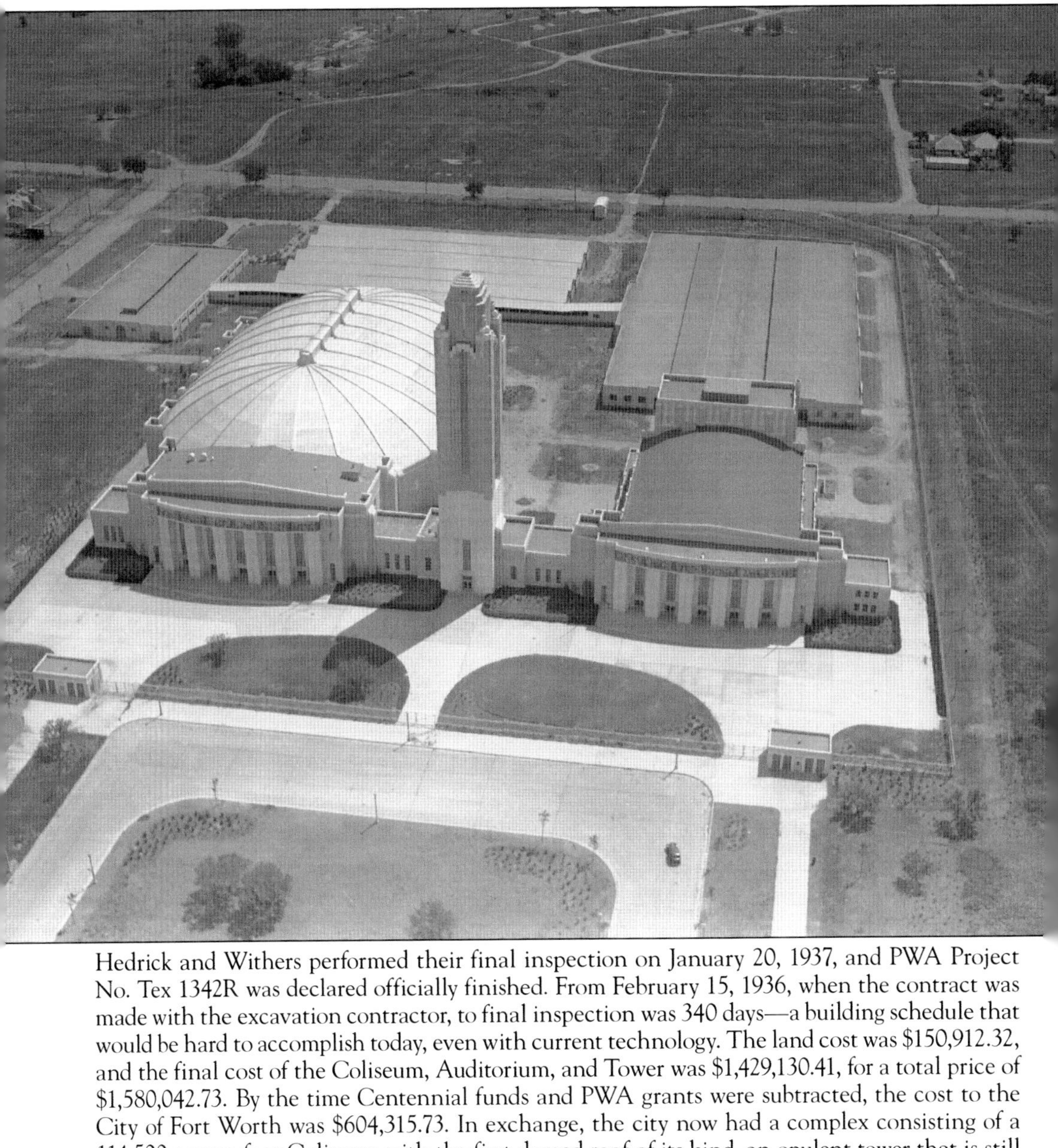

Hedrick and Withers performed their final inspection on January 20, 1937, and PWA Project No. Tex 1342R was declared officially finished. From February 15, 1936, when the contract was made with the excavation contractor, to final inspection was 340 days—a building schedule that would be hard to accomplish today, even with current technology. The land cost was $150,912.32, and the final cost of the Coliseum, Auditorium, and Tower was $1,429,130.41, for a total price of $1,580,042.73. By the time Centennial funds and PWA grants were subtracted, the cost to the City of Fort Worth was $604,315.73. In exchange, the city now had a complex consisting of a 114,500-sqaure-foot Coliseum with the first domed roof of its kind, an opulent tower that is still one of the most recognized landmarks of the city, and a 46,000-square-foot auditorium with the best available equipment for performances of all kinds. It is a monument to the determination of all who were a part of the construction. (FWST.)

Four

Cowboys and Culture

The first Fort Worth Fat Stock Show was held in 1896 under the oak trees along the side of Marine Creek. Town cattlemen Charles C. French and Charles McFarland saw the need to encourage meatpacking industries and cattle businesses to come to Fort Worth. The first show was pitiful at best, but it led to great things. By 1917, the show became known as the Southwestern Exposition and Livestock Show, and the following year, it included the world's first Western indoor rodeo in the North Side Coliseum. When the 1942 show ended, the question of whether or not there would be a show in 1943 because of the war was on everyone's mind. As it turned out, nature made the decision when days of torrential rain broke the Trinity River's natural dams and sent a five-foot wall of water followed by a seven-footer sweeping through the stockyards. The devastating damage amounted to over $100,000 to the North Side Coliseum, and all of the past records and awards were swept away or buried in the mud. The decision was made to move the show to the west side, into the Will Rogers Coliseum and barn facilities.

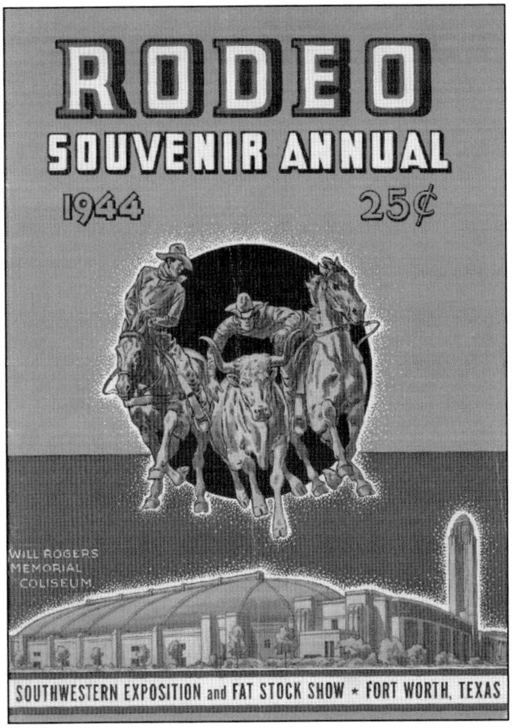

From March 10 to 19, 1944, the Southwestern Exposition and Fat Stock Show was held at the Coliseum for the first time, with a prize purse of $23,275. The producer was Verne Elliot, the codirector of "The Last Frontier" at the Centennial celebration. The president of the organization was John C. Burns, and Amon Carter was vice president. Along with entertainment, refreshments and dancing were offered at the Pioneer Palace—the venue left over from the Centennial celebration. (FWSS.)

Gene Autry was the first entertainer at the 1944 Fort Worth Stock Show. Shown here with his horse, Champion, Autry said that Will Rogers had encouraged him to pursue his musical career. Autry was working as a relief circuit worker at a telegraph office when Rogers came in and heard him singing. He arranged for Autry to meet people in the business, and his career was started. In 1946, Autry became the rodeo manager for a few years, replacing Verne Elliot. (FWSS.)

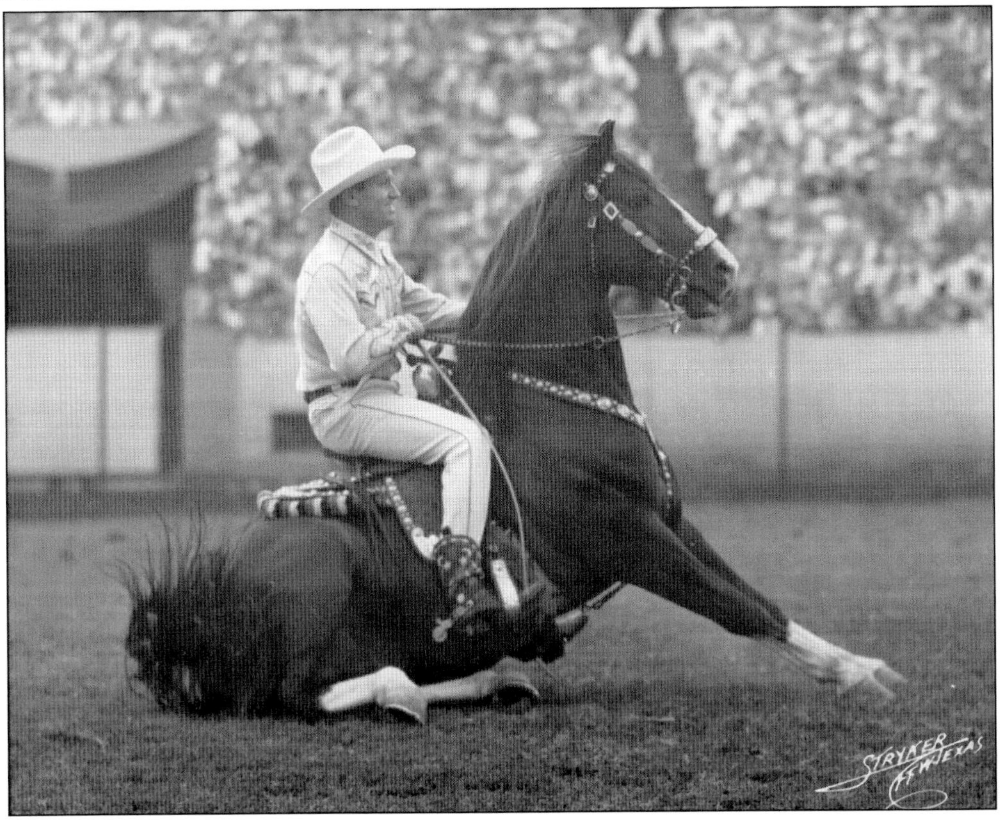

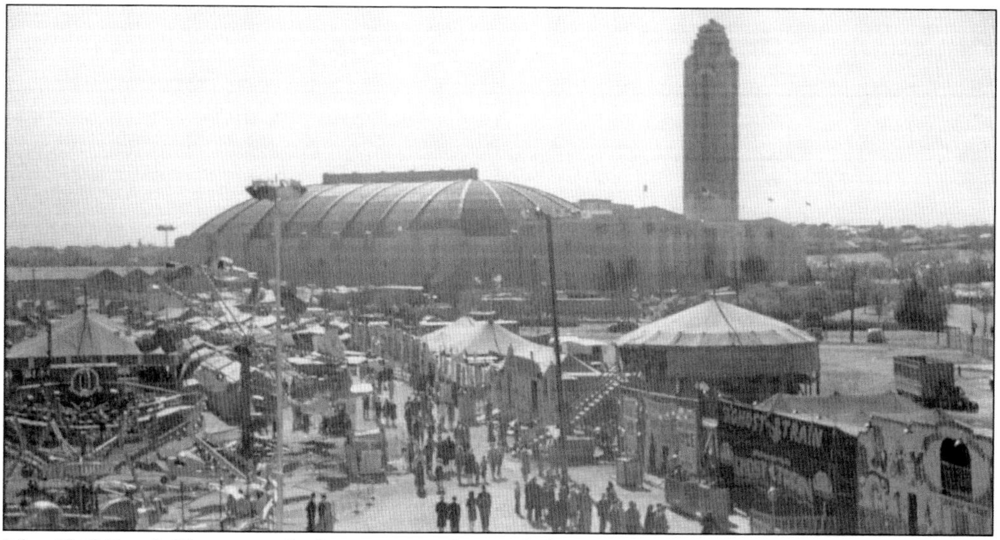

The 1947 Stock Show was the beginning of several changes. W.R. Watt became the president, a position he would fill until his death in 1977; the show moved from March to the end of January to create a better show circuit and to benefit cattle sales; and the financial structure of the organization changed, making it free from financial control from any other entity. Most Stock Show attendees were not aware of these changes; they just wanted to enjoy the show and the midway. (FWSS.)

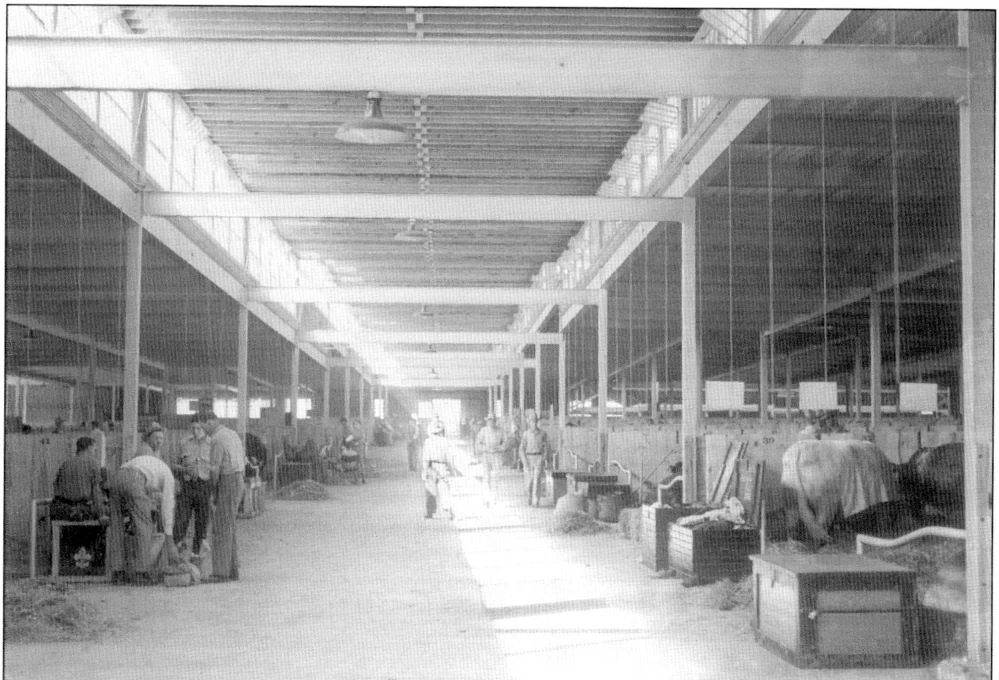

When the complex was constructed in 1936, a horse show building and horse and stock buildings were also constructed for $207,733.79. Later, these buildings would prove to be too small and inefficient for the needs of all the vendors and exhibitors, but they served their purpose in the early years. (FWST.)

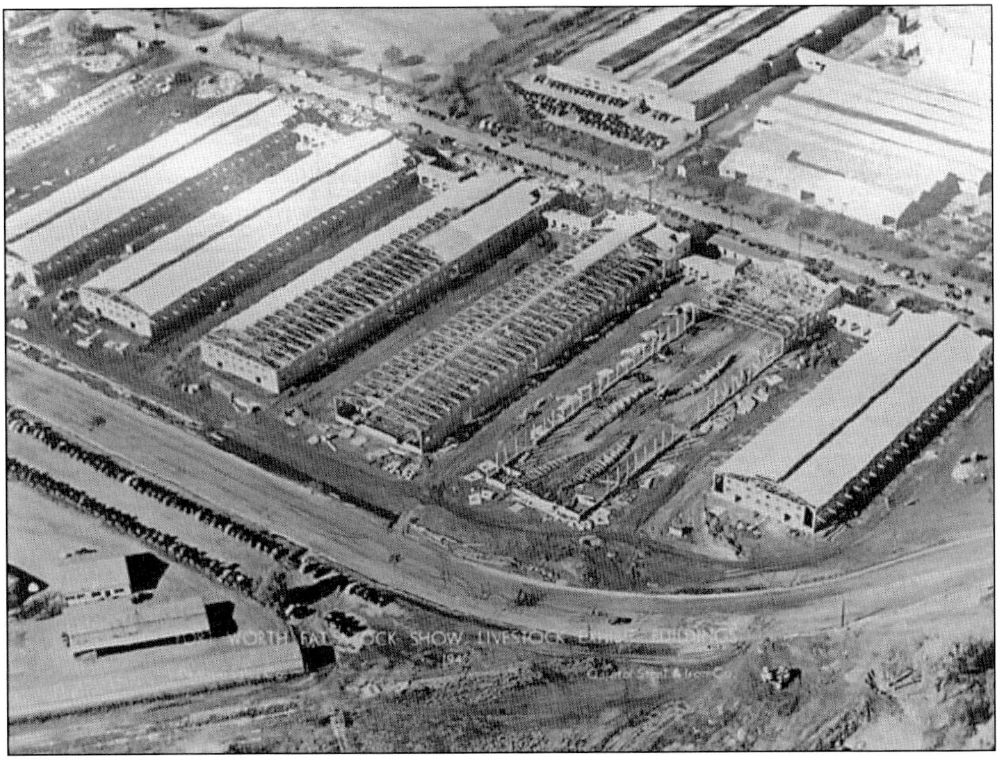

The days of setting up tents and weathering the brutal conditions of snow and ice came to an end with the addition of six new stock barns in 1948. Measuring 100 feet by 400 feet, the new facilities, connected by covered walkways, also came with gas heat, running water, ventilation, and covered unloading areas. The progression of the building phases is seen in this photograph taken at the request of Capitol Steel and Iron, who supplied the materials. (Capital Steel and Iron, LLC.)

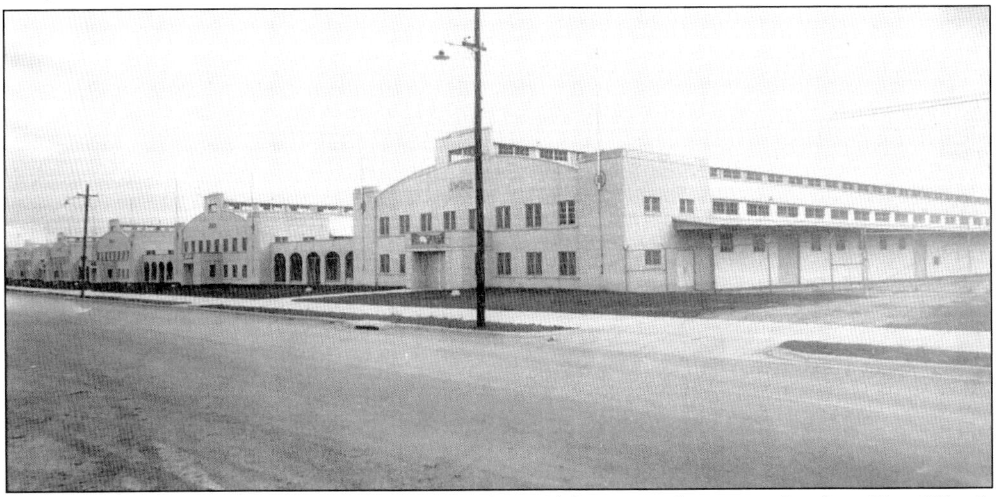

Built with municipal bonds, the barns were the collaborative design work of six Fort Worth architects, including Wyatt C. Hedrick, who had been the main architect of record in 1936. Also in 1948, the Fort Worth City Council declared that Will Rogers Coliseum would be the permanent home of the Stock Show. (Dalton Hoffman.)

On January 29, 1949, ten-year-old Rodney Spencer proudly showed his Reserve Champion shorthorn bull, Privee Peter Standard. By 1955, there were almost as many youths entering the Stock Show through organizations such as the 4-H club and Future Farmers of America (FFA), as there were adults. Young Rodney's legs are barely longer than the bull's, but the bull is significantly shorter than him. (FWSS.)

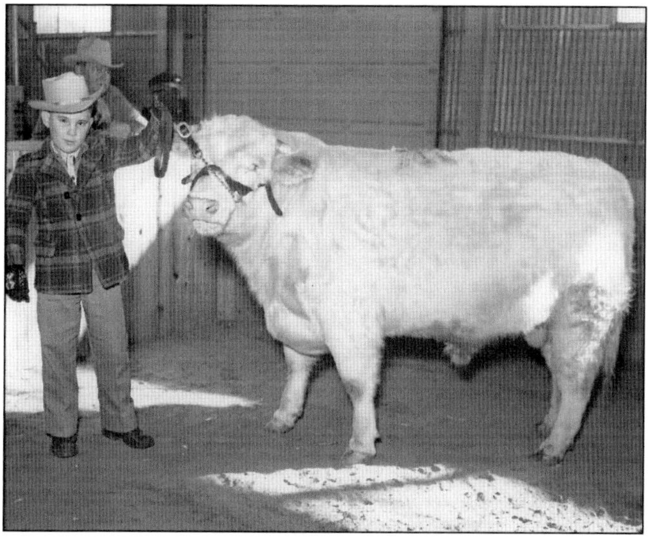

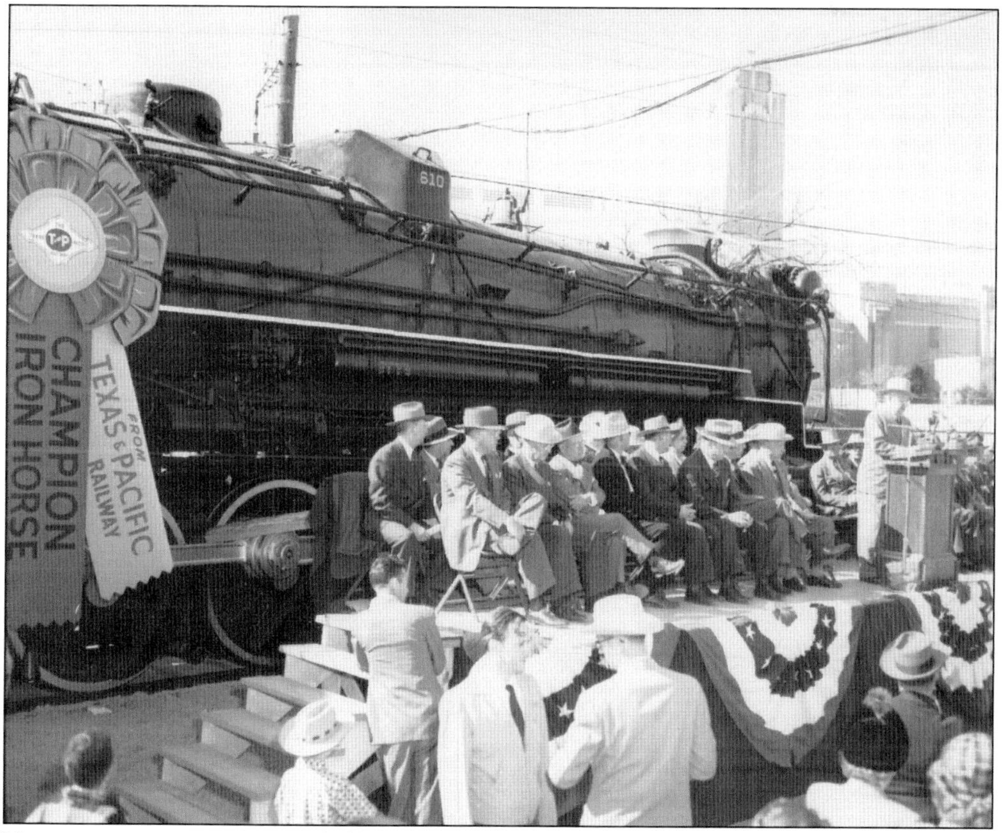

Hoping to continue to attract children, the Stock Show dedicated January 26, 1951, as Children's Day. The Texas & Pacific Railway (T&P) donated a 23-year-old locomotive known as No. 610, and it was promptly named the *Will Rogers*. It arrived on its own newly installed set of lines and rested just west of the Pioneer Palace. T&P officials presented the train to the show and its children and stayed to give tours of it. Ever-present Amon Carter is on stage, to the right of the presenter. (Dalton Hoffman.)

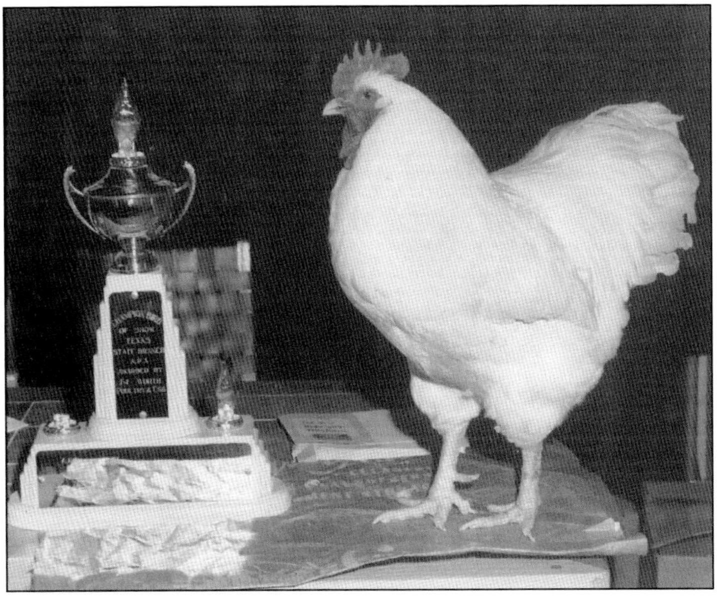

The 1952 Champion Bird of Show was a White Plymouth Rock owned by Carl Kelly of Stafford, Kansas. Livestock includes any animal raised for the home or farm. Cattle and horses are not the only judged categories; there is fierce competition in the rabbit, turkey, sheep, and goat divisions. (FWSS.)

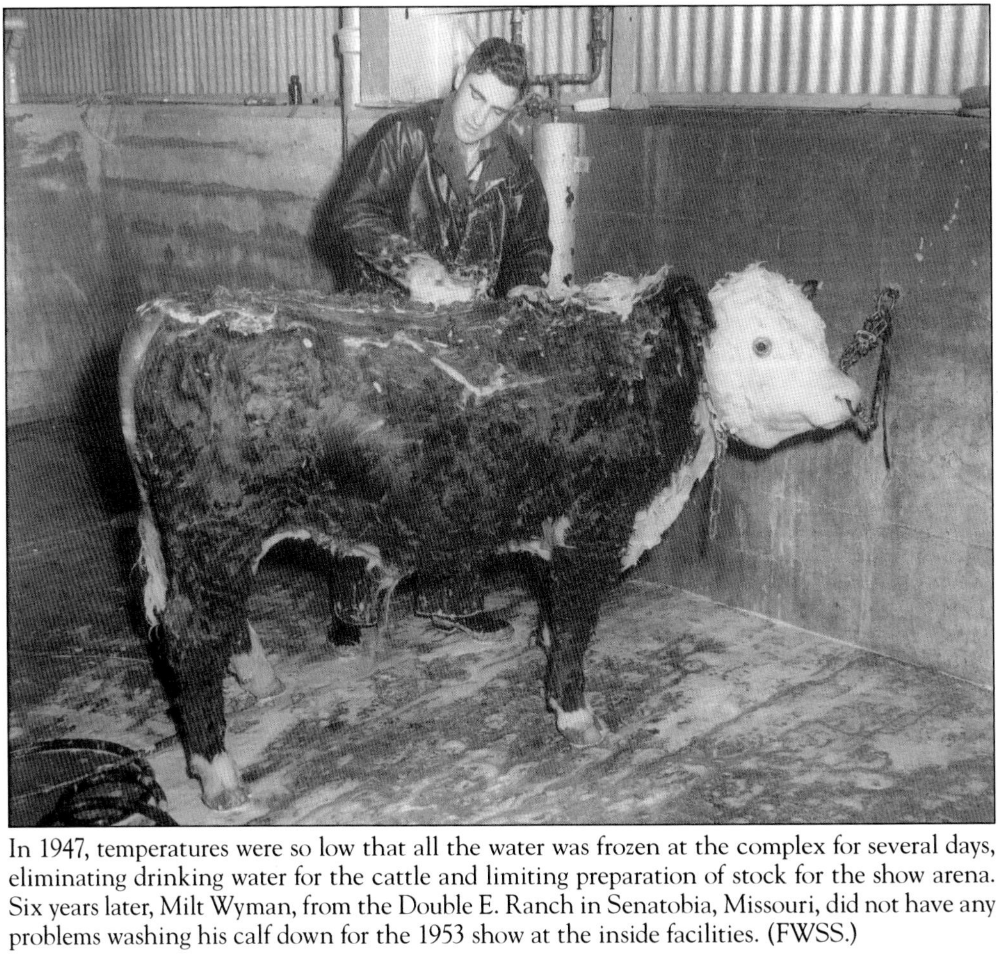

In 1947, temperatures were so low that all the water was frozen at the complex for several days, eliminating drinking water for the cattle and limiting preparation of stock for the show arena. Six years later, Milt Wyman, from the Double E. Ranch in Senatobia, Missouri, did not have any problems washing his calf down for the 1953 show at the inside facilities. (FWSS.)

Exhibitors set up their merchandise under tents until the early 1950s. After many years of enduring the weather without being able to use public facilities, they were finally moved into a temporary space between Cattle Building No. 1 and the Sheep Building. (FWSS.)

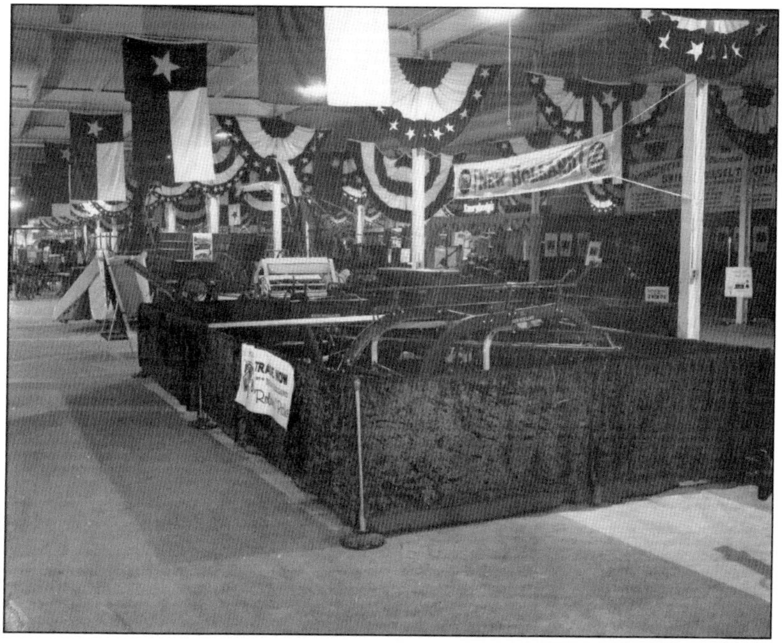

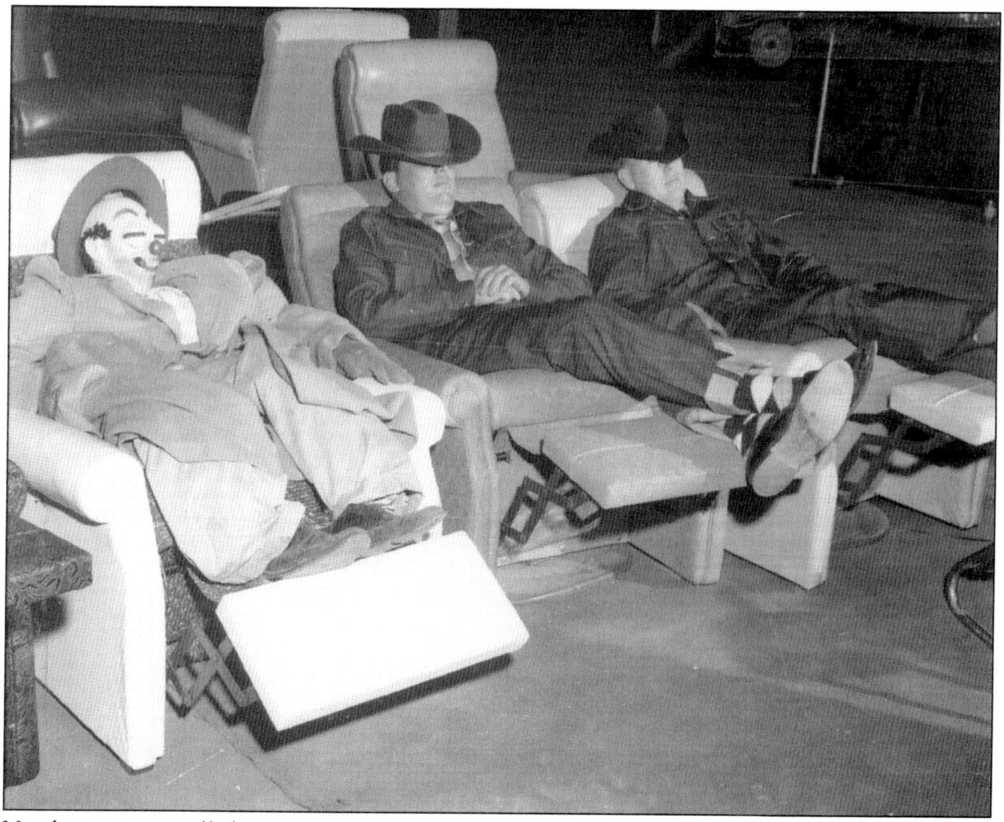

Vendors came in all shapes and sizes, with many different items to sell, such as tractors, farm equipment, cattle feed, and Western attire. Some vendors, like La-Z-Boy, appealed to everyone and allowed exhibitors and attendees of the rodeo to get some much-needed rest. (FWSS.)

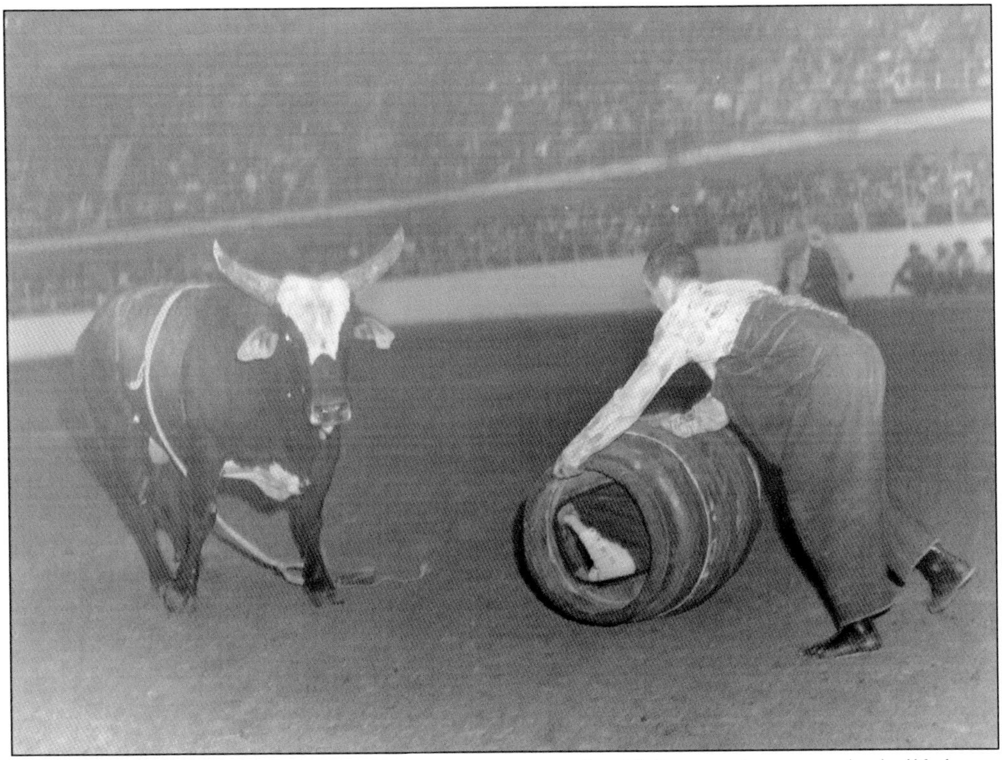

By the mid-1950s, clowns were not just entertaining crowds with humor, they were also bullfighters. Clay Reynolds wrote that they were "essential for the safety of competing cowboys during the bull-riding event. Familiar with the habits of the animals they work with, bullfighting clowns taunt and tempt bulls into extraordinary displays of temper, making the event all the more thrilling." Two clowns are pictured here. One of them is inside the barrel. (FWSS.)

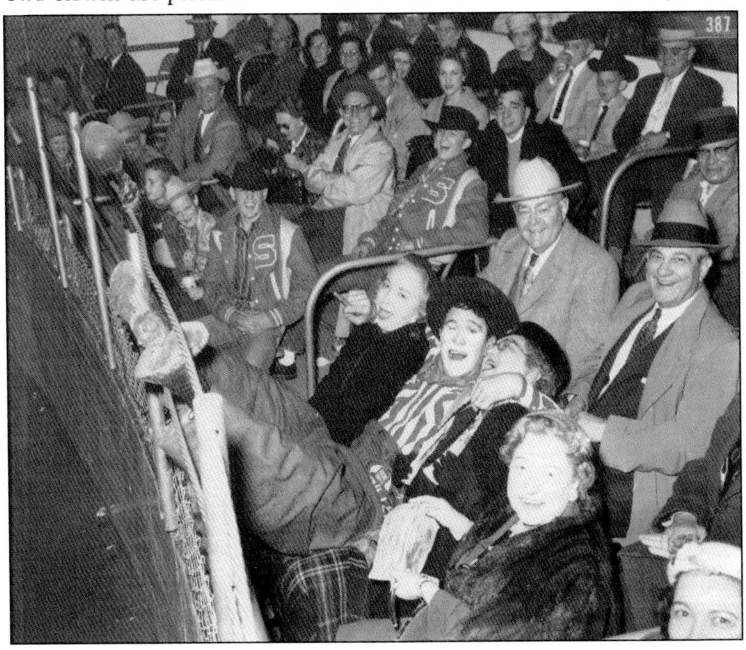

There are only 156 box seats at the Coliseum, and they are highly treasured. People have been known to wait as long as 20 years to purchase them, but they are virtually impossible to obtain, as they are generally handed down within families. Box members not only get the ringside experience, which often includes a little tossed-up dirt, but they often get unexpected visitors. (FWSS.)

A young Tom Watt Jr. shakes the hand of Roy Rogers during the 1958 Stock Show. Rogers and Dale Evans were guests at NBC's *Dinah Shore Chevy Show* on February 2, 1958, which was broadcast live from the Coliseum. Watt Jr. went on to be the president of the organization when his father passed away in 1977, serving until 2010. (FWSS.)

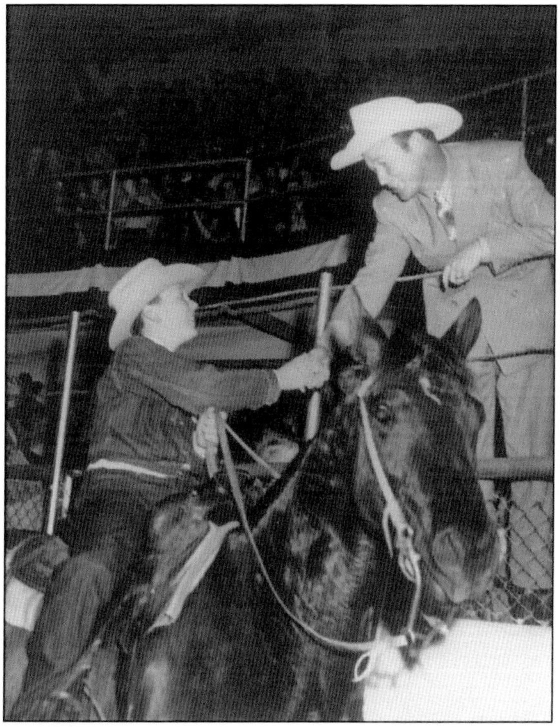

In the barn designs, a single span reached the whole width of the barn so all the available room could be used. This interior photograph of Cattle Barn No. 2 shows the advantage of the open design and the metal trusses that make up the roof. Visible also are the clear panels that let in light and provided ventilation. Among the many participants at the 1958 show was Louisiana State University, whose sign is visible on the far right wall. (FWSS.)

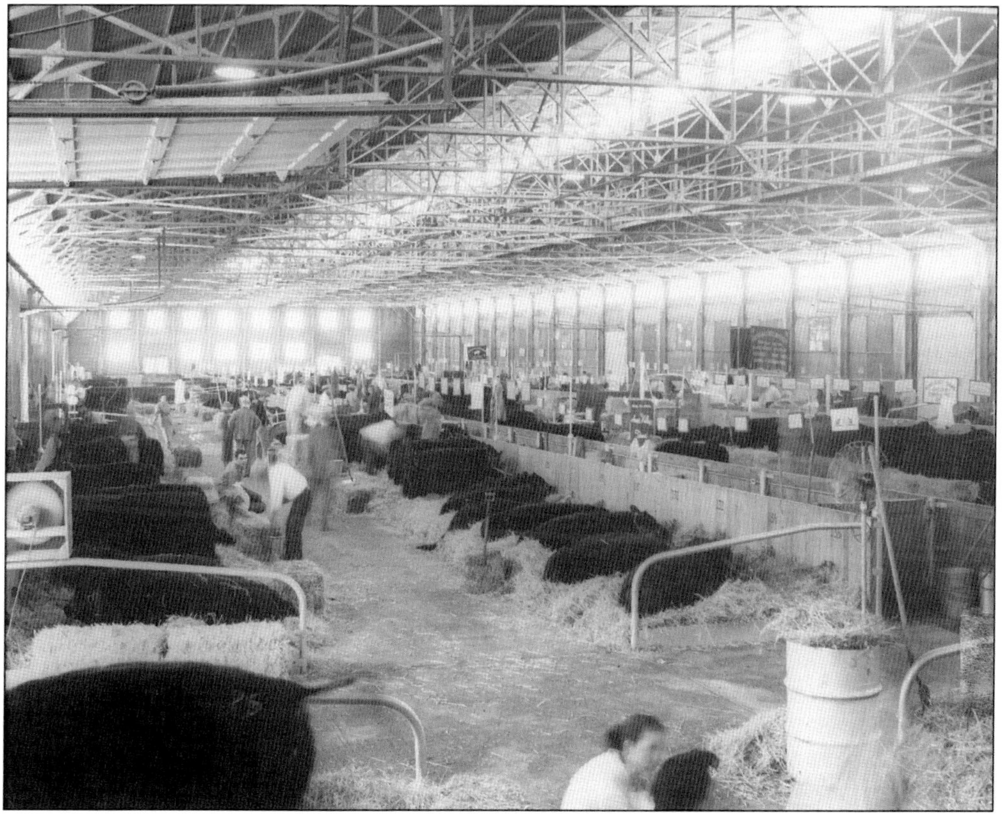

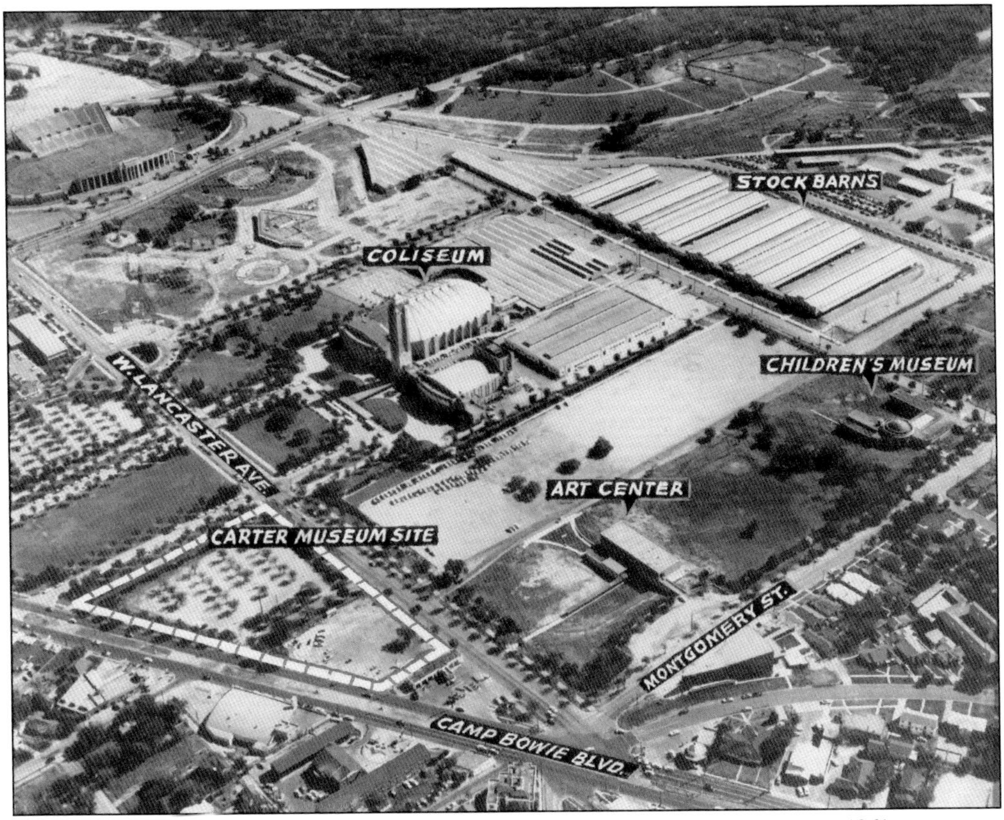

In this aerial study executed for the Amon Carter Museum before its construction in 1961, expansion of the Will Rogers Complex due to the Stock Show is visible. Added to the initial buildings are a series of barns that overflowed onto the Centennial grounds. Visible in this shot are the Pioneer Palace, which was still being used; the remains of Casa Mañana's stage; the cleared housing area once occupied by the bomber plant workers; and the beginnings of the Fort Worth Museum of Science and History. (ACM.)

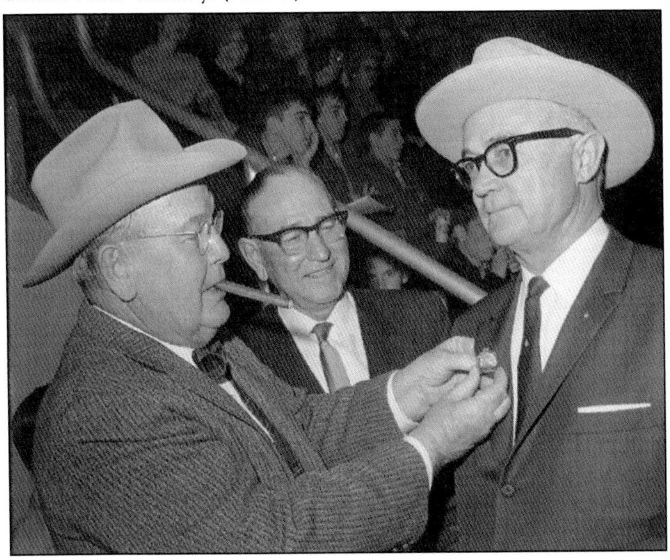

At one of the rodeos in the 1960s, W.R. "Billy Bob" Watt, the president and manager of the Shock Show, pins a visitors badge on to Lt. Gov. Preston Smith, one of many notable figures who attended the show. In the background, the audience is much more entertained with the rodeo than the political figure beside them. (FWSS.)

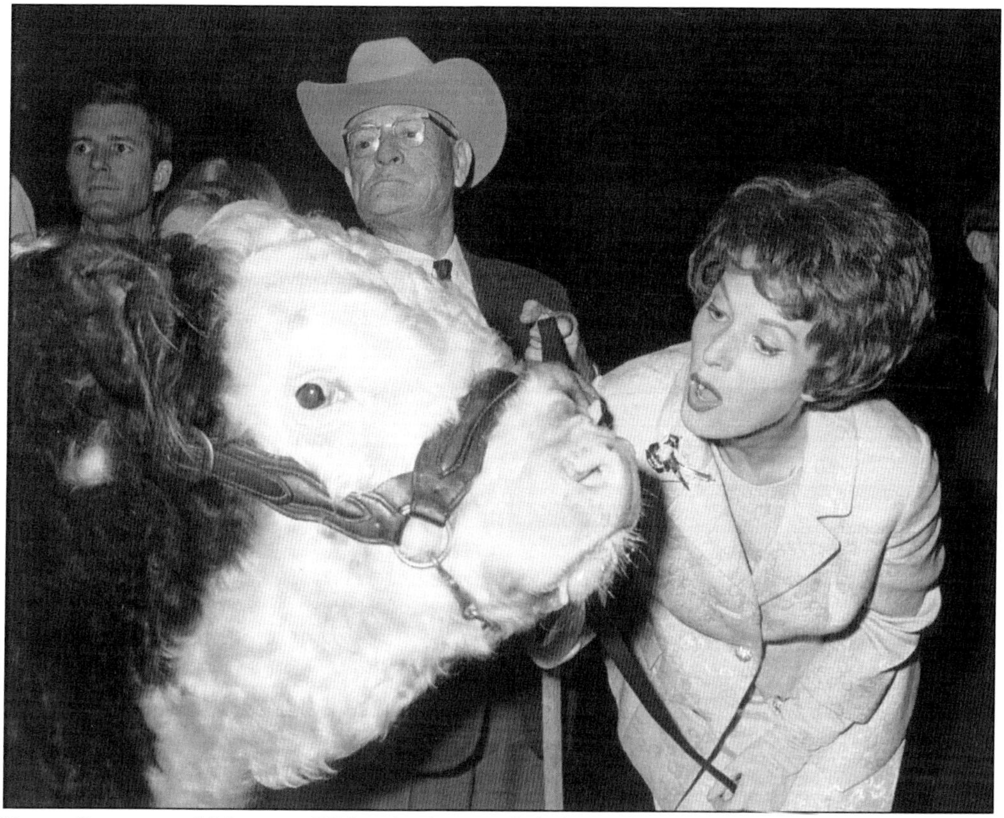

Jimmy Stewart and Maureen O'Hara both attended the 70th Southwestern Exposition and Fat Stock Show in 1966. They were in Fort Worth for the premiere of their movie *A Rare Breed*, about the arrival of the Hereford breed in Texas during the 1880s. Shown here, O'Hara seems quite comfortable with her new friend. (FWSS.)

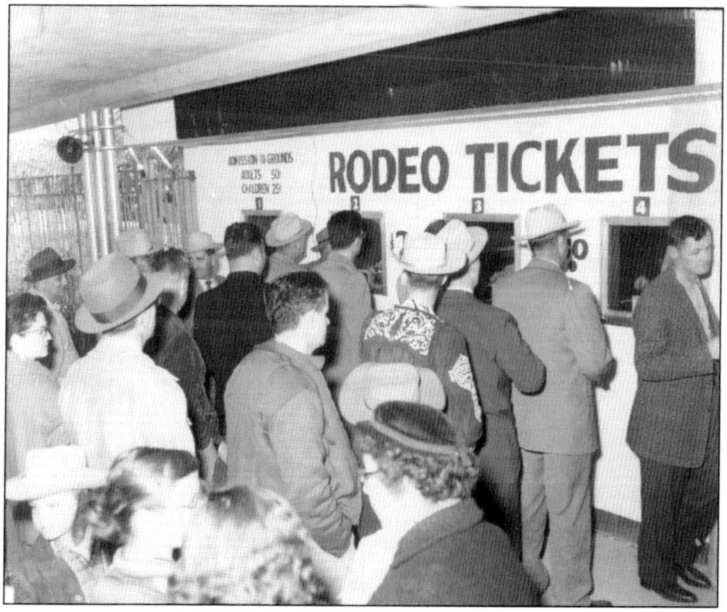

Before the $2.2-million visitor's center and ticket office was built in 1998, tickets were sold in a much less elaborate setting. The excitement, however, was surely equal in anticipation. (FWSS.)

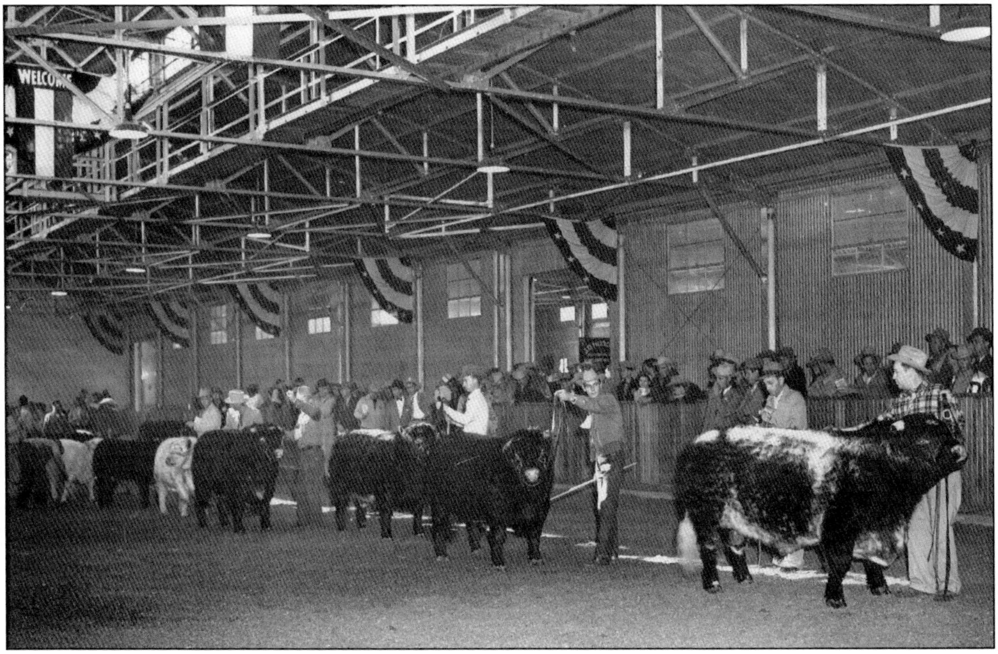

Hopeful exhibitors line their shorthorn bulls up for judging in the designated area between the barns as the audience watches. Judges look for the correct form and shape of an animal and for traits showing it is able to efficiently perform its intended function. (FWSS.)

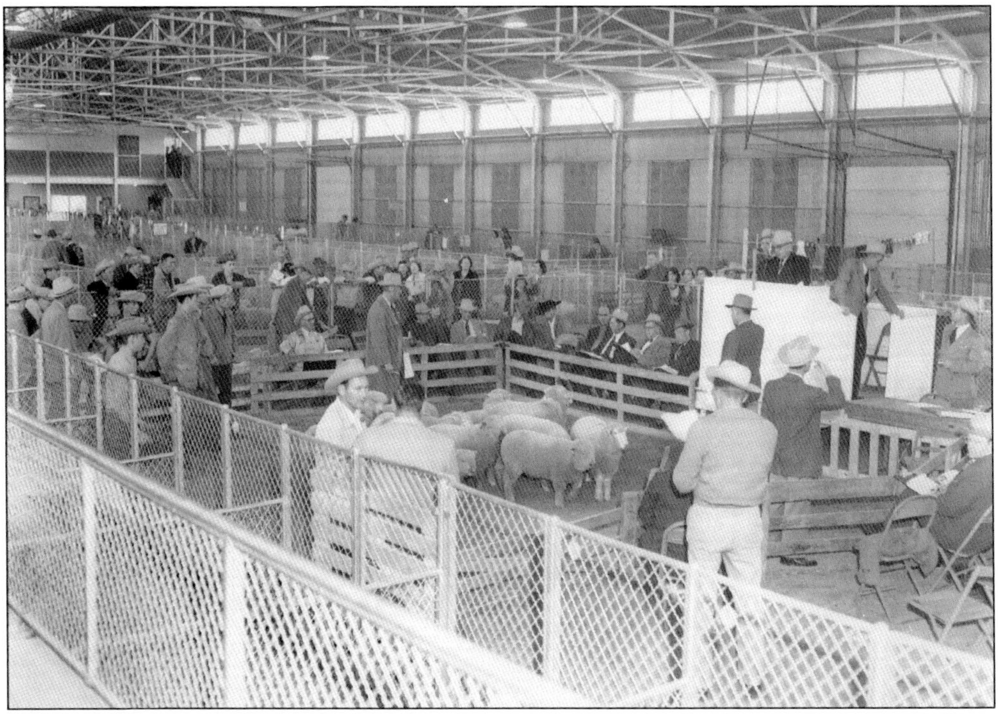

Sheep are auctioned off by lot in this 1953 photograph. More than 10 different breeds of sheep have been shown at the Stock Show, including Shropshires, Lincolns, Karakules, Karalinos, Merinos, Hampshires, Cotswolds, Southdowns, Oxford Downs, Rambouillets, and Montadales. (FWSS.)

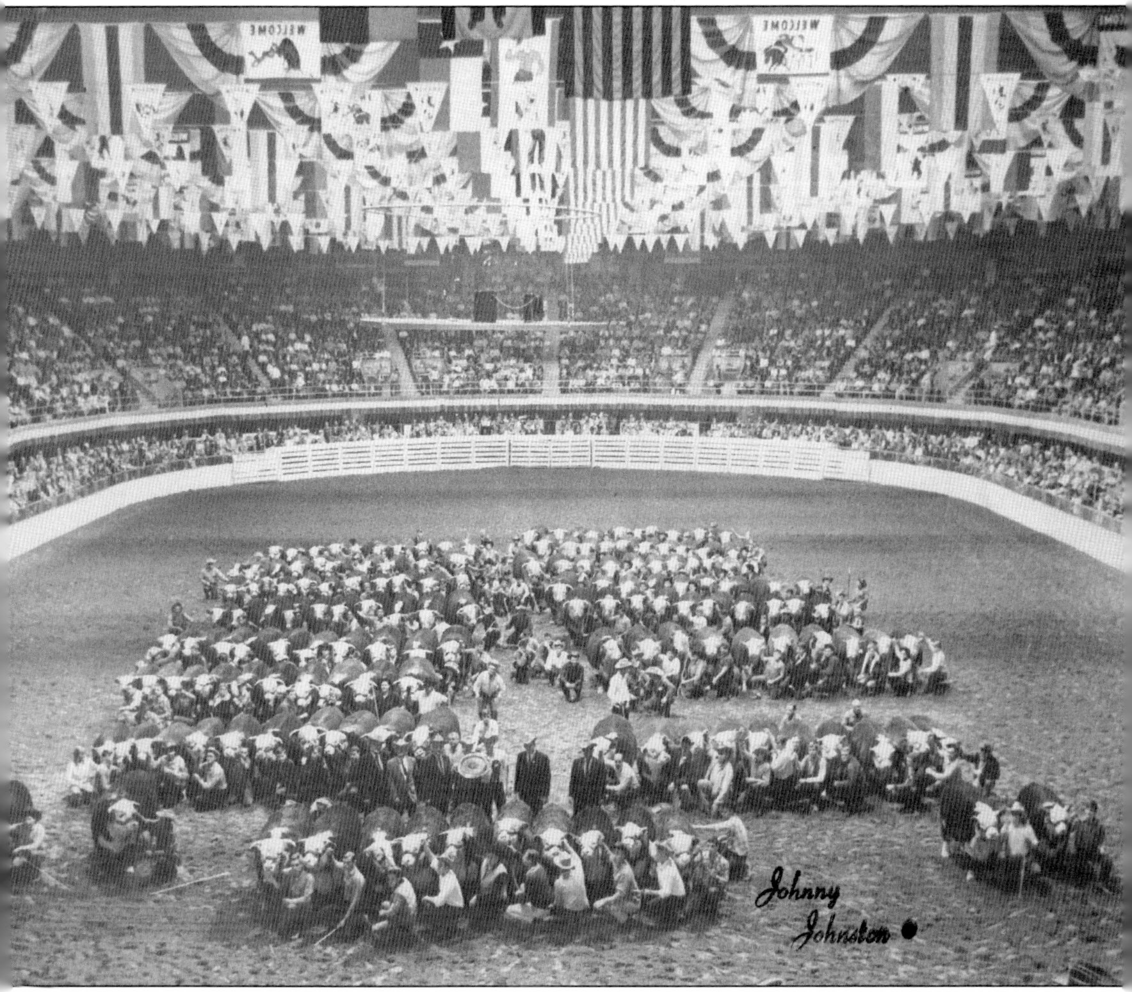

Until the 1960s, Best of Ten Head was a category in which 10 of the best of a herd were selected by judges. Under consideration for evaluation were structural correctness, volume, composition, balance or quality, growth, and sexual characteristics. These Herefords in the Coliseum were short, wide, and deep-bodied, noticeable by looking at the exhibitors who are kneeling to the same height as the standing cattle. After the 1960s, the call for leaner beef led to today's taller, leaner animals. (FWSS.)

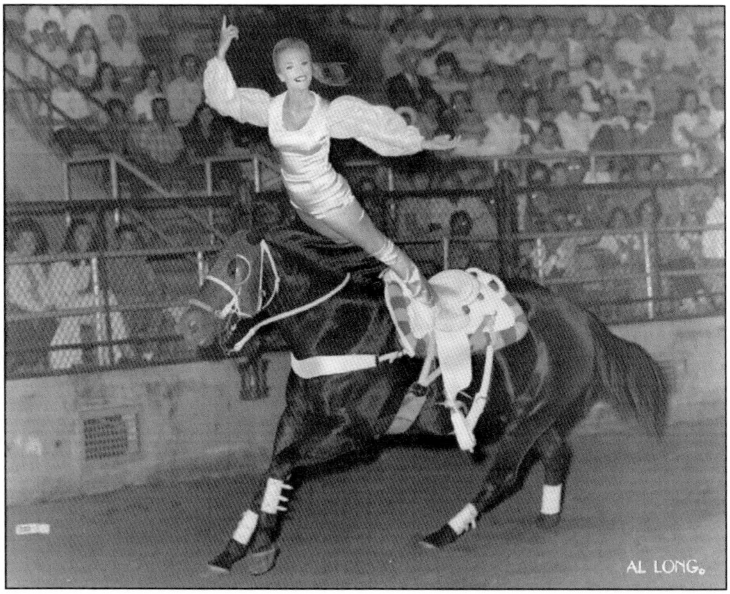

Stock show entertainment comes in all shapes and sizes, and with multiple levels of daring. Janette Plunkett Lee was a trick rider who toured America and Canada performing for rodeo crowds. In this photograph, she flawlessly executes the hippodrome. (FWSS.)

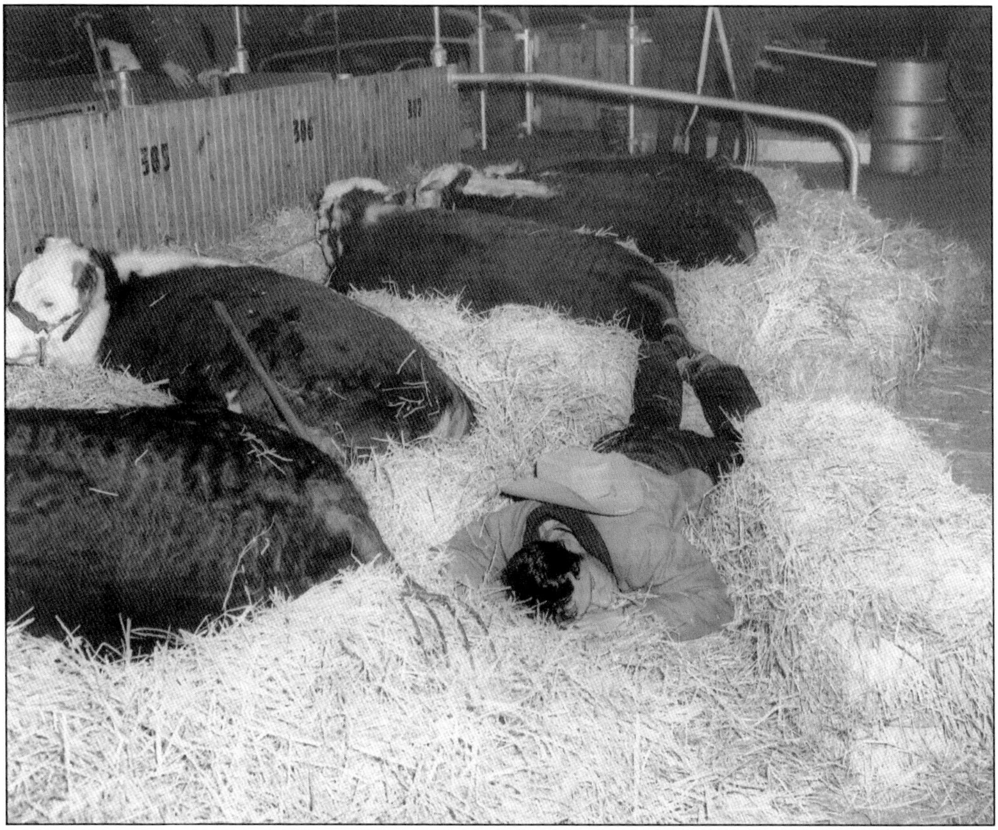

Of the many photographs of cowboys sleeping in the hay, this one of Doyle Fonder, of Merkel, Texas, shows how comfortable cowboys are with their stock. As he rests with the cows, his head is precariously close to both a pitchfork and a cow's rear end. (FWSS.)

Cattle and exhibitors wait to enter the auction arena in 1955 as the audience spills into the hallway. (FWSS.)

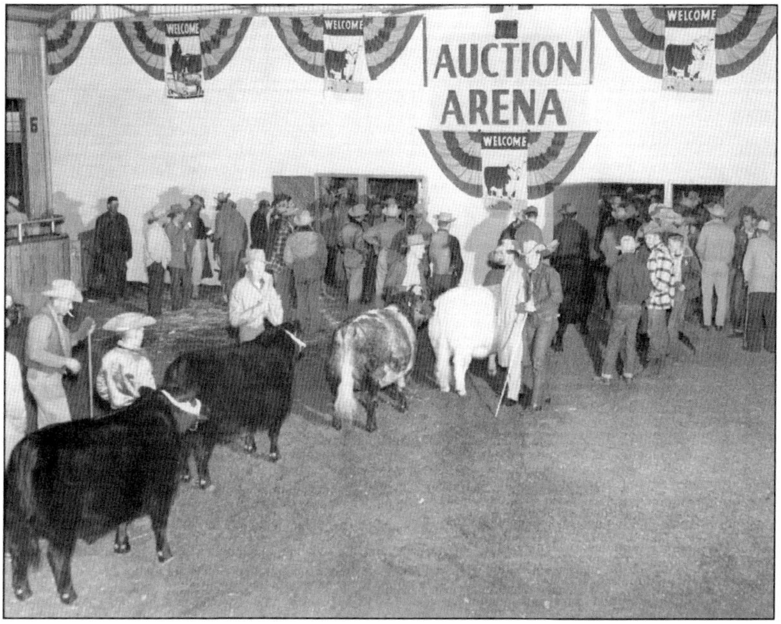

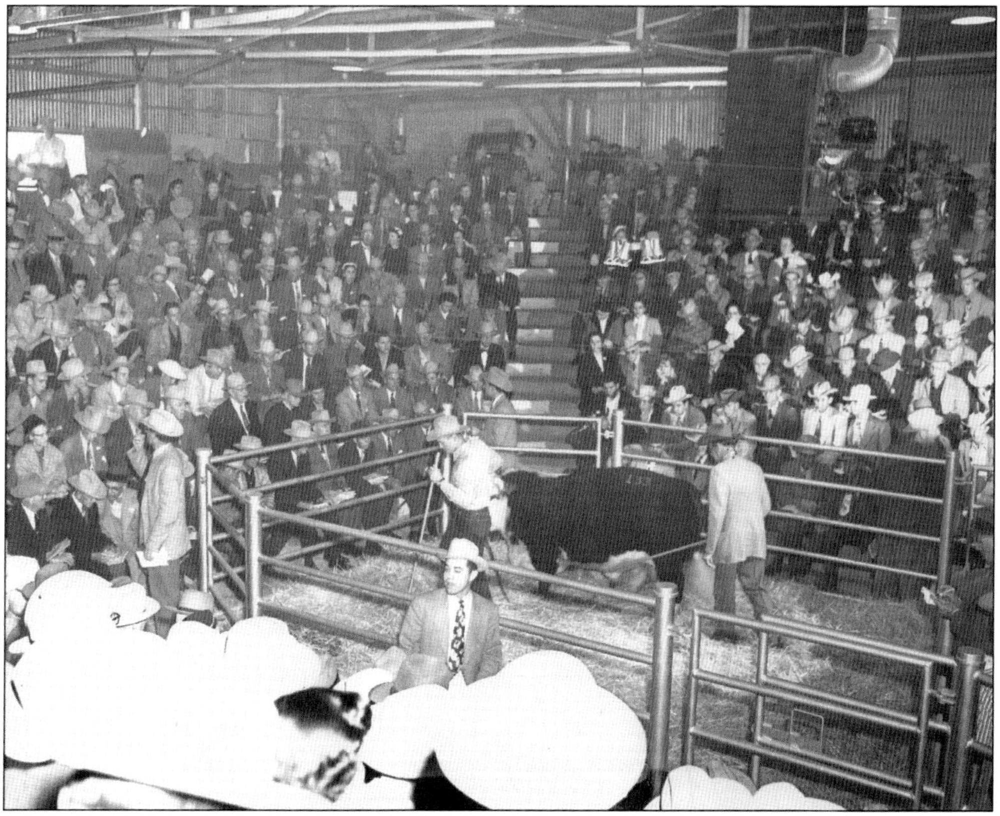

The fast pace of the auction attracts spectators as well as participants. Along with the regular auction, there is the Junior Livestock Auction, which raises funds generally used for college scholarships. (FWSS.)

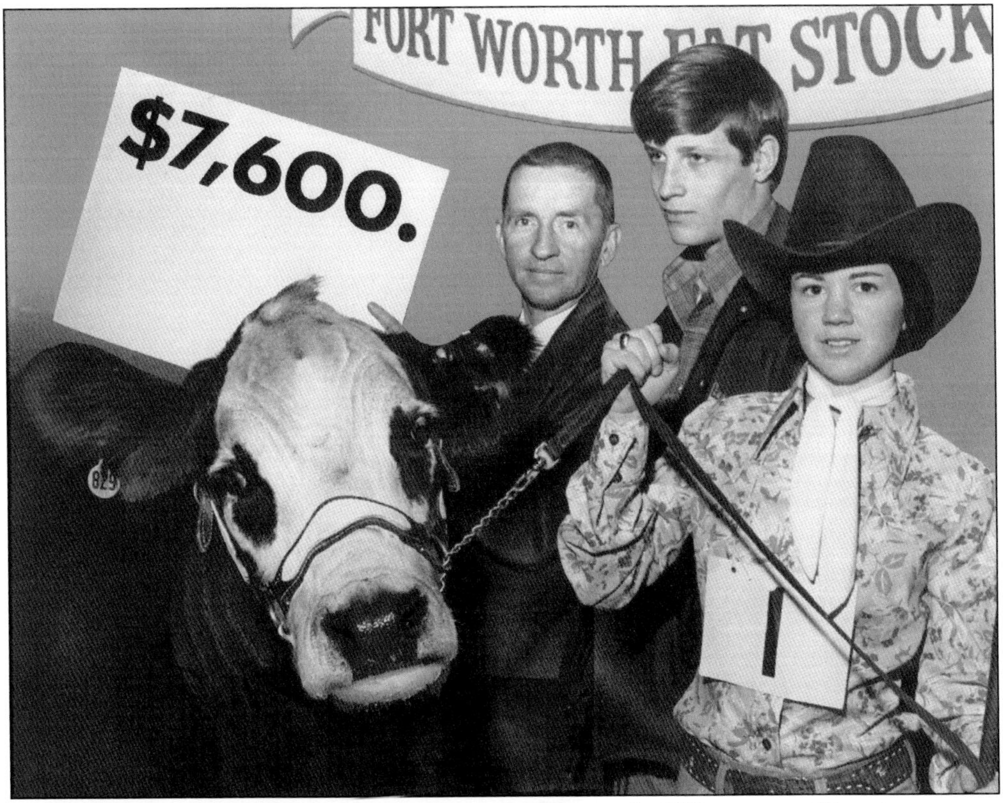

In 1976, young millionaire computer magnate H. Ross Perot bought the Grand Champion, Old Black Baldy, for an unprecedented $7,600 from 13-year-old Sherry Koenig of Cross Plains, Texas. Perot planned to ship the 1,230-pound Hereford-Angus steer to Texas Tech University for use in a training program. Koenig planned to buy more steers with her money. (FWSS.)

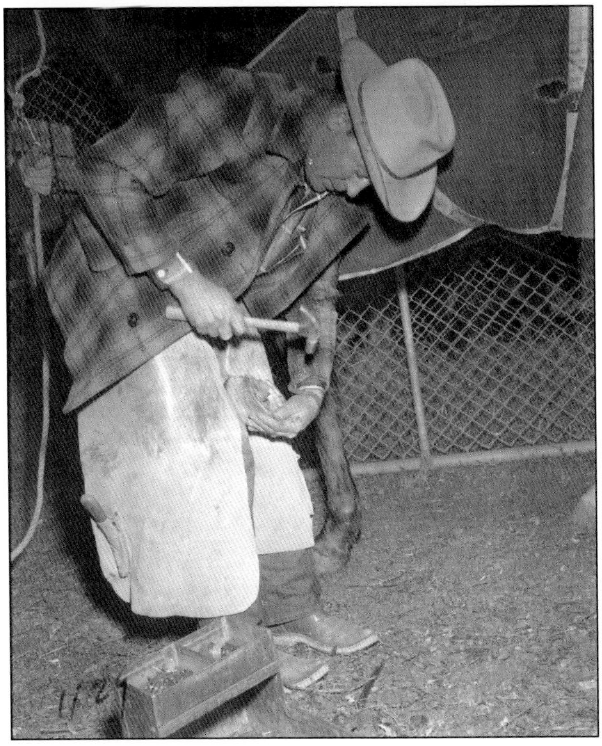

The services of farriers are extremely important at the Stock Show. A shoe that is properly formed and attached not only protects the horse and rider from injury but enables the best possible performance of the team. (FWSS.)

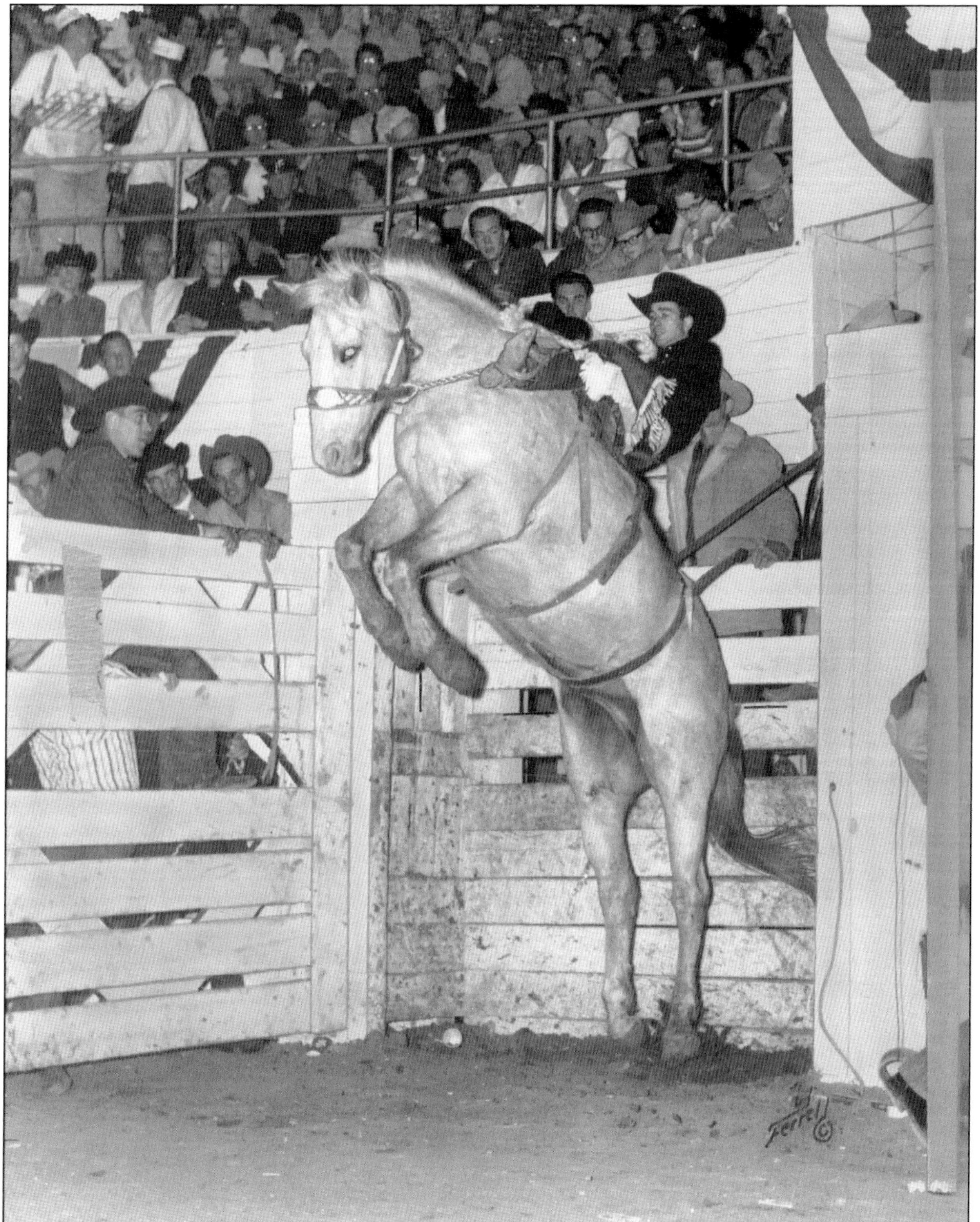

This image of Larry Kane at the 1962 rodeo captures the amazing power of a rodeo horse as it comes out of the chute. Cowboy rules state that when he leaves the chute he must be spurring his horse and have daylight between his rein hand and the animal's neck. Also, he may not switch the reins between hands. Disqualification occurs if the rider grabs the saddle horn, if he gets his spur caught in the cinch, or if his foot comes out of the stirrup. In the stands (top left), a vendor calmly sells drinks to the watching crowd. (FWSS.)

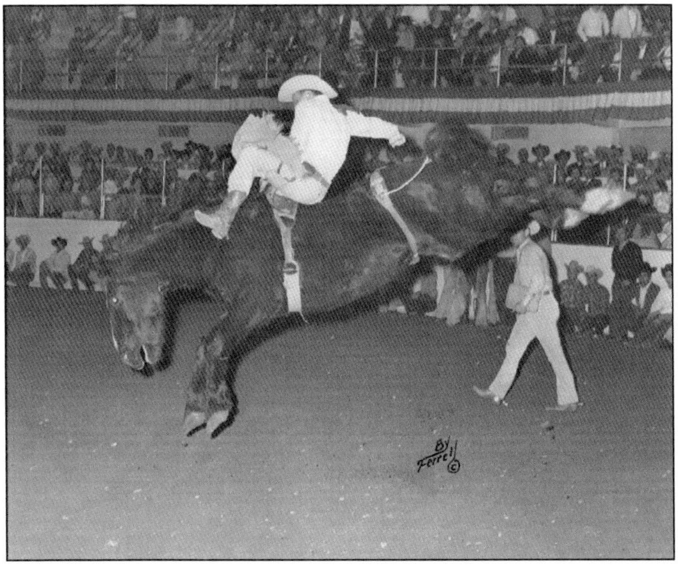

Jack Buschbom was a three-time world champion bareback bronc rider—in 1949, 1959, and 1960—and a member of the inaugural class of the Pro Rodeo Hall of Fame in 1979. Buschbom began his rodeo career as a bull rider when he was 17, but he soon began concentrating on bareback bronc riding. His style, which involved wild-spurring, was soon imitated by other competitors. (FWSS.)

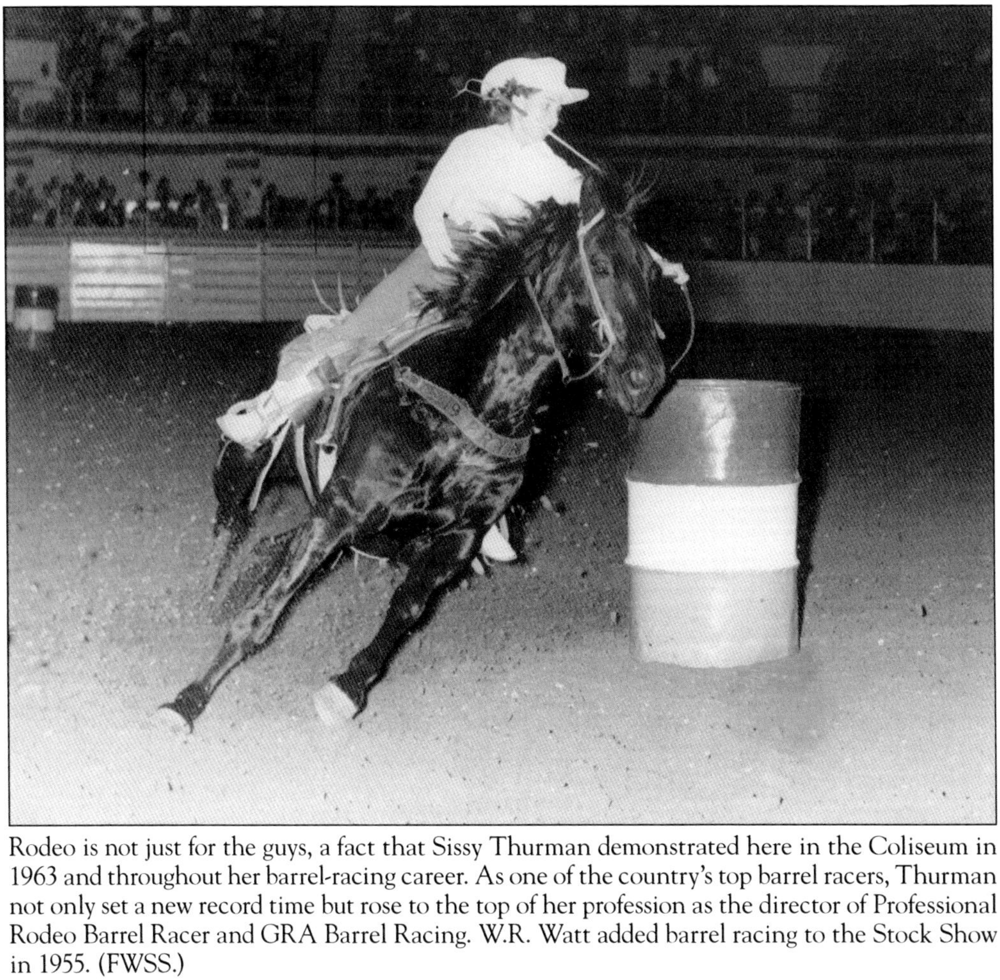

Rodeo is not just for the guys, a fact that Sissy Thurman demonstrated here in the Coliseum in 1963 and throughout her barrel-racing career. As one of the country's top barrel racers, Thurman not only set a new record time but rose to the top of her profession as the director of Professional Rodeo Barrel Racer and GRA Barrel Racing. W.R. Watt added barrel racing to the Stock Show in 1955. (FWSS.)

Watching cutting horses perform was a side show to the bigger event until 1949. At this time, W.R. Watt decided that it needed to have a bigger place in the schedule, and by 1952, there were 86 contestants in the competition. Cutting is still a part of the Stock Show but has grown so much in the past years that the National Cutting Horse Association holds its own show at the Will Rogers Complex. (FWSS.)

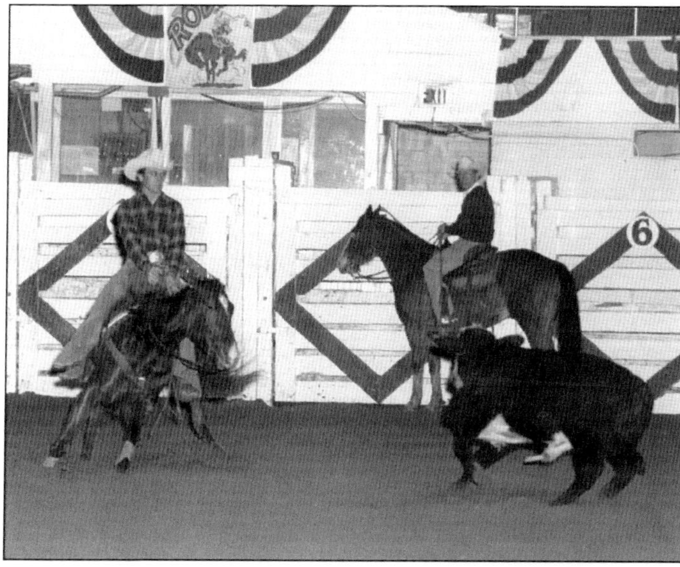

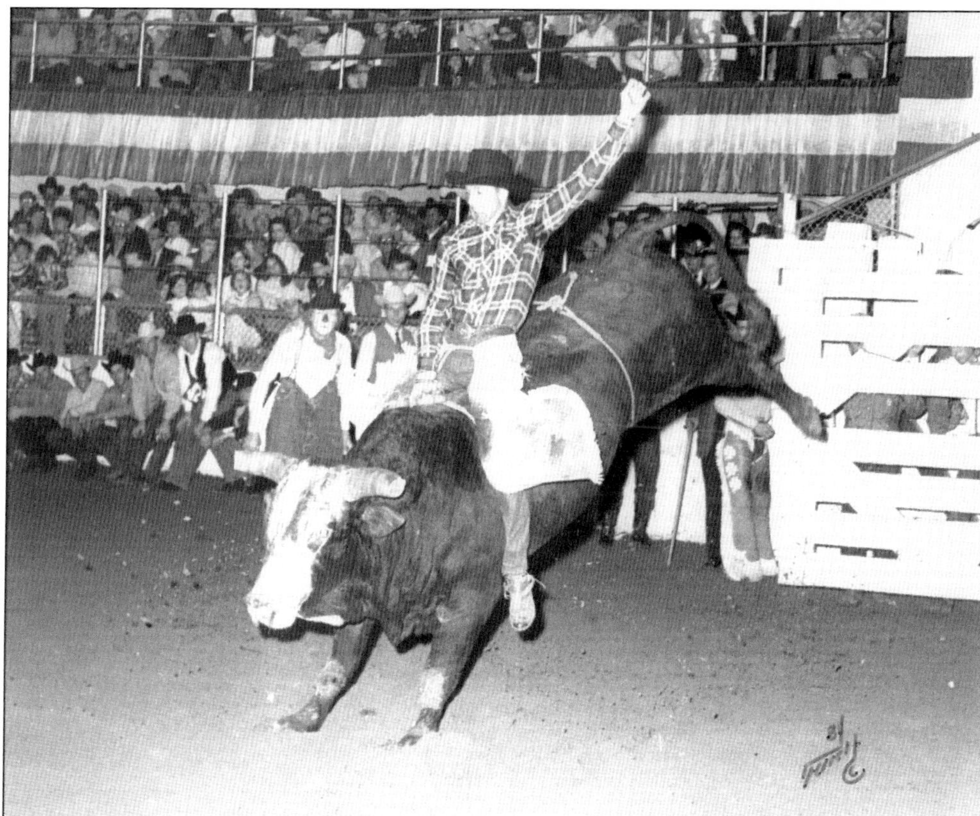

Brahma bull riding was introduced to the Stock Show in 1920 by Verne Elliot. By the time the Stock Show moved into the Will Rogers Coliseum, bull riding was a regular part of the show. As part of an effort to move the show from the North Side Coliseum, Van Zandt Jarvis held a private rodeo for youth participants from the FFA and 4-H clubs in the Will Rogers Coliseum in 1940, four years before the Stock Show first appeared at the facility. (FWSS.)

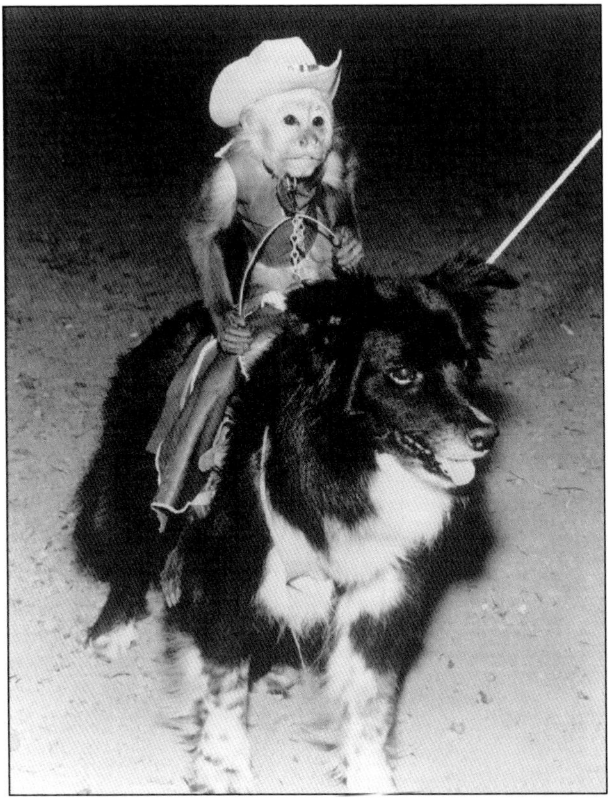

Whiplash the cowboy monkey continues to entertain fans of all ages at rodeos all over the country, including the Stock Show. Saddled up on his trusty dog, Whiplash herds Barbados sheep and toys with the crowd with stunts of all descriptions. (FWSS.)

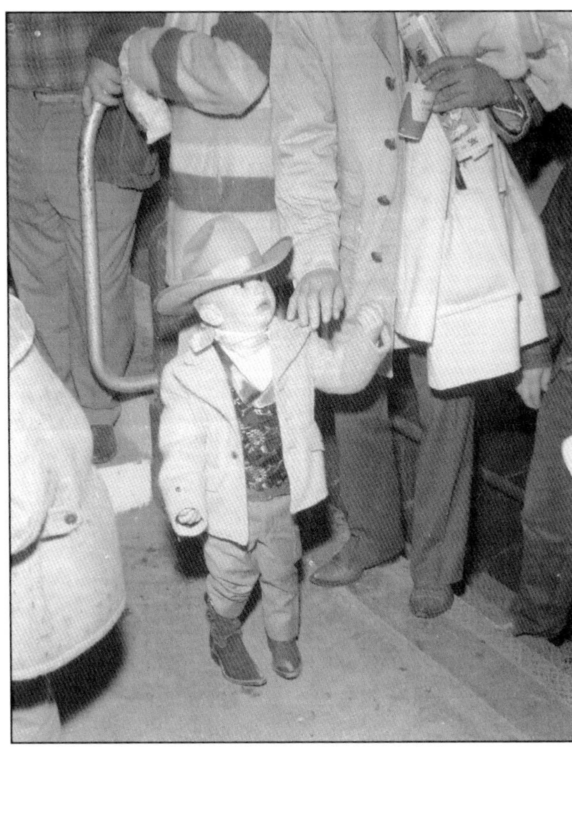

One of the littlest cowboys, all dressed up in his finest Western gear, attends the Stock Show in 1957. In a city that has long depended on its Western heritage and way of life, the future is secure as these traditions are continuously passed down. (FWSS.)

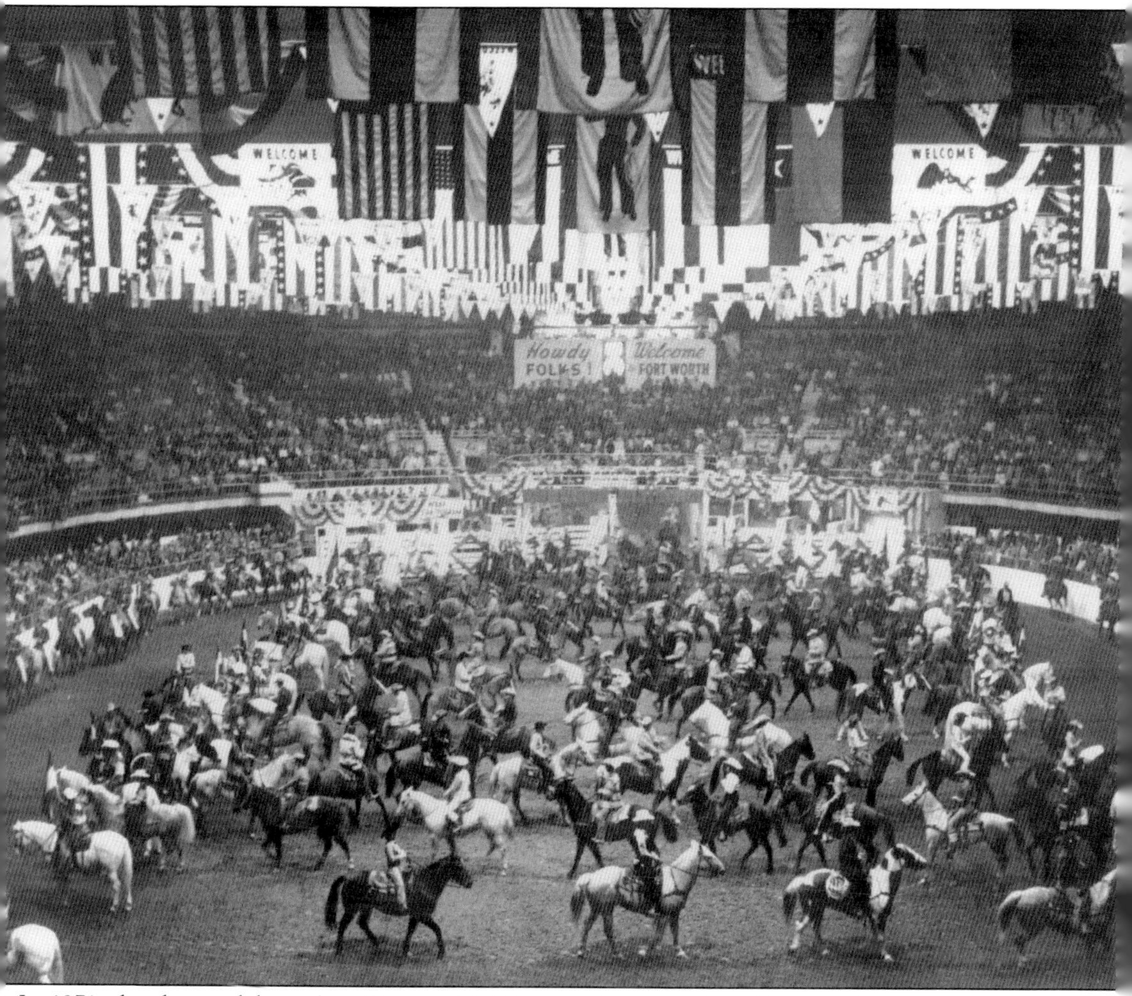

In 1971, the show celebrated its Diamond Jubilee Anniversary. W.R. Watt and Amon Carter Jr.—who stepped in after his father died in 1955 and served as chairman of the board until his death in 1982—made sure the show was ready. Filled with promise, cowboys and girls started the show with the Grand Entry, in a Coliseum all dressed up in its finest banners. The 1970s were great for attendance, and in 1979, the Grand Champion sold for $52,000. The following year, the market dropped out of the cattle industry and the Grand Champion only brought $16,300. (FWSS.)

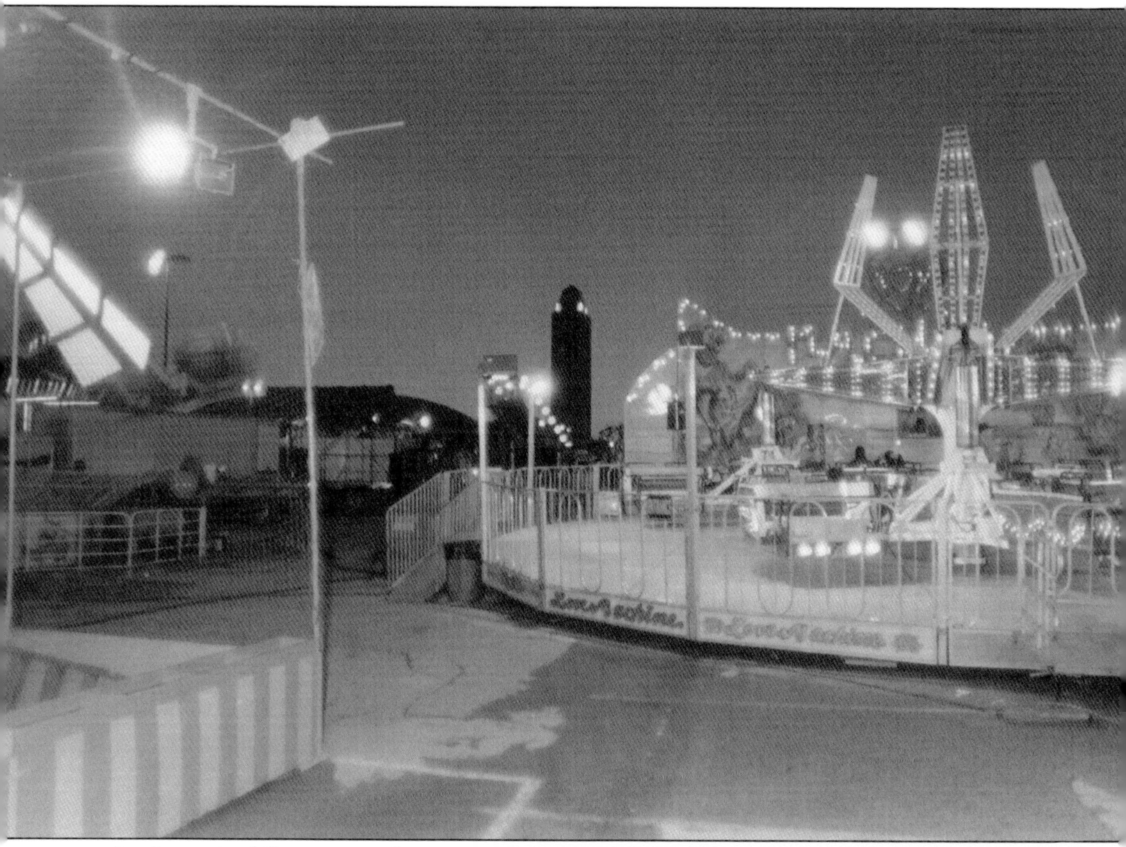

As the night falls over another successful year of the Fort Worth Stock Show, the future of the event is constantly in motion. In 2008, the Fort Worth Stock Show and Rodeo was inducted into the Pro Rodeo Hall of Fame. At the 2010 Stock Show, over 22,000 animals were shown, over $5 million in livestock sales were conducted, a million visitors attended, 1,287 rodeo contestants competed for $594,000, and the Grand Champion steer sold for $210,000. In addition to the original buildings, the Stock Show—which rents the buildings from Fort Worth—has paid for the Amon G. Carter Jr. Exhibits Hall, the Will Rogers Equestrian Center, the Richardson-Bass Building, and the Charlie and Kit Moncrief Building. In their wildest dreams, Charles C. French and Charles McFarland could never have conceived of such success. (FWSS.)

Five

The Perfect Venue

The Coliseum and Auditorium have played hosts to thousands of shows of all varieties. The ability of the Coliseum to be transformed from concrete to ice rink, to grass lawn, and to a pad of specialized dirt has made it the perfect location for many organizations and shows throughout the years. While some events are a single occurrence, many associations come back year after year, including the Fort Worth Kennel Club, the Golden Gloves, the Miss Texas pageant, Moslah Shrine Circus, and the Ice Capades. Among the events not captured in this chapter are Texas Christian University and Harlem Globetrotters basketball, high school and college graduations, Boy-Scout-a-ramas, dance recitals and competitions, horse shows, rodeos, futurities, children's concerts, and on and on. Thousands of performances have awed, inspired, captivated, and stuck in the memories of multiple generations inside the walls, and under the dome, of the Coliseum and Auditorium.

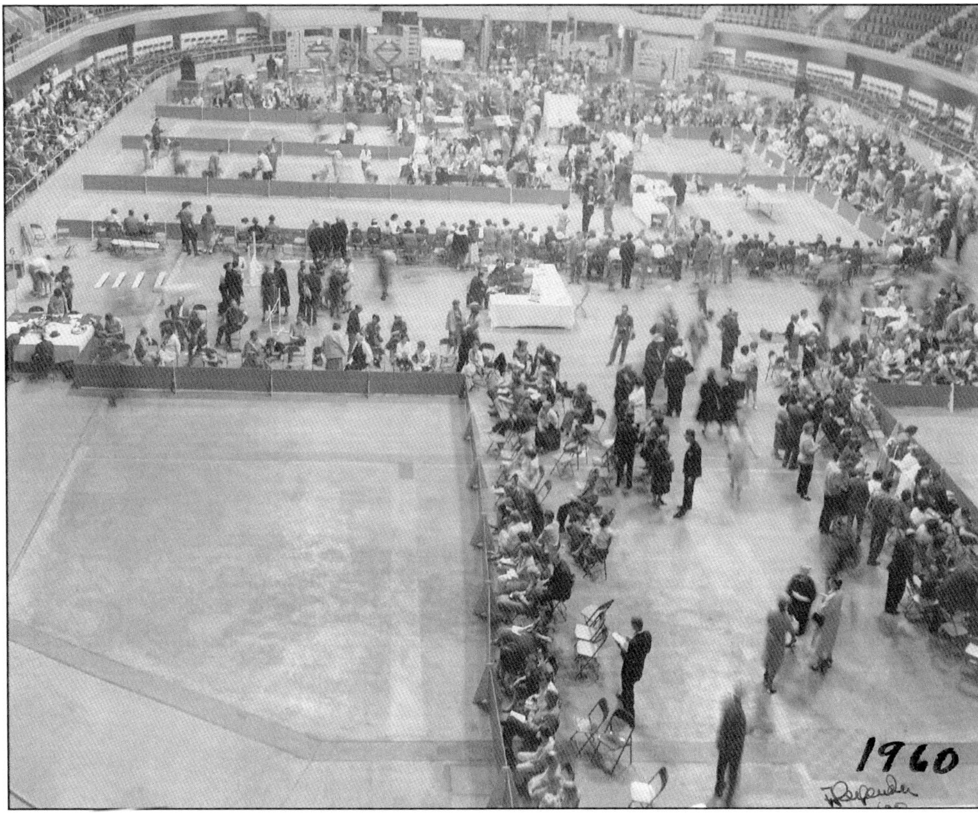

The Fort Worth Kennel Club held its first show in the Coliseum on October 28–29, 1936, a little over a month after the facility had been dedicated. The poster pup for the first show was 16-month-old Ash Waldman Schneid, a German dachshund. This 1960 photograph shows how the floor of the Coliseum was separated into different areas of competition, with spectators and owners seated at eye level. (Fort Worth Kennel Club.)

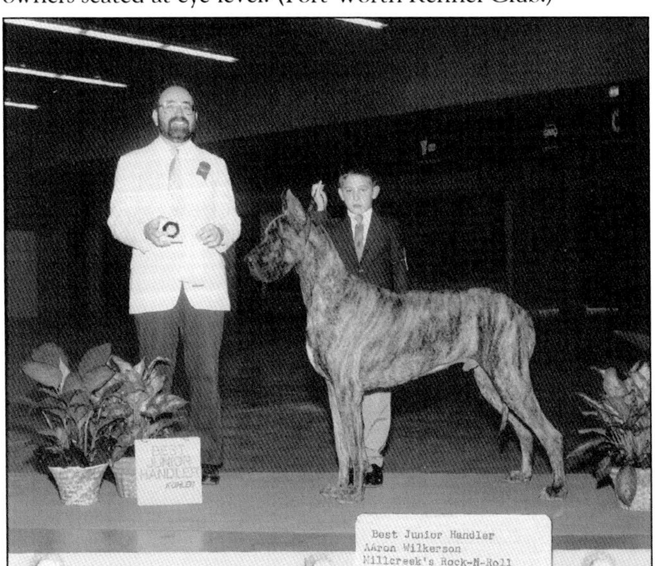

The Kennel Club encourages youth participation in the competition. Seven groups of dogs, Sporting, Hounds, Working, Terrier, Toy, Non-Sporting, and Herding, are judged by looks and by their ability to do the job they were bred to do. With as many as 3,000 dogs in a show, there is serious competition for the judges to pick from. (Fort Worth Kennel Club.)

When the show first began, the exhibitors were mostly men. But Mildred Bryant (right) changed that, winning top breeder and becoming an exhibitor, a judge, and the president and chair of different clubs. (Fort Worth Kennel Club.)

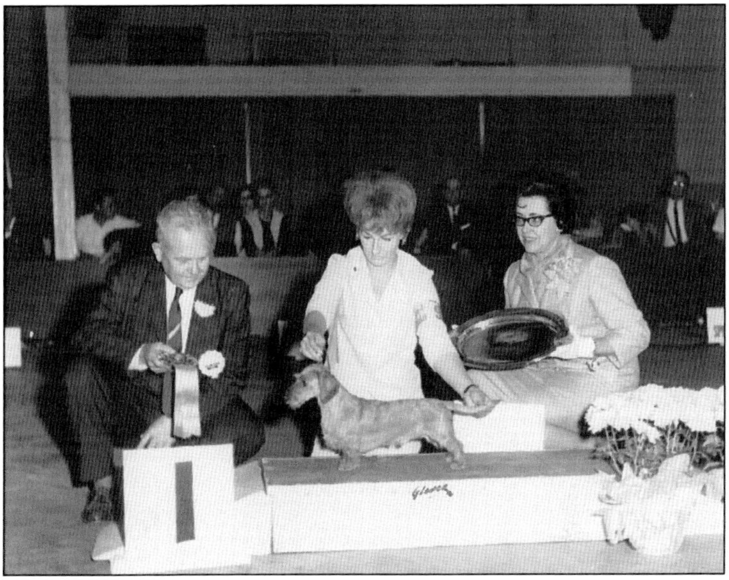

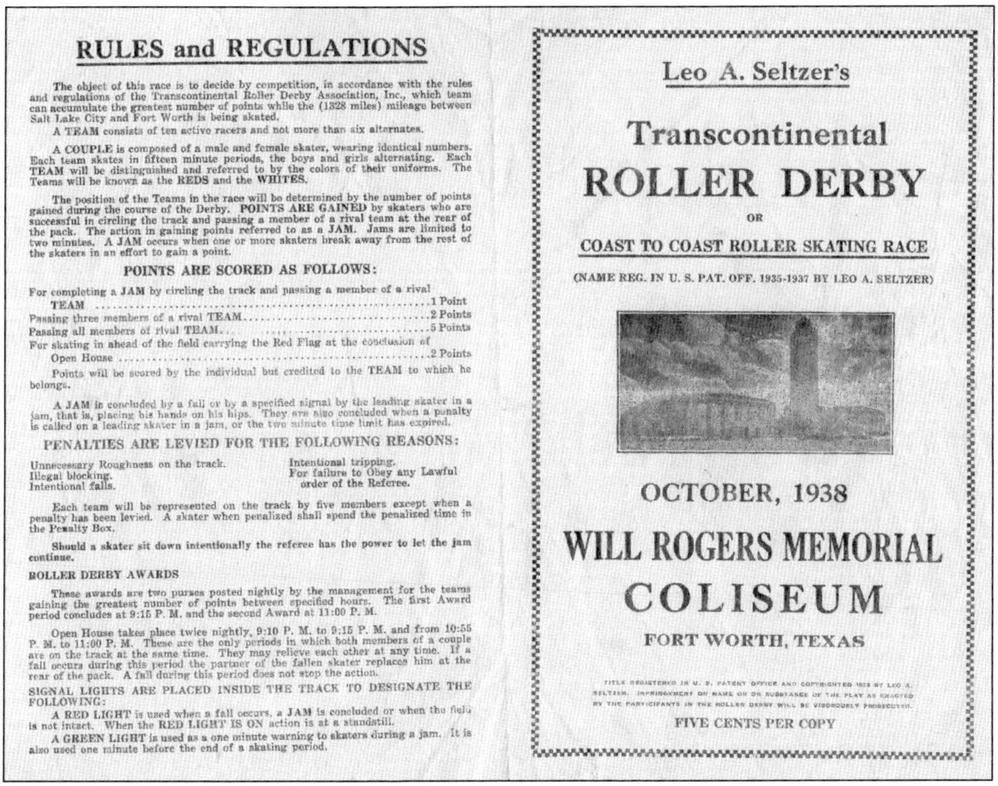

RULES and REGULATIONS

The object of this race is to decide by competition, in accordance with the rules and regulations of the Transcontinental Roller Derby Association, Inc., which team can accumulate the greatest number of points while the (1328 miles) mileage between Salt Lake City and Fort Worth is being skated.

A **TEAM** consists of ten active racers and not more than six alternates.

A **COUPLE** is composed of a male and female skater, wearing identical numbers. Each team skates in fifteen minute periods, the boys and girls alternating. Each **TEAM** will be distinguished and referred to by the colors of their uniforms. The Teams will be known as the **REDS** and the **WHITES**.

The position of the Teams in the race will be determined by the number of points gained during the course of the Derby. **POINTS ARE GAINED** by skaters who are successful in circling the track and passing a member of a rival team at the rear of the pack. The action in gaining points referred to as a **JAM**. Jams are limited to two minutes. A **JAM** occurs when one or more skaters break away from the rest of the skaters in an effort to gain a point.

POINTS ARE SCORED AS FOLLOWS:

For completing a **JAM** by circling the track and passing a member of a rival TEAM .... 1 Point
Passing three members of a rival TEAM .... 2 Points
Passing all members of rival TEAM .... 5 Points
For skating in ahead of the field carrying the Red Flag at the conclusion of Open House .... 2 Points

Points will be scored by the individual but credited to the **TEAM** to which he belongs.

A **JAM** is concluded by a fall or by a specified signal by the leading skater in a jam, that is, placing his hands on his hips. They are also concluded when a penalty is called on a leading skater in a jam, or the two minute time limit has expired.

PENALTIES ARE LEVIED FOR THE FOLLOWING REASONS:

Unnecessary Roughness on the track.
Illegal blocking.
Intentional falls.
Intentional tripping.
For failure to Obey any Lawful order of the Referee.

Each team will be represented on the track by five members except when a penalty has been levied. A skater when penalized shall spend the penalized time in the Penalty Box.

Should a skater sit down intentionally the referee has the power to let the jam continue.

ROLLER DERBY AWARDS

These awards are two purses posted nightly by the management for the teams gaining the greatest number of points between specified hours. The first Award period concludes at 9:15 P. M. and the second Award at 11:00 P. M.

Open House takes place twice nightly, 9:10 P. M. to 9:15 P. M. and from 10:55 P. M. to 11:00 P. M. These are the only periods in which both members of a couple are on the track at the same time. They may relieve each other at any time. If a fall occurs during this period the partner of the fallen skater replaces him at the rear of the pack. A fall during this period does not stop the action.

SIGNAL LIGHTS ARE PLACED INSIDE THE TRACK TO DESIGNATE THE FOLLOWING:

A **RED LIGHT** is used when a fall occurs, a **JAM** is concluded or when the field is not intact. When the **RED LIGHT IS ON** action is at a standstill.

A **GREEN LIGHT** is used as a one minute warning to skaters during a jam. It is also used one minute before the end of a skating period.

Leo A. Seltzer's

Transcontinental

ROLLER DERBY

OR

COAST TO COAST ROLLER SKATING RACE

(NAME REG. IN U. S. PAT. OFF. 1935-1937 BY LEO A. SELTZER)

OCTOBER, 1938

WILL ROGERS MEMORIAL

COLISEUM

FORT WORTH, TEXAS

FIVE CENTS PER COPY

Roller derbies were held in many places during the Depression. Leo Seltzer staged derbies in different cities across the country using a portable track and was famous for his Transcontinental Derby, which represented the mileage between San Diego and New York City. Points were given for various tasks throughout the race. Skaters would compete for the most points throughout the night in order to win prize money. The Coliseum hosted his Transcontinental Derby in 1938. (Doug Harman.)

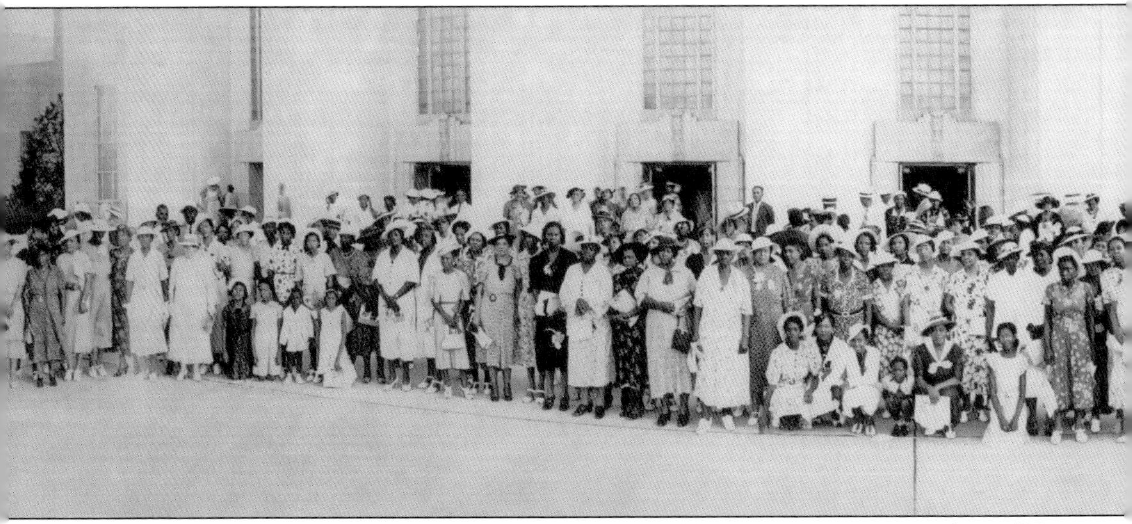

In 1937, the National Association of Colored Women held it biennium meeting at the Will Rogers Auditorium. The women worked to remove barriers of racism and stressed how their mostly middle-class membership could help those less fortunate. Their motto "Lifting as We Climb" said a lot about the organization. The 1937 meeting had over 300 attendees, who discussed the threat

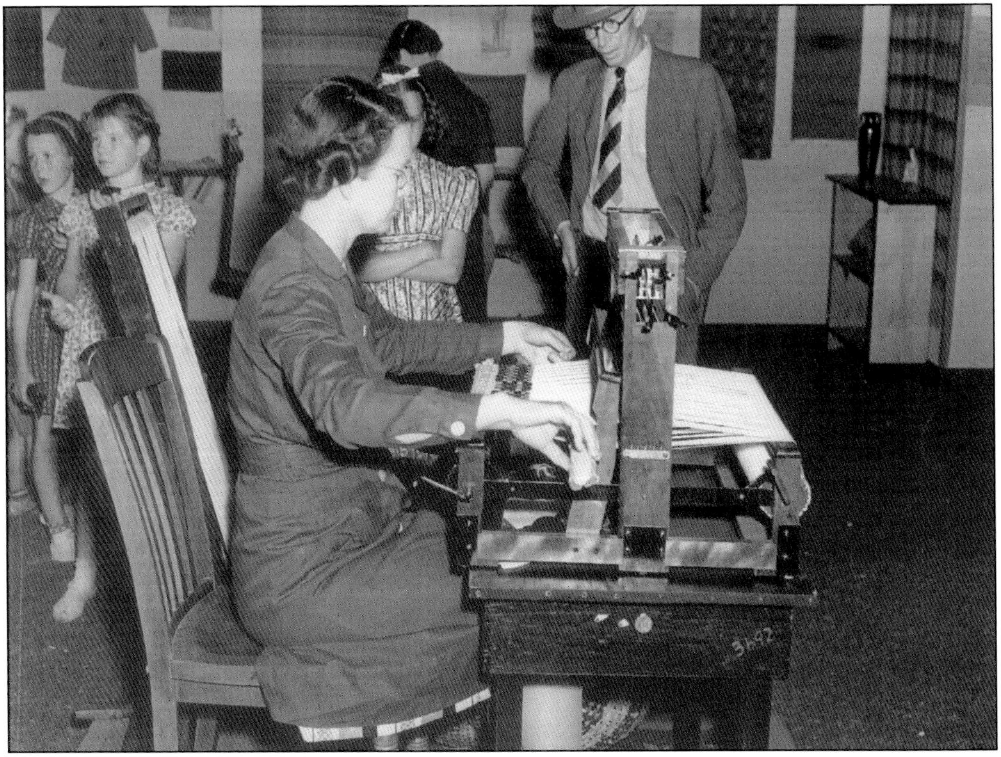

From April 23 until May 13, 1939, the WPA held an exhibit at the Coliseum titled "American Hands at Work." This program highlighted the merits of non-construction activity such as photography, mapmaking, woodworking, and weaving. (Works Progress Administration "American Hands in Action" Album, Special Collections, University of Texas at Arlington Library, Arlington, Texas.)

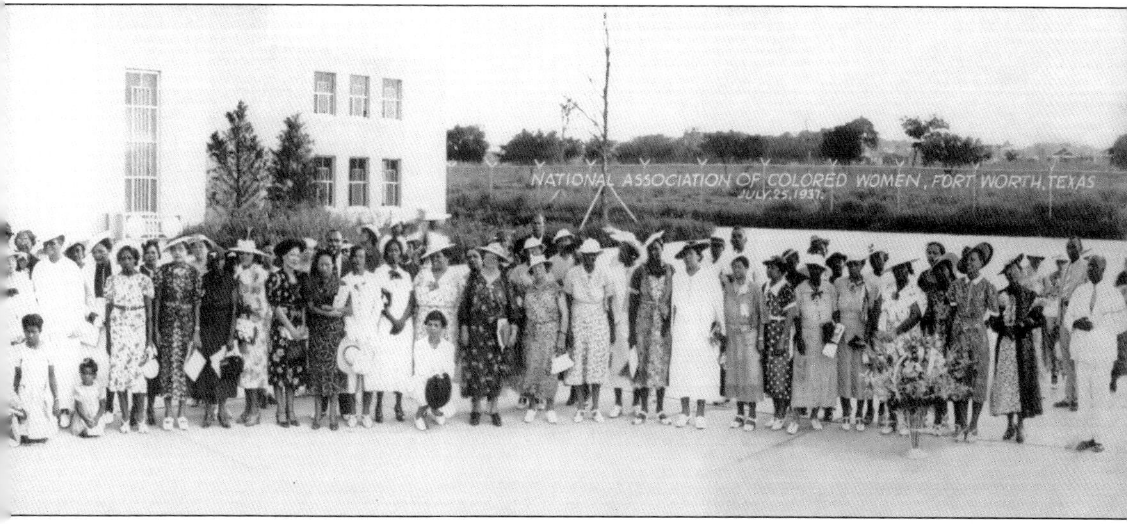

of the war and how they needed to band together to fight for peace. In a time of segregation, the women were permitted to meet at the facilities but had to use the far right-hand door, which was designated for people of color. This entrance also had access to the back of the ticket booth, which served African Americans. (Doug Harman.)

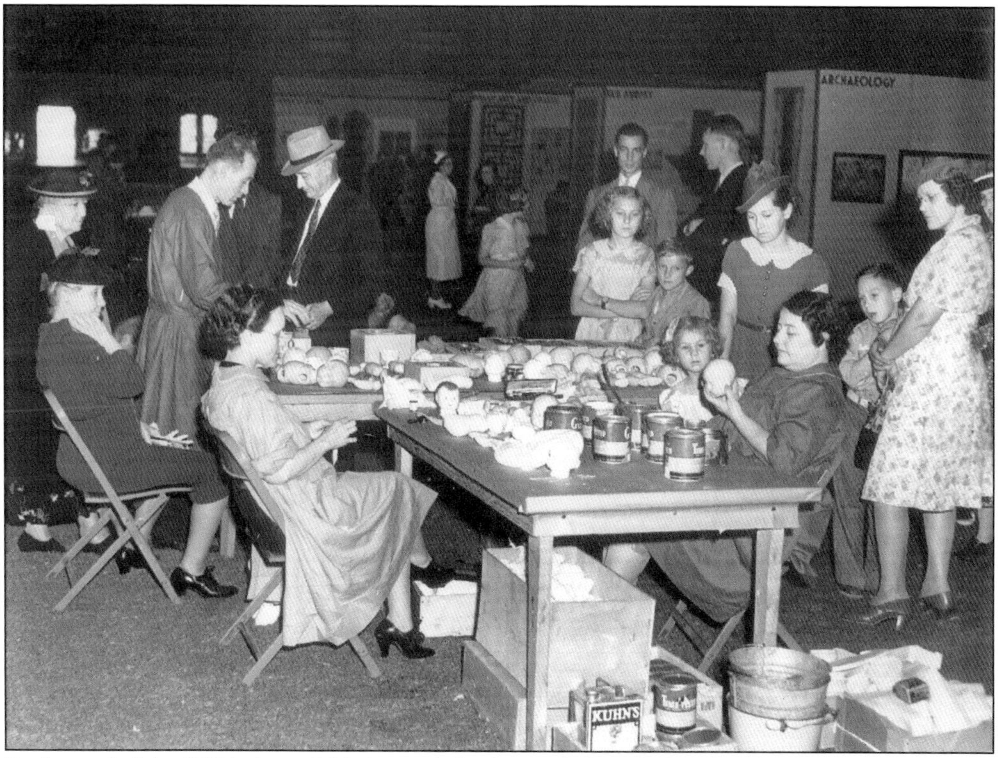

By the end of the WPA show, 26,349 people had attended, including hundreds of schoolchildren. The goal was to show how "millions of Americans had been taken from idleness and relief rolls by the Federal Works Program and put to work and useful tasks." The women shown here made dolls. (Works Progress Administration "American Hands in Action" Album, Special Collections, University of Texas at Arlington Library, Arlington, Texas.)

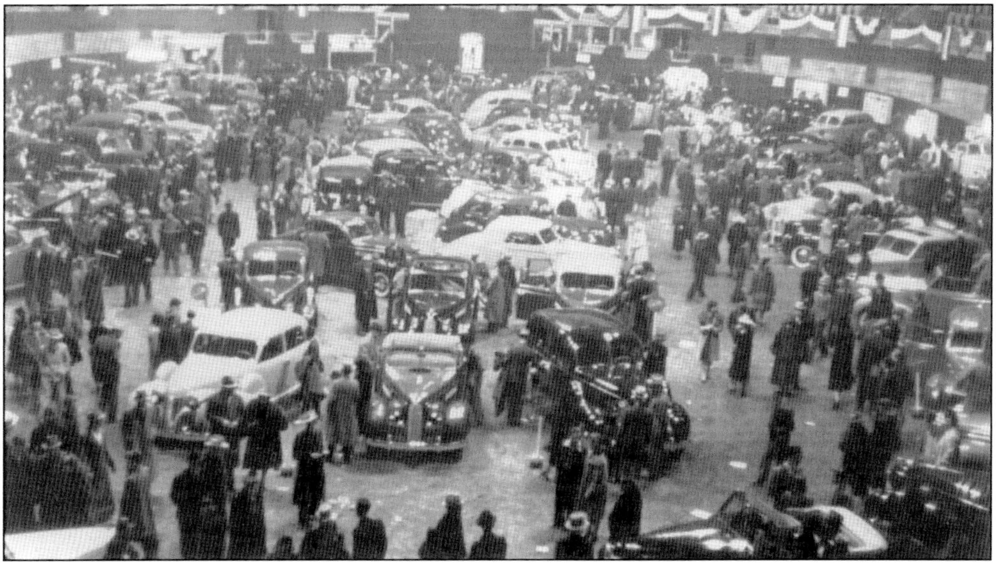

Car shows have long been a favorite, and in March 1939, the enthusiasm was high as the beautiful new models were on display in the Coliseum. The banners around the arena suggest that the show might have taken place during the Fort Worth Stock Show. Countless car shows have been held at the Coliseum. (FWPL.)

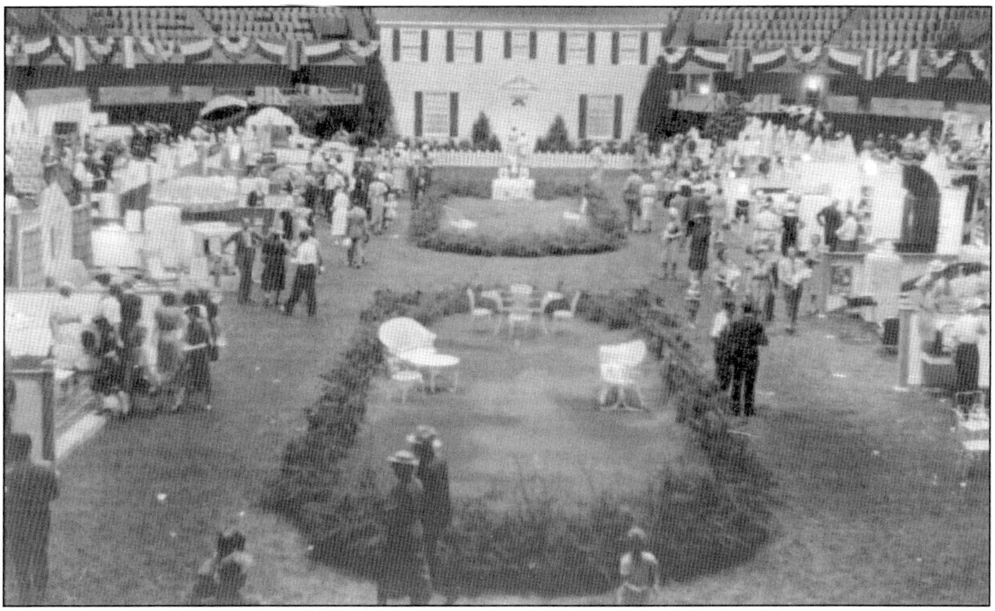

In 1939, near the end of the Great Depression, the Fort Worth *Star-Telegram* held one of its many home shows. Featuring all of the newest and best items a home should contain, vendors set up in the Coliseum on what appears to be a grass lawn. The "home" in between the draped chutes was a facade installed over the entrance to the barn. (FWPL.)

Ice hockey is another of the many different sporting events hosted by the Coliseum. In 1939, a group of local financiers proposed turning the Coliseum into an ice skating rink for a period of six months each year. The immediate benefit was that Fort Worth could become a part of the professional ice hockey circuit, which included Tulsa, St. Louis, Kansas City, Minneapolis, and Wichita. By 1941, the Fort Worth Rangers played at the Coliseum, often in front of full houses. The team played for five seasons, taking the war years off, and folded in 1949 with two second-place titles to their credit. (FWPL.)

To turn the Coliseum into an ice rink, the dirt is removed—up to 16 cubic yards—from the interior oval, the floor is painted white, and markings, such as centerlines for the hockey rink, are put in place. The 90-foot-by-200-foot space is then flooded with approximately three-quarters of an inch of water—more for events that include high jumps—and left to set for 24 hours. (Historic Fort Worth.)

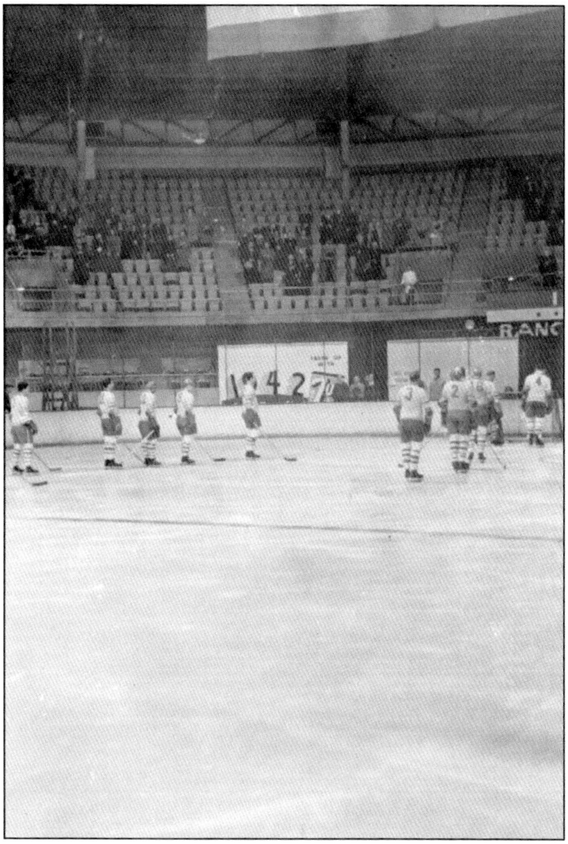

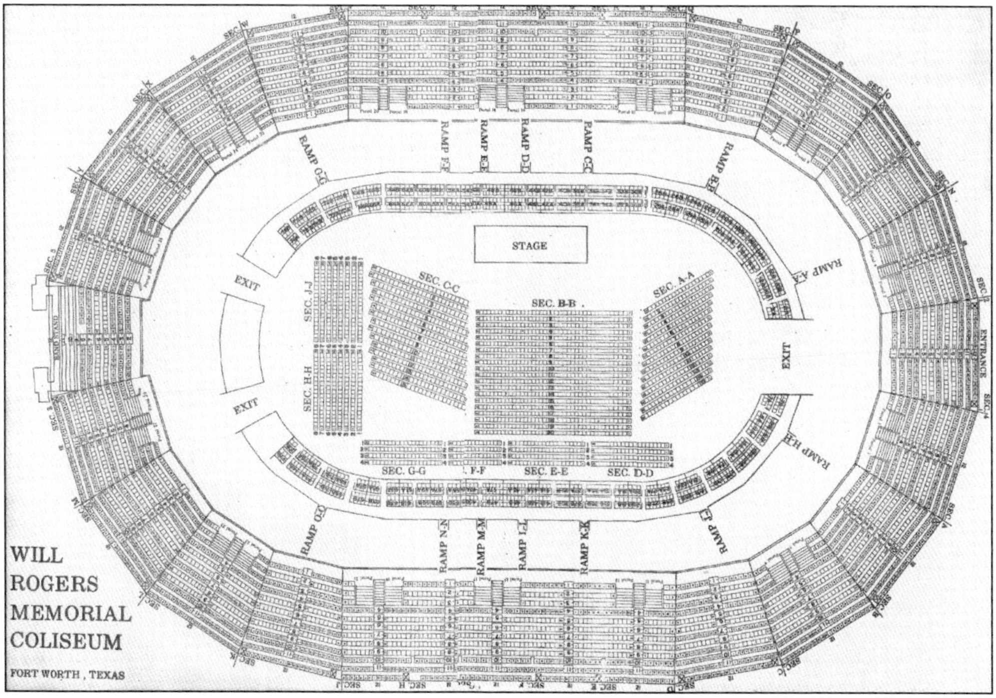

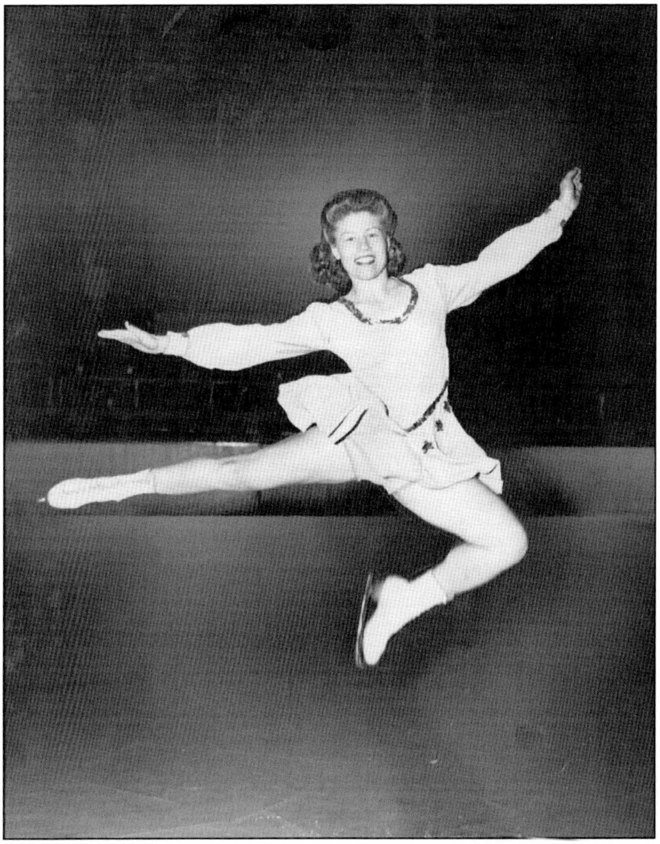

In 1946, Betty Jane Courtright was a professional ice skater, instructor for the Coliseum, and director of the Fort Worth Figure Skating Club's production of "Melody on Ice." (FWST.)

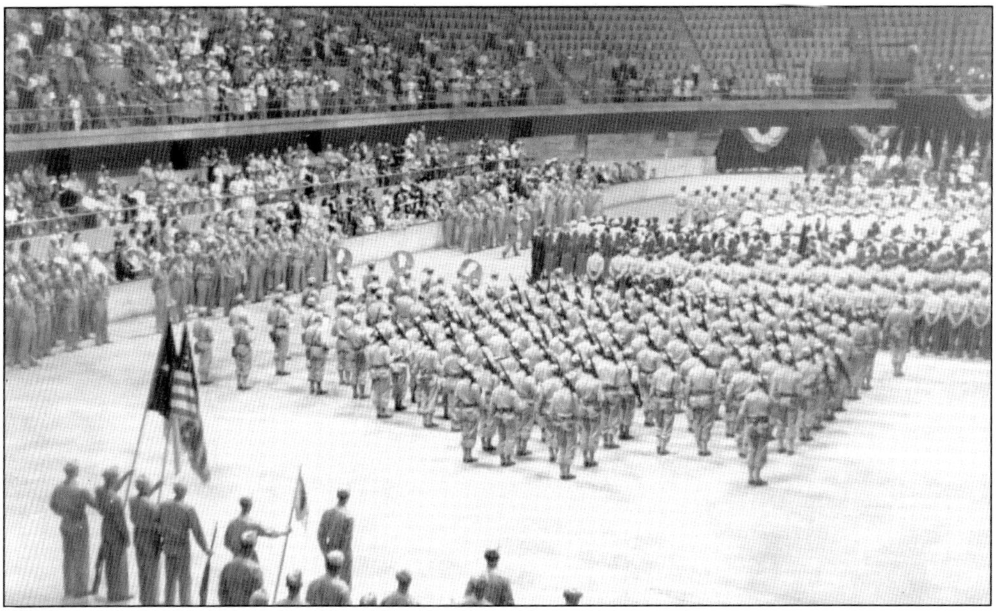

The closing ceremonies for the 1942 Memorial Day ceremony surely contained a lot of emotions, as the nation honored the sacrifices of those from the past and thought about the war that had just recently begun. (FWPL.)

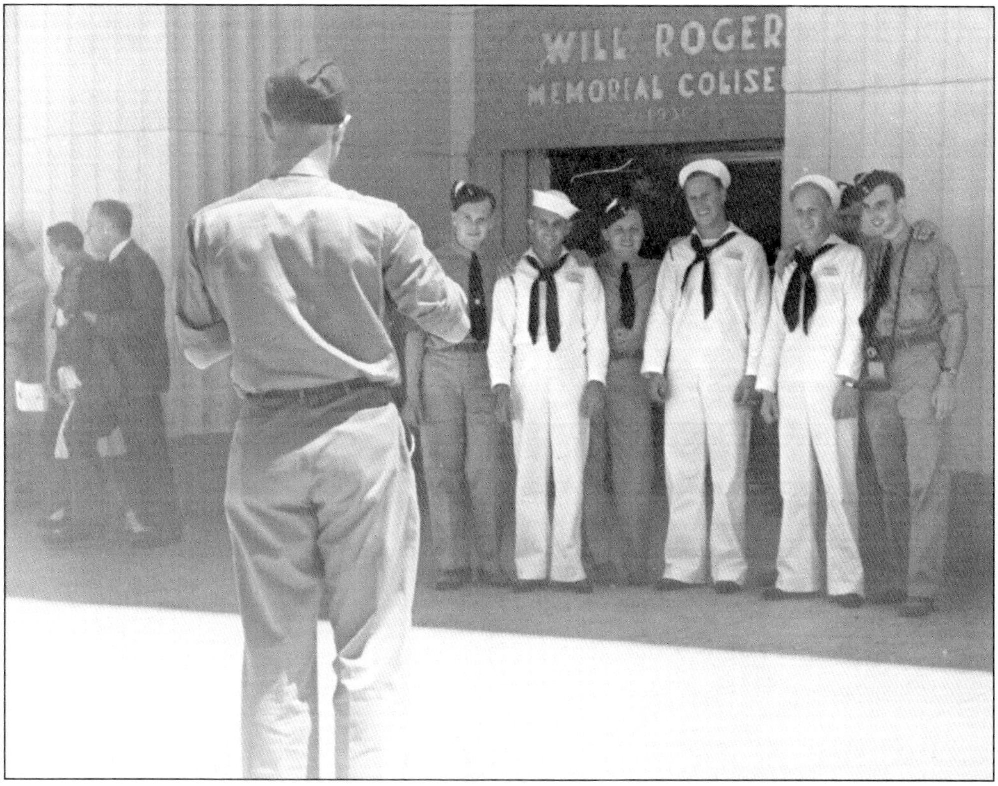

Members of the Exchange Club pose in 1942. The granite lintel over the door is inscribed with the words "Will Rogers Memorial Coliseum 1936." The cost of the carving and gold-leafing was $303.50. The Auditorium also has its own lintel, but it was not added to the building until much later. (FWPL.)

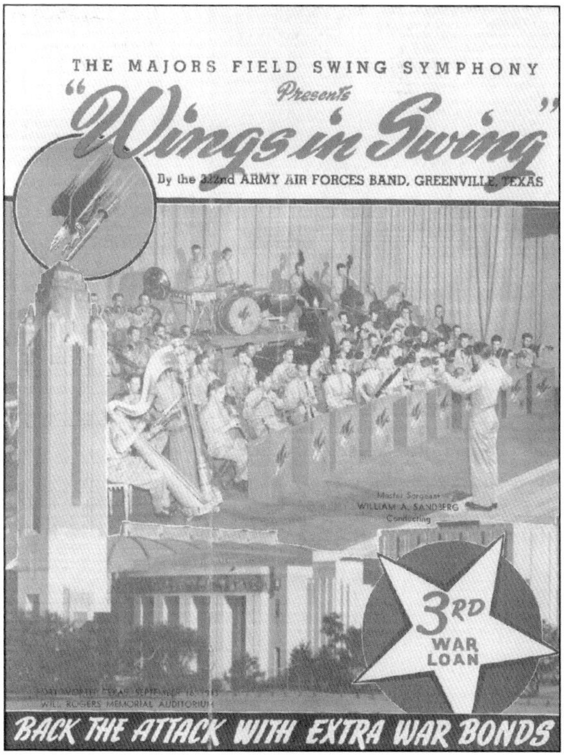

As part of his speech encouraging Americans to invest in War Bonds, Pres. Franklin Delano Roosevelt encouraged the people to show the enemy the faith they had in their men and country by investing all they could in the cause. As a result of the "Back the Attack" program, the "Hollywood Cavalcade" performance at Will Rogers Coliseum helped raise $13 million. (FWPL.)

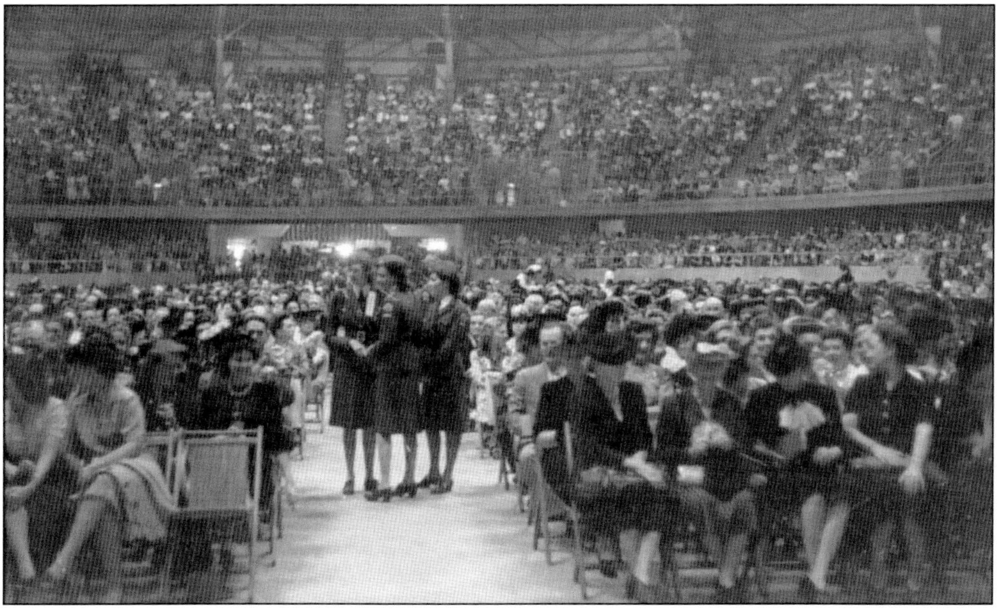

There were eight different bond drives to raise money. The third began on September 9, 1943, and ran until October 2, 1943, with the goal of raising $15 billion. Hollywood stars participated in a 20-city tour, raising $19 billion for the war. A crowd of more than 10,000 joined the fine men and women in uniform to see the stars. (FWPL.)

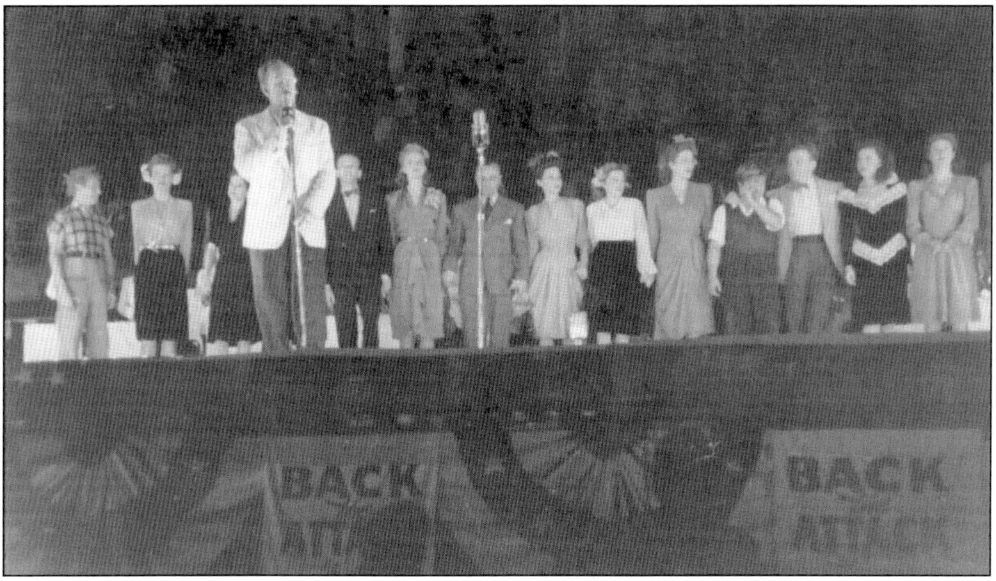

When the Hollywood Cavalcade arrived in Fort Worth, several of the stars had contracted food poisoning in New Orleans. Betty Hutton was so ill that she did not perform, Judy Garland fainted after arriving at the Coliseum, and both Lucille Ball and Kay Kyser felt terrible during the show. The large group included several big names, including James Cagney, Mickey Rooney, Margie Stewart, Dorothy Merritt, Kay Kyser, Doris Merrick, Paul Henried, Greer Garson, Judy Garland, Betty Hutton, Kathryn Grayson, Jose Iturbi, Rosemary LaPlanche, Harpo Marx, Lucille Ball, Fred Astaire, Georgia Carroll, Harry Babbitt, Diane Pendleton, Ruth Bardy, Muriel Goodspeed, and Dick Powell. (FWPL.)

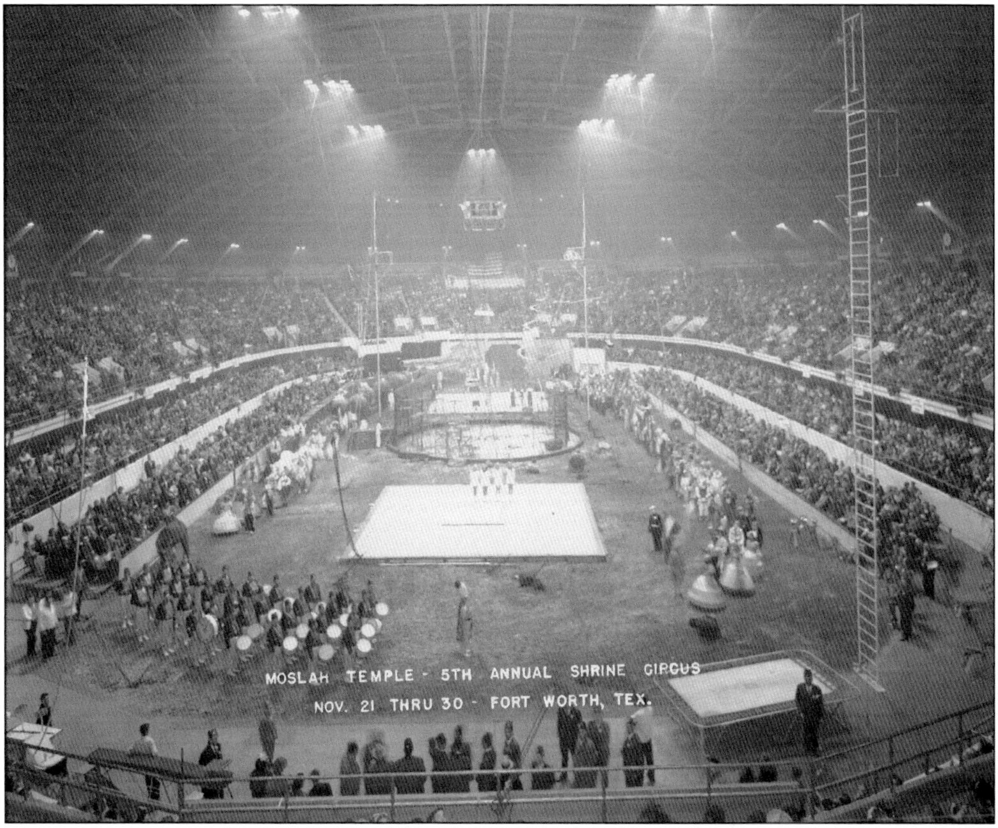

The Moslah Shrine Circus has been held at the Coliseum since 1942. Proceeds from the event support the Shrine Center, helping the Moslahs to conduct their many philanthropic services. Many other circuses have also been held in the Coliseum over the years. (WDS.)

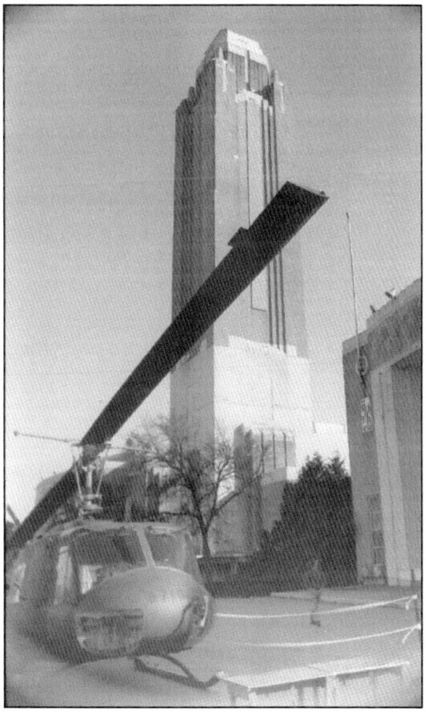

In March 1946, 2nd Lt. Kenneth R. Bloom and Pvt. Robert S. Unk from Sheppard Air Force Base balanced their helicopter on top of the Tower for several minutes. The pilots were part of an aviation exposition being held in conjunction with the Stock Show and gave daily demonstrations of their abilities. (FWPL.)

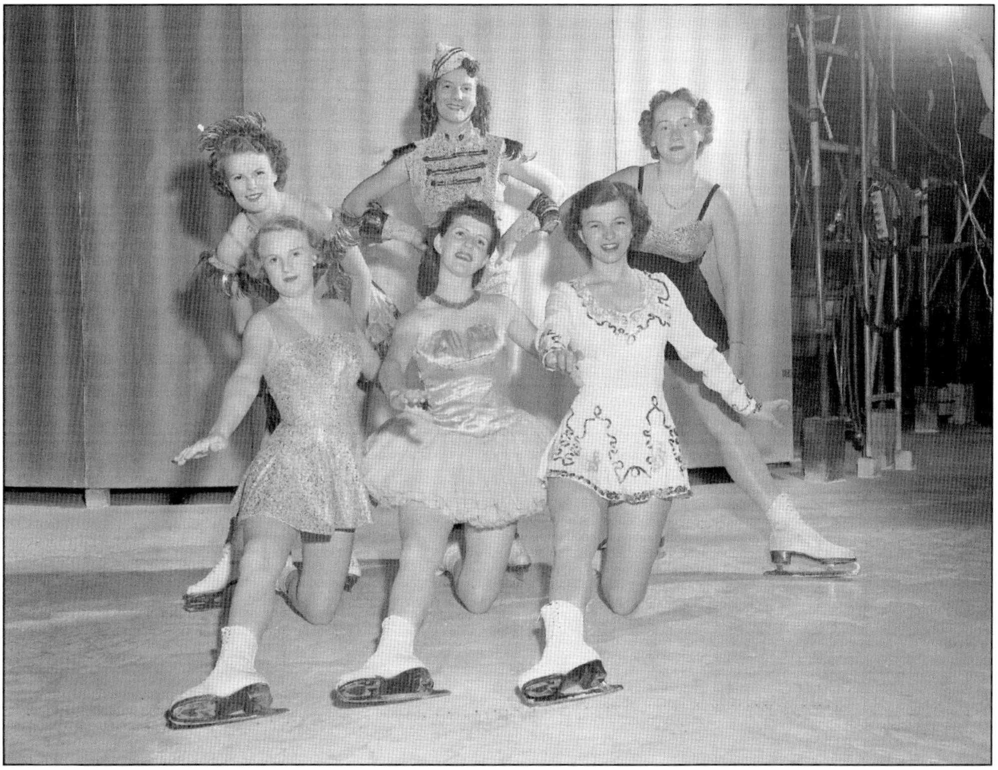

The Ice Capades, a carnival on ice, began in 1940 when John H. Harris realized the value of an ice-skating show featuring everything from clowns to professional skaters. From 1940 until 1995, they consistently entertained large crowds in venues throughout the United States and Canada, regularly returning to Will Rogers Coliseum. In competition to be crowned Fort Worth's "Queen of the Ice" in 1950 were, from left to right, (first row) Joyce Atchison, Janis Adams, and Patsy Norcross; (second row) Laura Lee Hoskins, Billie Arlene Biggs, and Dorothy Ann Kirsch. (FWST.)

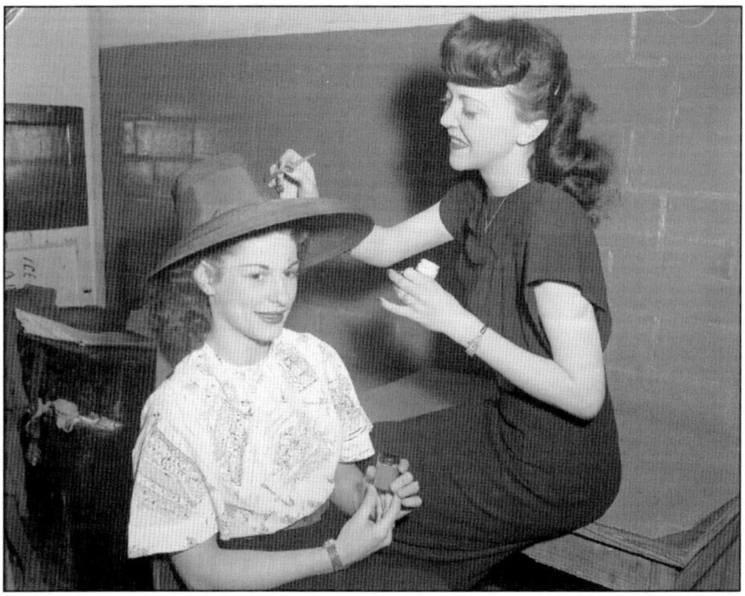

Feature performers Ann Robinson (left) and Edythe Walley touch up before an event. Robinson began skating at the age of 12 and was the National Novice Ladies Champion and Mid-Western Junior Ladies Champion in 1944. Edythe and her husband, Nat Walley, were the famous skating parents of Deborah Walley, who played the role of Gidget in the 1960s. (FWST.)

The most popular female act of the Ice Capades was Donna Atwood, who joined the show in 1941 when the Olympics were cancelled due to the war. After 15 years of touring and well over 6,000 shows, Atwood retired, leaving her husband, the show's owner and producer John H. Harris, and her skating partner, US National Champion Bobby Specht, to continue without her. Here, Atwood is in costume for the *Student Prince* show on April 9, 1951, at the Coliseum. (FWST.)

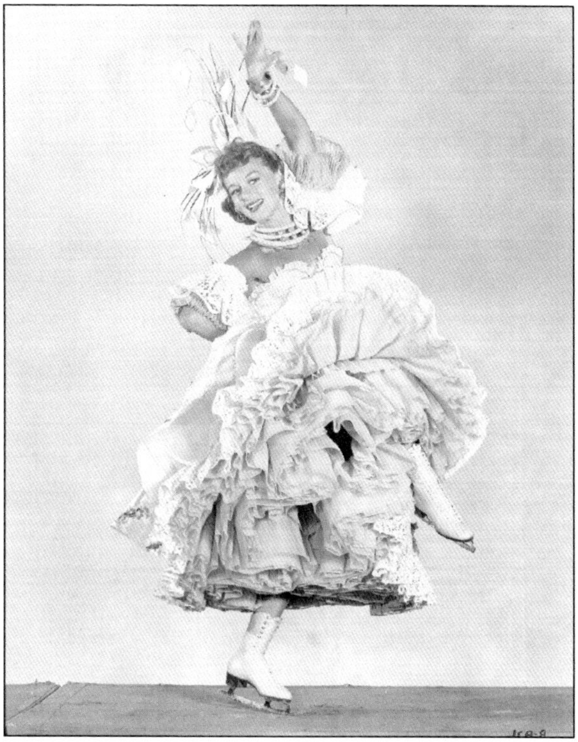

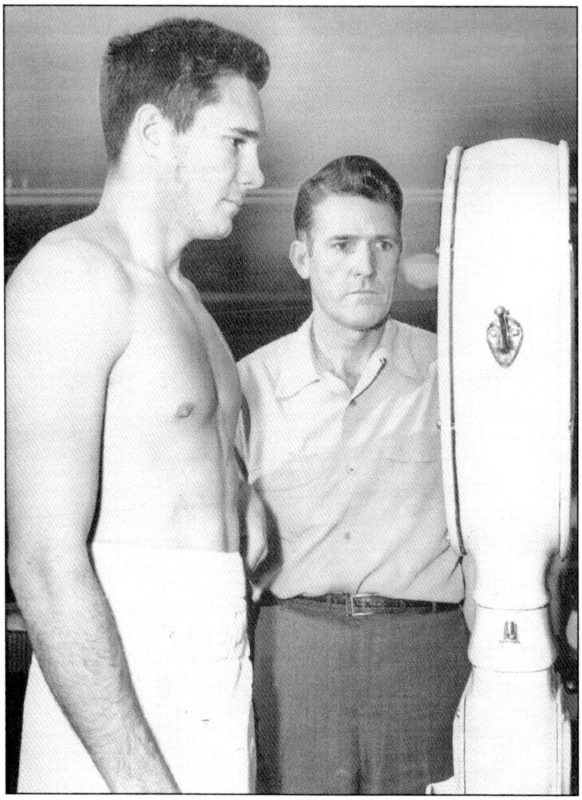

The oldest lessee at Will Rogers Coliseum is the Texas Golden Gloves, who signed on at the beginning of its 1936–1937 season. Tom Adams, the defending Light Heavyweight Champion in 1948, weighs in with tournament superintendent Walter Connelly. There once were 11 weight classes, and now there are 10: Pinweight, Flyweight, Bantamweight, Featherweight, Lightweight, Welterweight, Middleweight, Light Heavyweight, Heavyweight, and Super Heavyweight. (Fort Worth Golden Gloves.)

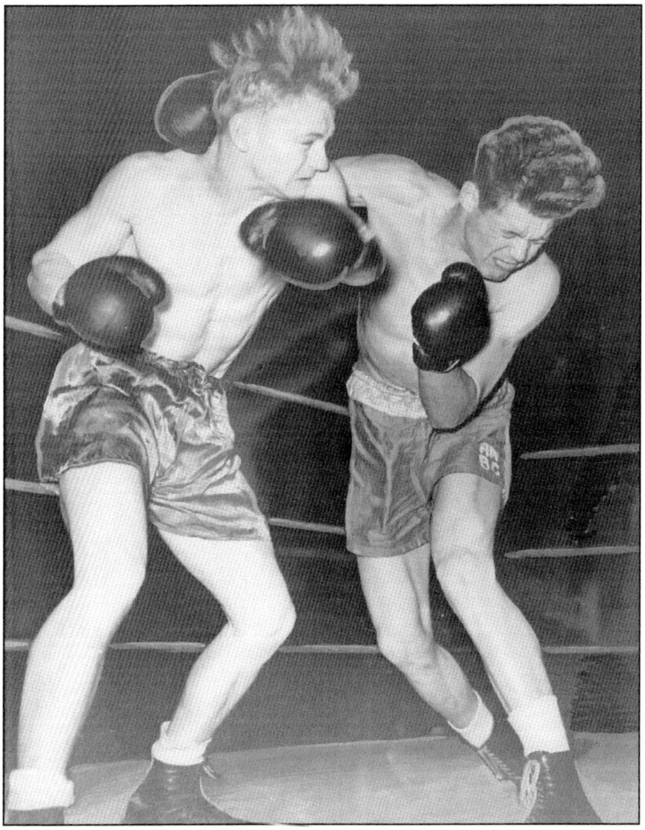

The fighters at the Golden Gloves give all they have. Bill Sanders and Jerel Walker duked it out in this 1949 bout. While neither of these fighters went on to national fame, many winners have continued to professional careers. (Fort Worth Golden Gloves.)

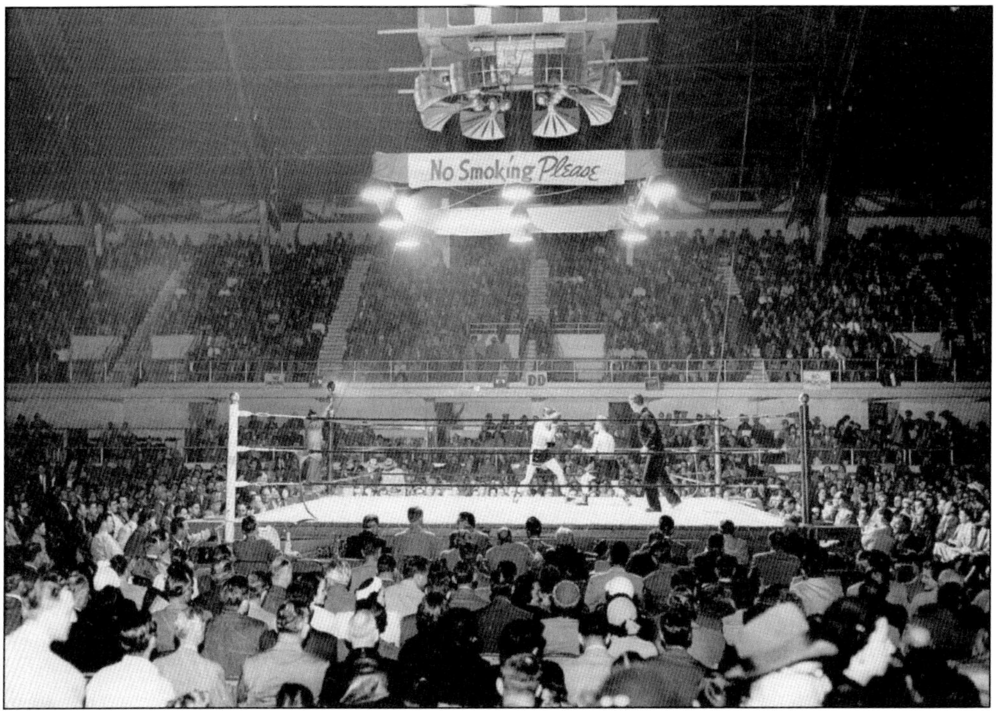

Before smoking was restricted anywhere, the Golden Gloves asked their audience to refrain. This image, taken some time in the 1950s, was used on many of the brochures and promotional materials. (Fort Worth Golden Gloves.)

Many boxers got their start in the Golden Gloves, and many of them returned to coach, sponsor, or encourage other youths to get involved with the competition. Here, in February 1957, former National Champion Richard Menchaca encourages Victor Graffio of Beaumont in the state competition at Will Rogers Coliseum. (Fort Worth Golden Gloves.)

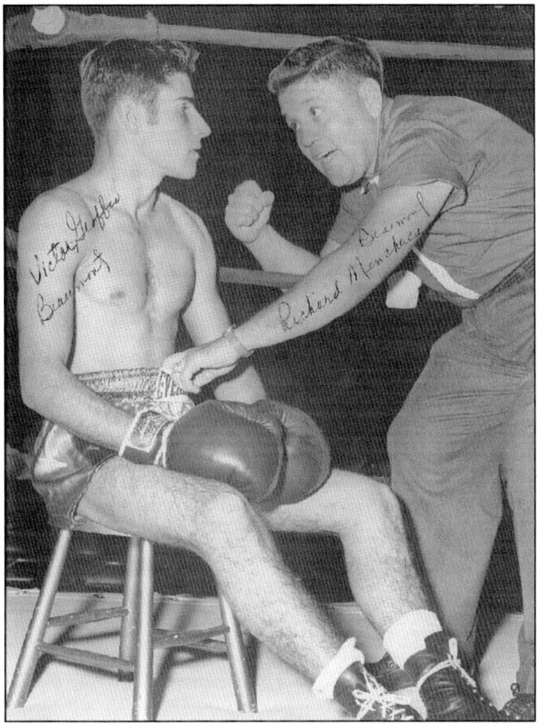

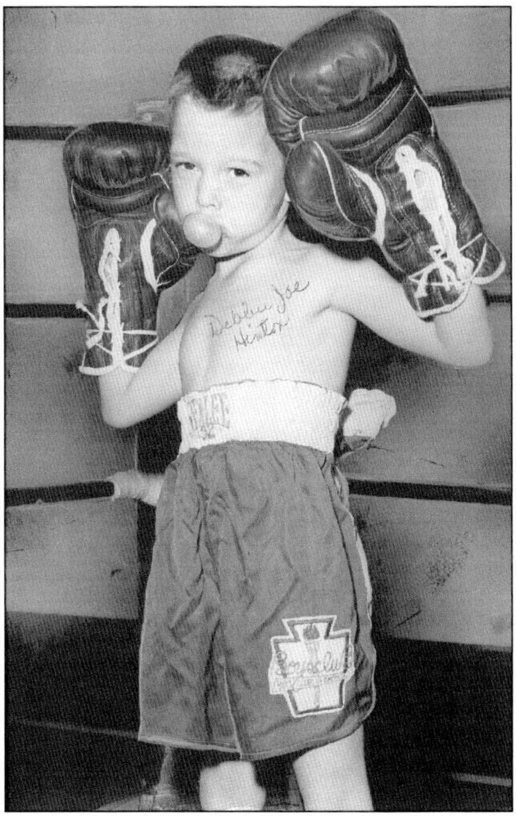

Golden Gloves sponsors amateur boxing programs for young athletes from ages eight and up. Winners of 10 different weight levels at the state competitions go to the national competition, and many of the participants go on to major boxing careers. Debbie Joe Hinton, age seven and weighing 65 pounds, poses in 1958 with gloves that are bigger than his head. (Fort Worth Golden Gloves.)

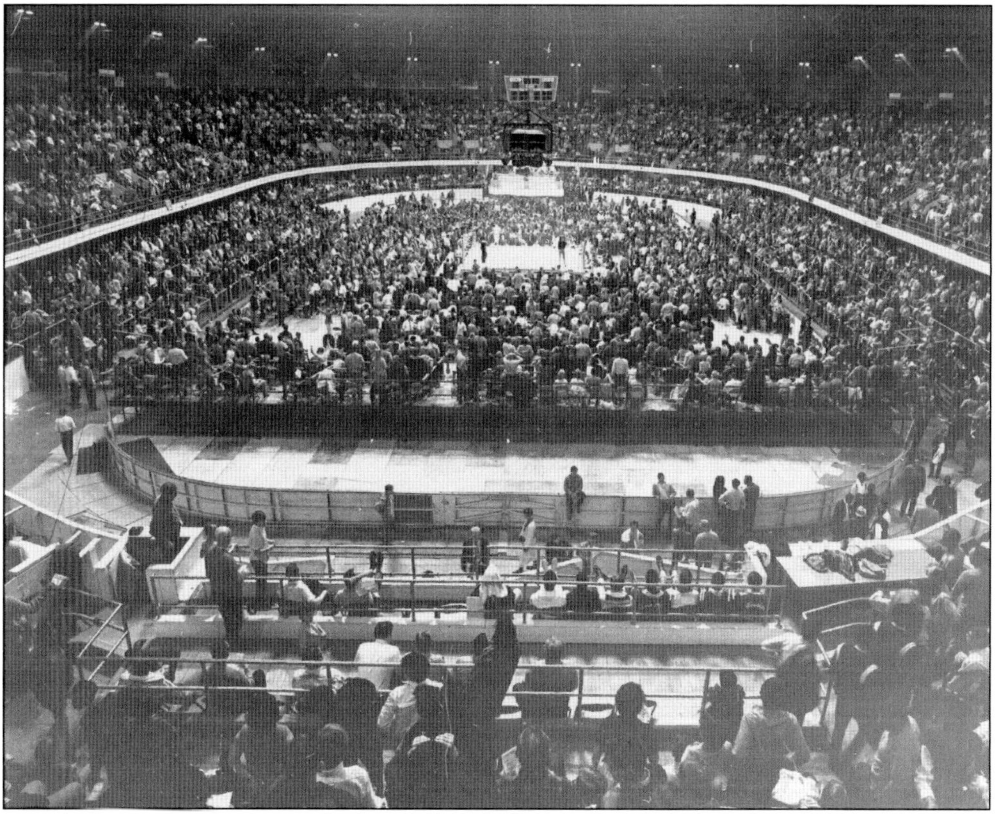

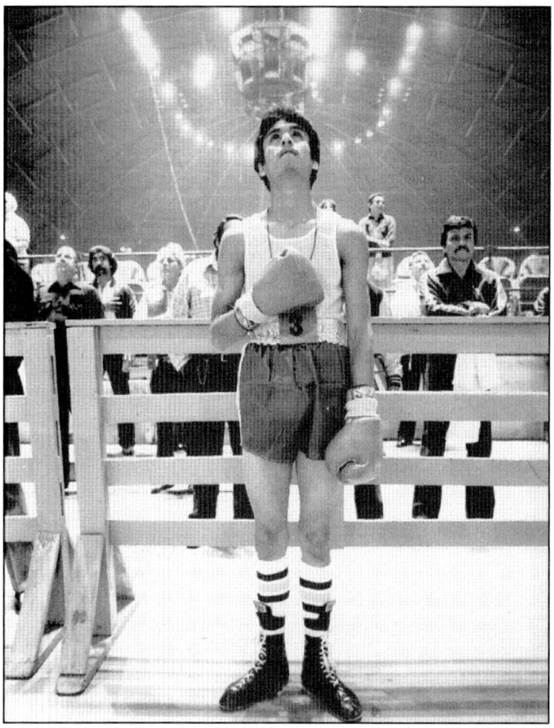

The Texas branch of the Golden Gloves has benefitted several charity programs throughout the years. Beneficiaries included the Fort Worth *Star-Telegram* Free Milk and Ice Fund, the Goodfellows—another Fort Worth *Star-Telegram* program that provided clothes, shoes, and toys to underprivileged schoolchildren—and the Youth Development Fund, which provided a free gymnasium for boys where they could train with free equipment and instructors. The event drew capacity crowds like this one from the 1960s. (Fort Worth Golden Gloves.)

Before the state championship, Juan Payan of El Paso was caught in a moment that truly captures the hope and promise of the Golden Gloves: the National Anthem played as he stood in the bullpen awaiting his chance at victory. (Fort Worth Golden Gloves.)

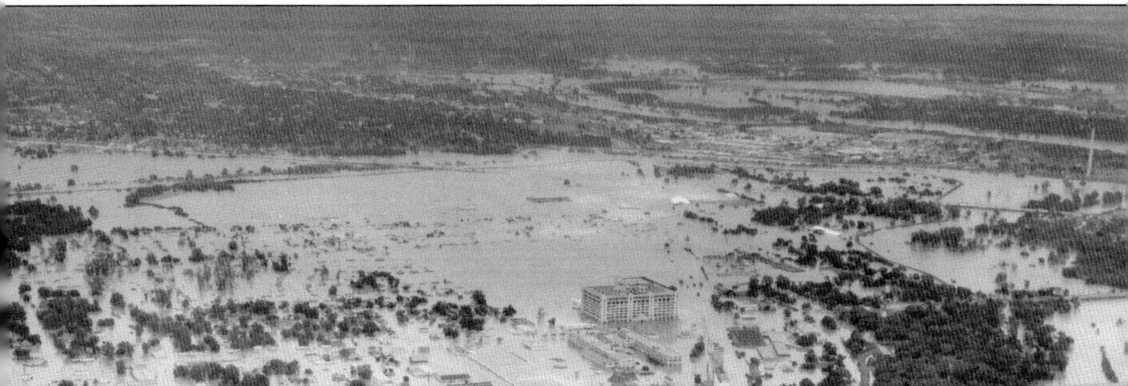

The flood of May 1949 was responsible for 11 deaths and $11 million in damages. Because of prior flooding of the Trinity River in 1908 and 1922, the Galveston District of the Army Corps of Engineers approved the construction of several lakes in the area in 1945, including Benbrook Lake, and a proposed Trinity River shipping channel, but construction had barely started when the 1949 flood occurred. The widespread devastation caused on the west side of Fort Worth can be seen in this photograph. The water almost reached the second floor of Montgomery Ward (center right). Farther left, the grass inside Farrington Field's is submerged, but just across University Drive, the remains of the Centennial grounds and Will Rogers Coliseum (not in photograph) remained dry. When which land was best suited for the permanent structure that became Will Rogers Memorial Center was being debated, several wise citizens wrote to the city council and pointed out that the portion of the Van Zandt track was a high enough piece of land that it would be protected from such a flood. This photograph shows that they were correct. (FWST.)

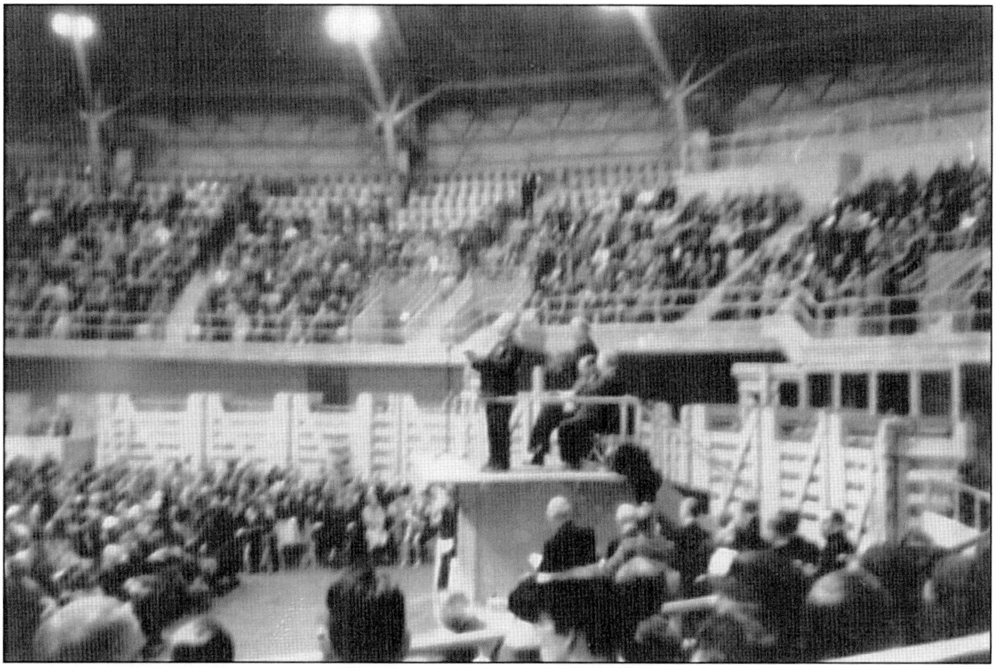

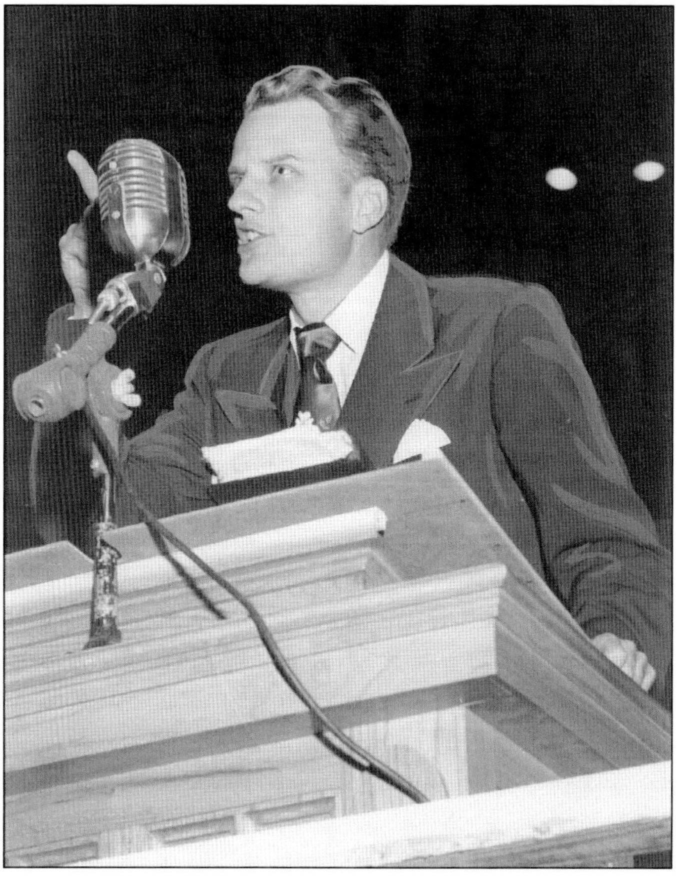

Before Rev. Billy Graham, there was the Rev. Rodney "Gypsy" Smith Jr., who, like his father, was one of the most famous evangelists in the world. During one of his trips to Texas, Smith preached to crowds of 12,000 every day for an entire season in the Coliseum. (Doug Harman.)

Rev. Billy Graham held his first and second open revivals in Texas at Will Rogers Coliseum. The first, on November 9, 1950, filled the Coliseum and much of the Auditorium, where the crowd listened through a public address system. It was the largest crowd Fort Worth had ever recorded at an indoor event. (FWST.)

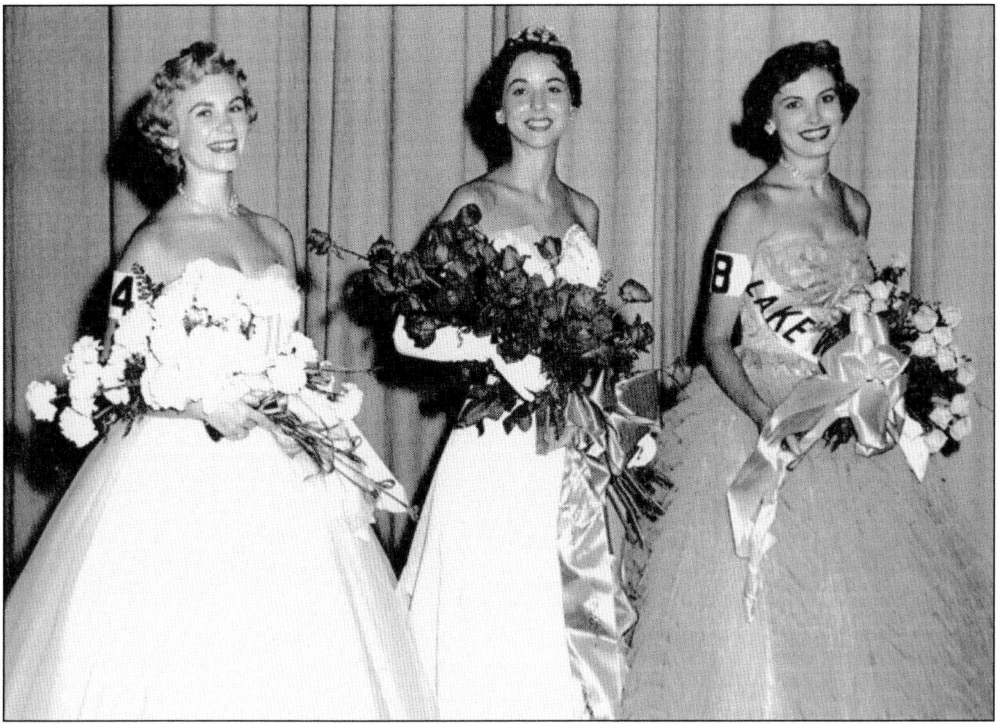

Miss America started in 1921 as a way to keep summer tourists in Atlantic City; two years later, three Texas women were in the pageant. In 1954, the nonprofit organization moved the Miss Texas competition into Will Rogers Auditorium, where it stayed until 1971. The winner in 1954, Yvonne Erwin, pictured in the center, was a senior at Southern Methodist University. (Randy Pruett.)

From left to right, Lynda Ferguson (Miss Louisiana), Karen Hansmeier (Miss Nebraska), Linda Varley (reigning Miss Texas), and Sandi Curtis (Miss Oklahoma) visited the 1965 Miss Texas Pageant at Will Rogers Coliseum on July 28, 1965. Two years before their visit, the pageant was broadcast statewide from the Will Rogers Auditorium for the first time. (FWST.)

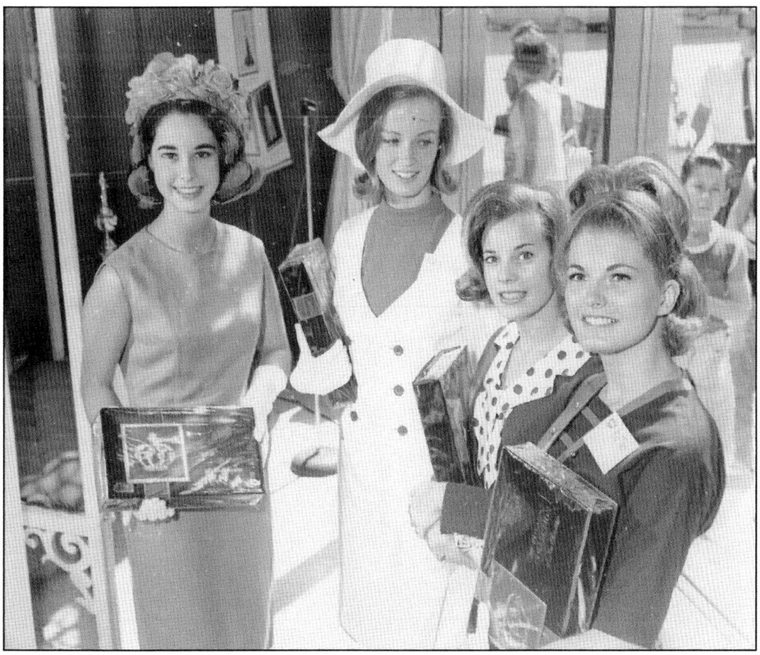

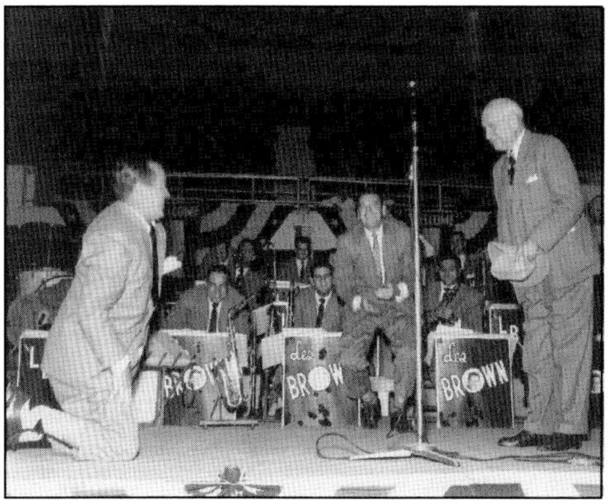

On November 29, 1950, Bob Hope gave a free show for Carswell Air Force Base military personnel and their families. Performers included Jerry Colonna, Jimmy Wakely, and Marilyn Maxwell—stars who had entertained the troops with Hope in Korea. It was a huge success and had one of the largest crowds ever at the Coliseum. Hope was the master of ceremonies and chief entertainer, but Amon Carter made a splash when he presented Hope with a new 21-jewel watch. Hope thanked Carter and told the crowd, "He's a grand guy, I don't care what Dallas says." (TCU.)

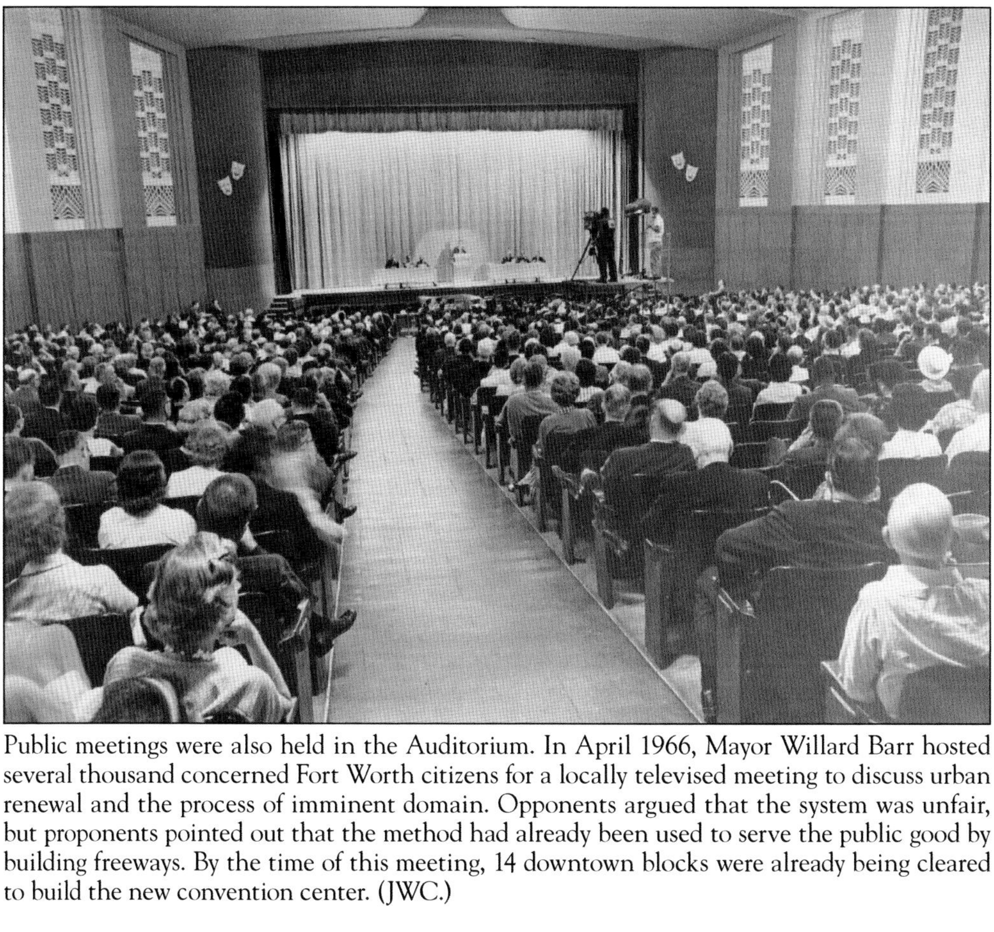

Public meetings were also held in the Auditorium. In April 1966, Mayor Willard Barr hosted several thousand concerned Fort Worth citizens for a locally televised meeting to discuss urban renewal and the process of imminent domain. Opponents argued that the system was unfair, but proponents pointed out that the method had already been used to serve the public good by building freeways. By the time of this meeting, 14 downtown blocks were already being cleared to build the new convention center. (JWC.)

Six

Masterpiece Performances

In order for a structure to serve the public good, it must appeal to people from all walks of life, with many different interests. The Auditorium has hosted many great performances other than those already mentioned. From classical music to rock 'n' roll, ballet to folk, generations of appreciative fans have been entertained with music and dance at the center. For the first 40 years, the Auditorium was home to hundreds of symphony, ballet, and orchestral performances, attracting the best from around the country. Rock 'n' roll concerts featured the most popular artists of the day entertaining capacity crowds. Many shows, like the 1978 Rolling Stones concert, went so well that they were made into albums, CDs, and even DVDs. People attended some shows in jewels and furs and other shows in blue jeans and tie-dyed shirts—all were welcome at the center built for the enjoyment of the people.

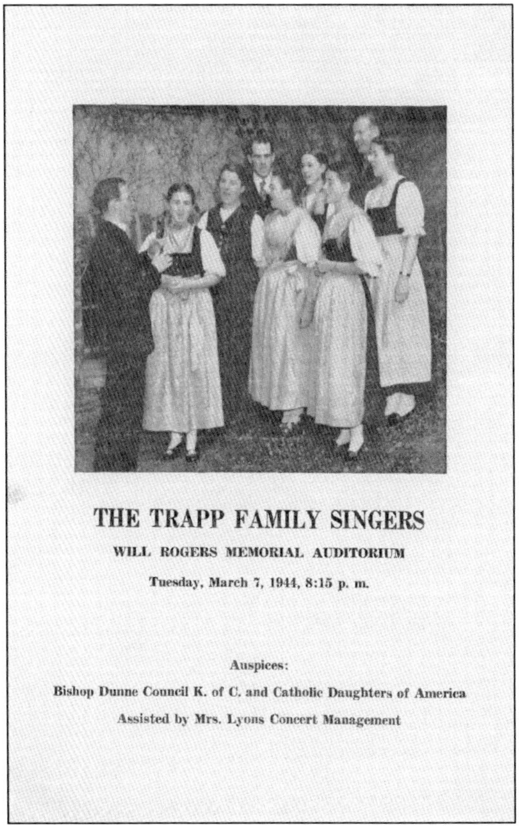

After Austria was annexed by Germany in 1938, the von Trapp family fled to Italy with their musical conductor, Dr. Franz Wasner. By September 1938, they had arrived in New York, where they began a concert tour. The family, made famous by the movie *The Sound of Music*, made an appearance at the Auditorium on March 7, 1944. (FWPL.)

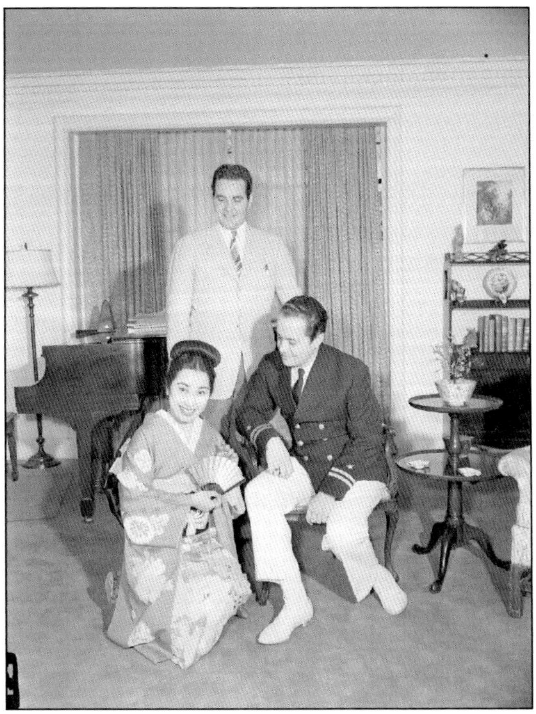

Begun in 1946 by Eloise Snyder, Betty Spain, Jeanne Axtell Walker, and hundreds of volunteers, the Fort Worth Civic Opera Association is the 14th-oldest opera company in the United States. Over the years, the Opera gave hundreds of performances in the Will Rogers Auditorium, including the Puccini opera *Madame Butterfly* in 1947. The main characters were played by Tomiko Kanazawa, an American-born Japanese soprano, as Cio-Cio-San; Melvin Dacus as Sharpless, the American consul at Nagasaki; and Gabor Carelli, a Hungarian-American tenor as B.F. Pinkerton. (FWST.)

The Chicago Symphony was founded in 1891 by Theodore Thomas and was the third-oldest orchestra in America at the time of this performance on February 1, 1948. The 1948 season was 30 weeks long, from October through April, with a total of 125 concerts. The conductor, Artur Rodzinski, was one of the best in the country, having previously conducted the New York, Los Angeles, and Rochester Symphony Orchestras, the Cleveland and Detroit Symphonies, and the Philadelphia and Metropolitan Opera Houses. (FWPL.)

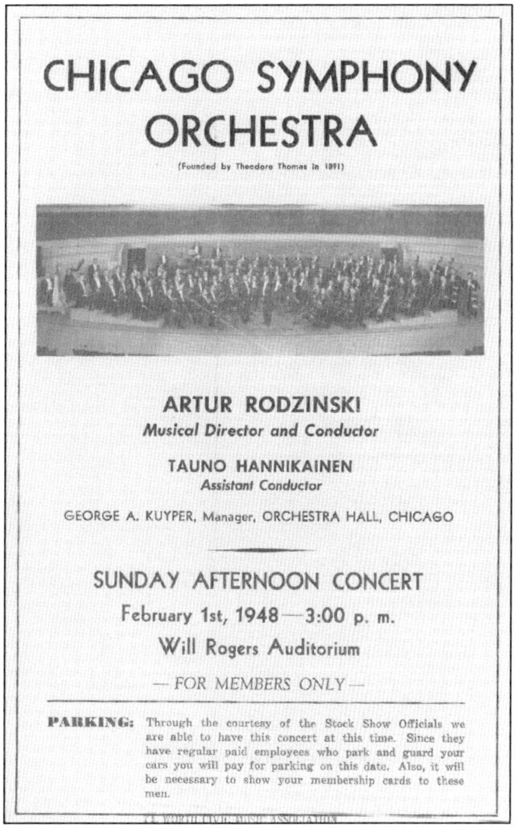

CHICAGO SYMPHONY ORCHESTRA

(Founded by Theodore Thomas in 1891)

ARTUR RODZINSKI
Musical Director and Conductor

TAUNO HANNIKAINEN
Assistant Conductor

GEORGE A. KUYPER, Manager, ORCHESTRA HALL, CHICAGO

SUNDAY AFTERNOON CONCERT
February 1st, 1948—3:00 p. m.
Will Rogers Auditorium
— *FOR MEMBERS ONLY* —

PARKING: Through the courtesy of the Stock Show Officials we are able to have this concert at this time. Since they have regular paid employees who park and guard your cars you will pay for parking on this date. Also, it will be necessary to show your membership cards to these men.

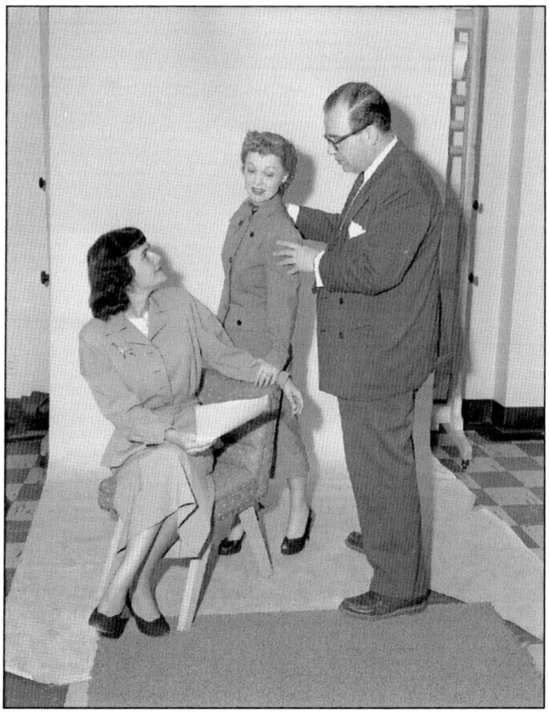

Dino Yannopoulos, the stage director for the February 1951 performance of *The Marriage of Figaro*, first began conducting at the age of 16. Here, he gives cues to Dorothy MacNeil (left), Figaro's bride, and Bettye Hairston (center), a mischievous page. Yannopoulos was the principal director of the Metropolitan Opera in New York until 1977. (FWST.)

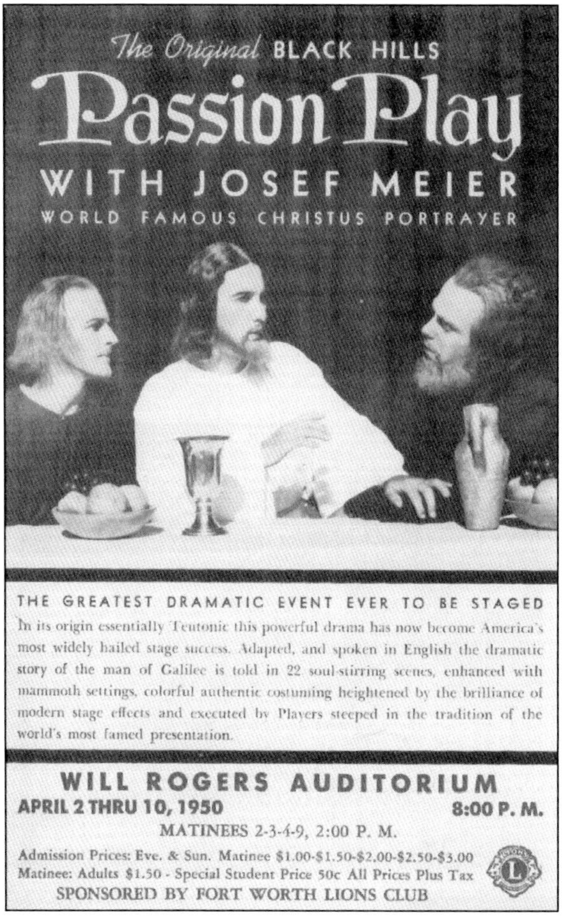

Originally from Westphalia, Josef Meier was one of the world's most outstanding portrayers of Christ, coming from a long line of German Biblical dramatists. He performed for more than 5,000 audiences in Europe, America, and Canada. This program is from *Passion Play*, performed at the Auditorium on April 2–10, 1950. (FWPL.)

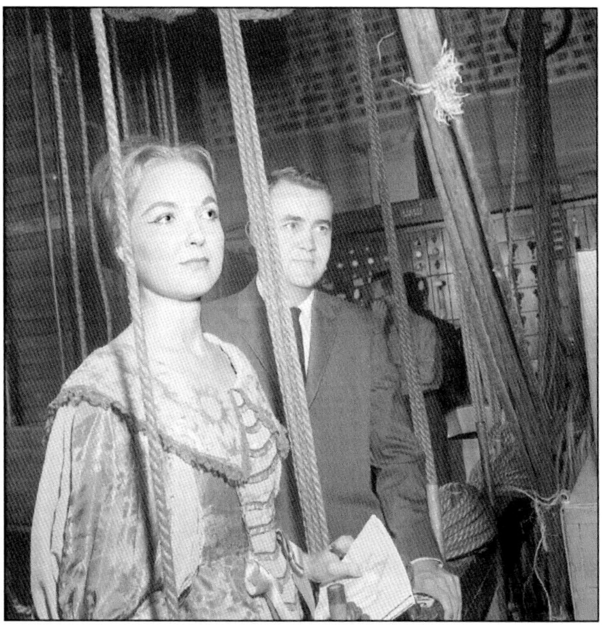

Cyrena McMurry waits backstage with her husband, Stan, before her performance as Alisa in *Lucia de Lammermoor* at the November 28, 1962, Auditorium show. After seven years of singing it in English, the 1962 production was sung in Italian, at the recommendation of soprano Lily Pons, the headliner. Other cast members included Joshua Hecht, Benjamin Rayson, Howard Fried, and, making his debut appearance in Fort Worth, Placido Domingo. Six years later, the April 7, 1968, production of *Lucia de Lammermoor* was the last operatic performance at the Auditorium before the Fort Worth Civic Opera Association moved to the Tarrant County Convention Center. (FWST.)

Fort Worth Pops was presented by the Symphony League of Fort Worth to benefit the Fort Worth Symphony Orchestra Association. Among the stars in the show were Don Wilson, Linda Loftis (Miss Texas 1961), and the Cowtown Chorus of the Society for the Preservation and Encouragement of Barber Shop Quartet Singing in America. (FWPL.)

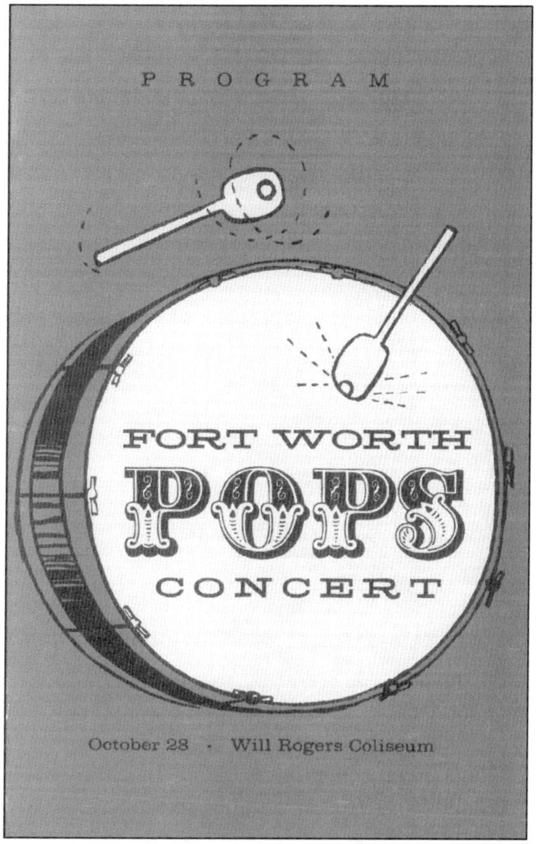

The next generation of fans of the Fort Worth Symphony Orchestra was treated to this free performance in January 1965 at the Auditorium. The majority of these young men and women seem captivated by the show. (FWST.)

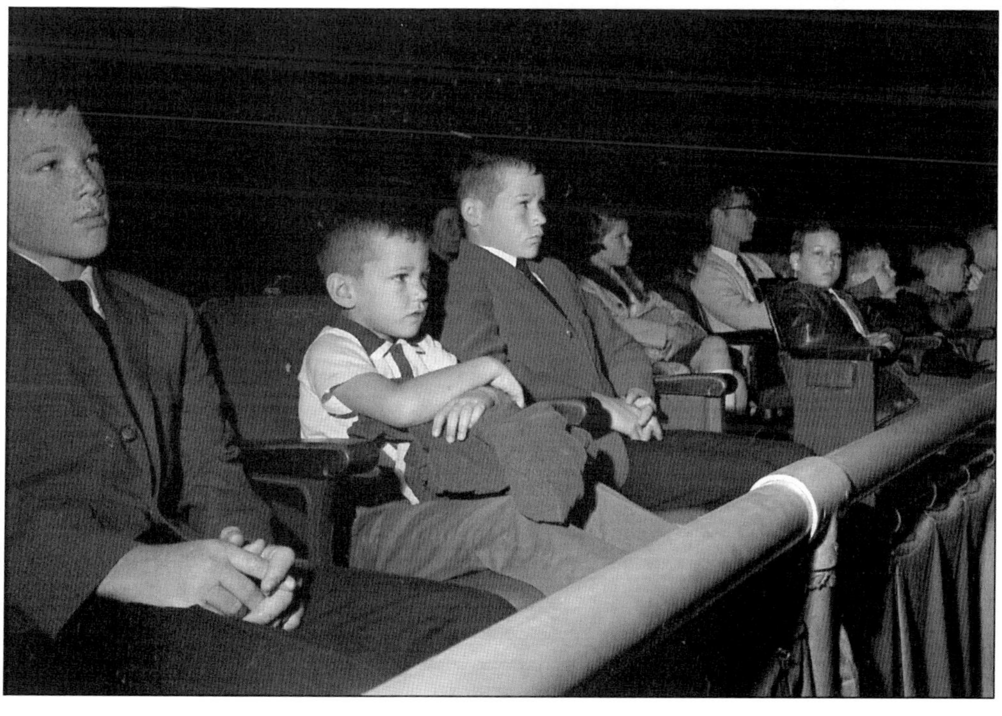

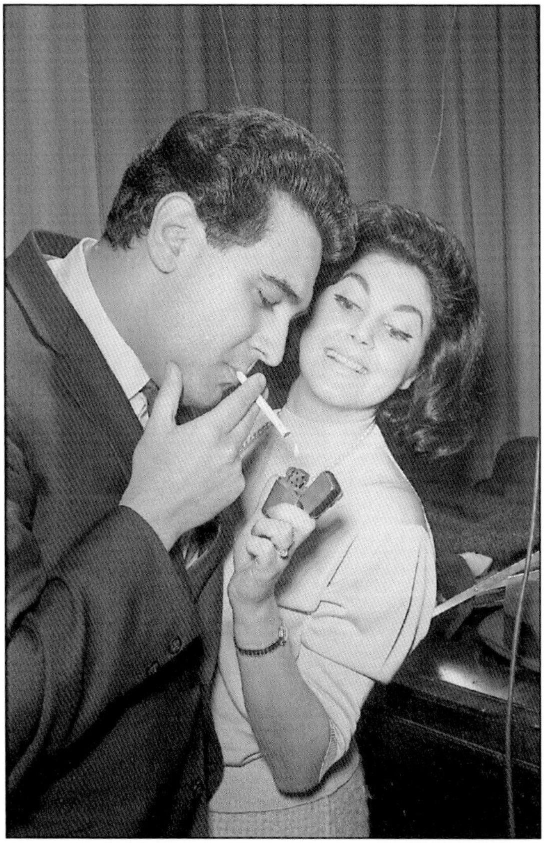

Humanitarian, award-winning opera star, and member of the Three Tenors Placido Domingo takes a smoke break at rehearsal with Joyce Blackham. Their performance of *Carmen* at the Auditorium on November 26, 1965, was a part of the Fort Worth Opera's 20th season. Domingo sang the role of the soldier Don Jose, and Blackham, a British mezzo-soprano, made her American debut as Carmen. (FWST.)

In the 1960s, the Fort Worth Symphony had to borrow money to pay its musicians; to help repay the loan from the Fort Worth National Bank, Jack Benny held a "Benny-fit." Below, Benny rehearses with the symphony and conductor Ezra Rachlin for his performance on February 24, 1966. Rachlin was past director and conductor of the Philadelphia Opera Company, and while he was in charge of the Fort Worth Symphony Orchestra from 1965 to 1971, he was also the musical director and conductor of the Austin Symphony Orchestra and chief conductor of the Queensland Symphony Orchestra in Australia. (FWST.)

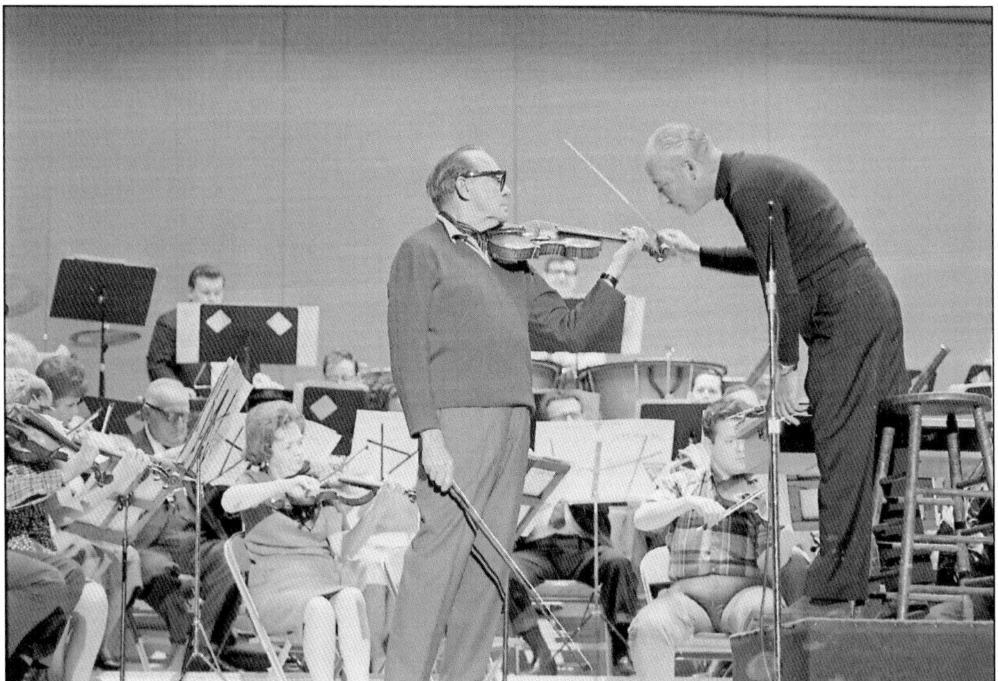

La Bohème was one of the most popular operas performed in the Auditorium. It was presented in 1966 by the Fort Worth Opera Association for its 20th anniversary season and was the association's 65th production. The 1966–1967 schedule also included Puccini's *Madame Butterfly*, Saint-Saëns's *Samson and Delilah*, Rossini's *The Barber of Seville*, and Verdi's *Otello*. (FWPL.)

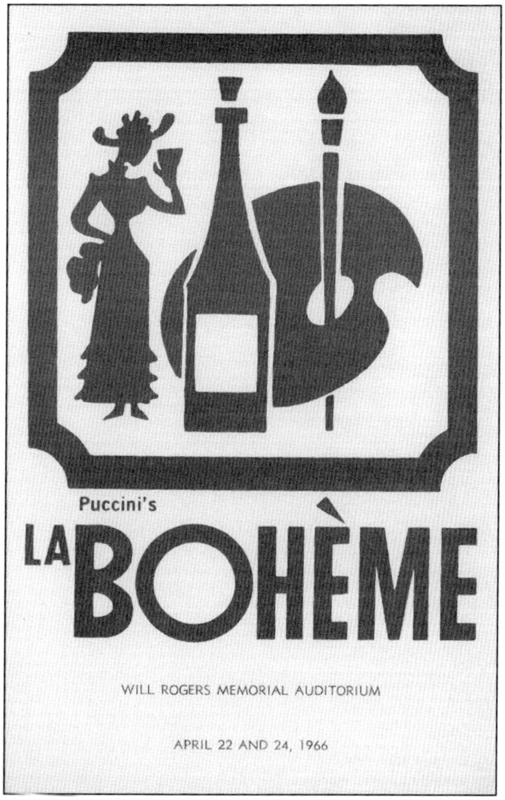

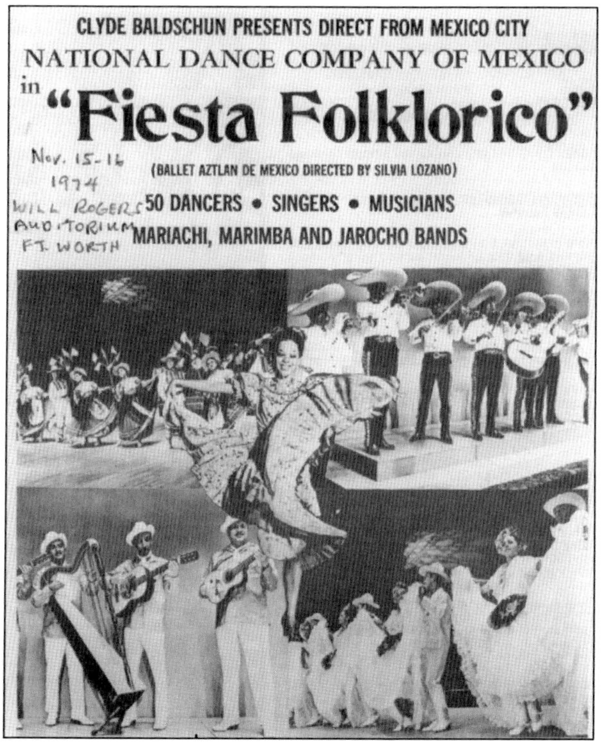

In 1974, *Fiesta Folklorico*, directed by Clyde Baldschun and Associates from Woodland Hills, California, brought its 50-member team to the Auditorium. Included in this group were Mexican singers, instrumentalists, dancers, and comedians who captivated their audiences with colorful costumes and expert performances. (FWPL.)

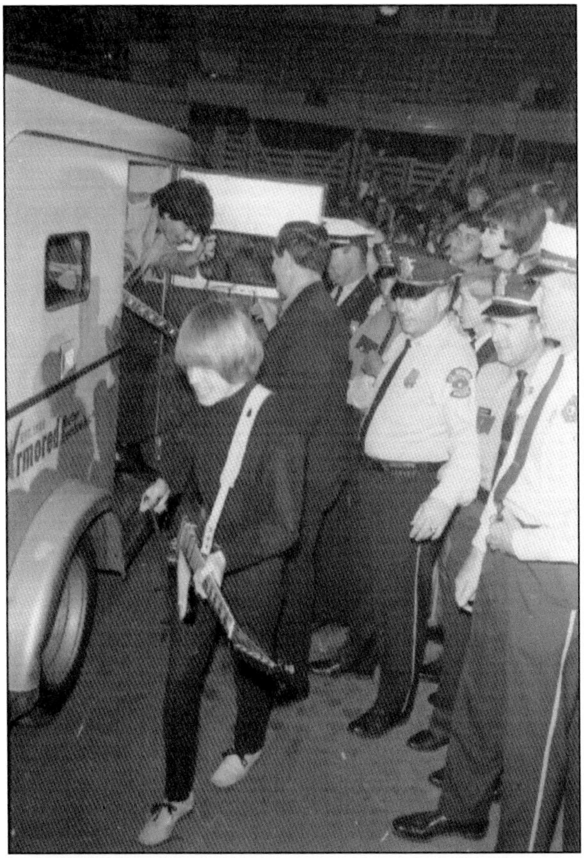

The concert series at the Auditorium featured an impressive collection of notable names. Photographs are surprisingly sparse, but the one at left, of the Rolling Stones getting out of an armored truck at the Coliseum on November 21, 1965, and below, of the crowd, captures the hysteria surrounding them and other performers from the 1950s through the 1980s. Included in the list of entertainers are the Everly Brothers; Chuck Berry; Buddy Knox; the Drifters; Paul Anka; Fats Domino; the Crickets; Eddie Cochran; Frankie Lymon; Clyde McPhatter; Iron Butterfly; the Doors; the Electric Prunes; the Seeds; the Box Tops; the McCoys; the Livin' End; the Exotics; the Jades; the Beach Boys; Steppenwolf; Jimi Hendrix; Sly and the Family Stone; Creedence Clearwater Revival; Emerson, Lake, and Palmer; the Kinks; Mahogany Rush; Stevie Ray Vaughan and Double Trouble; and Little Feat. (Both, FWST.)

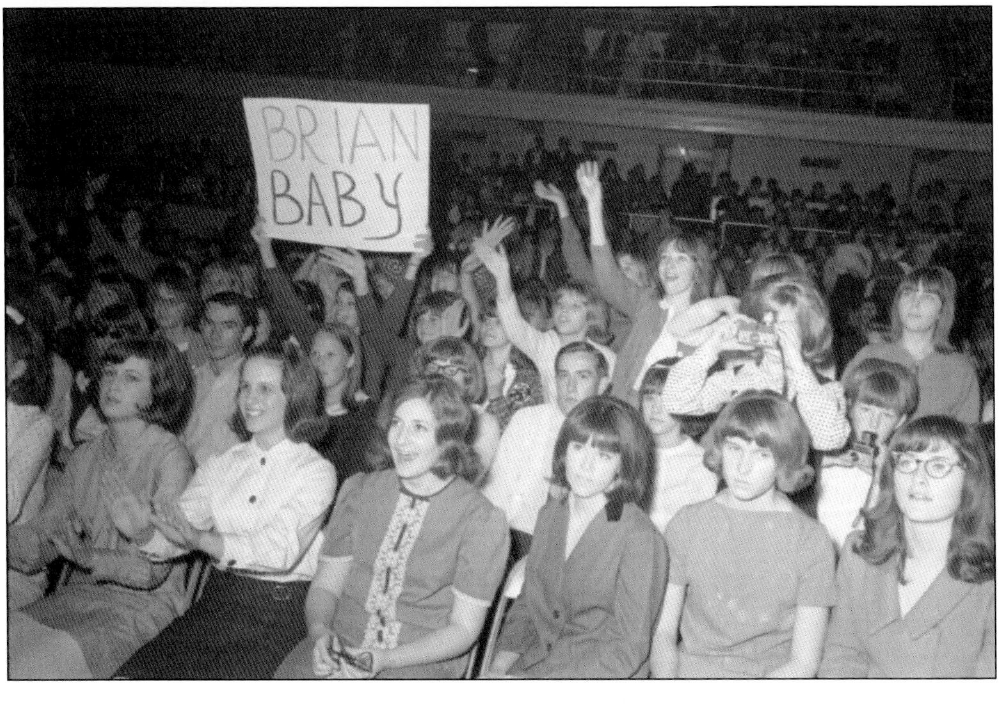

Seven

Art for the Ages

The Coliseum, Tower, and Auditorium represent the ultimate example of Art Deco architecture in Fort Worth and are works of art unto themselves. The tile friezes on the Coliseum and Auditorium represent the themes of the Centennial: history and economy. The Fort Worth *Star-Telegram* reported that they were "conceived from designs drawn by Kenneth Gale." Gale spent several weeks consulting with the architects, most probably Herman Koeppe, and others, possibly William Hammond and Samuel Peters Ziegler. After a full-size painting was presented, Koeppe prepared an architectural graph to be submitted to the WPA for approval. Women at the Mosaic Tile Company in Zanesville, Ohio, worked with full-sized patterns of the panel on the back wall of their studio as they hand-painted each tile. When completed, the two 150-foot panels were sent to Fort Worth in pieces and reassembled like a great big jigsaw puzzle. Three other distinctive art pieces complete the center: the bronze statue of Will Rogers on his favorite horse, Soapsuds, in front of the complex, the bronze bust of Rogers in the Tower rotunda, and the familiar painting of Rogers in the foyer of the Coliseum. They all combine to leave the indomitable signature of both Rogers and Carter on a center that was built for the city that they both loved so much.

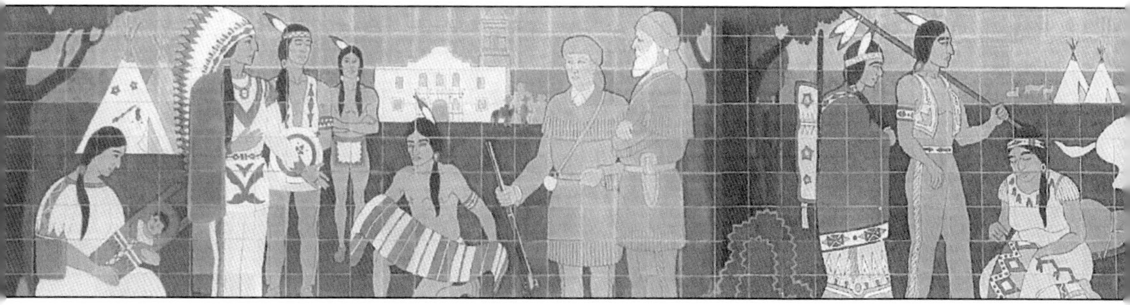

After these nine-inch-square tiles were made, they were painted, glazed, assembled, checked for errors or misfits, boxed, shipped to Fort Worth, reassembled on the workroom floor, and finally set in place. From left to right, the scenes show (above) Indians with Anglo traders in front of the Alamo,

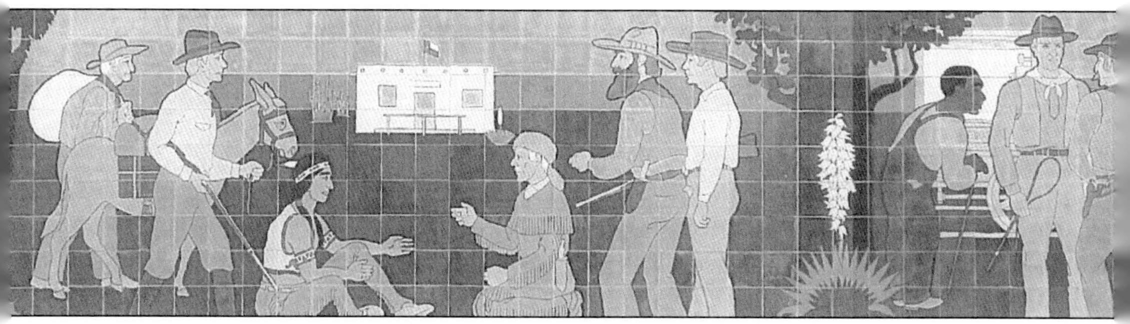

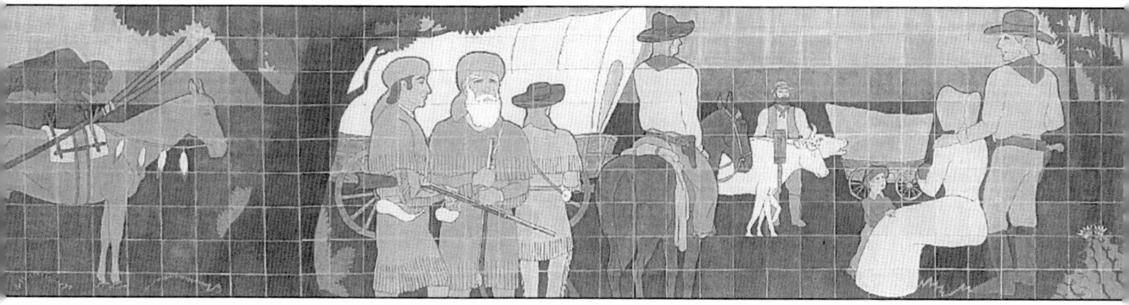

Indians hunting buffalo, and settlers arriving on the frontier; (below) Texas Rangers in front of Independence Hall, the coming of the railroad and a slave with his master, and cowboys at work on a ranch. (Courtesy of Joe Jopling for Fort Worth Public Art.)

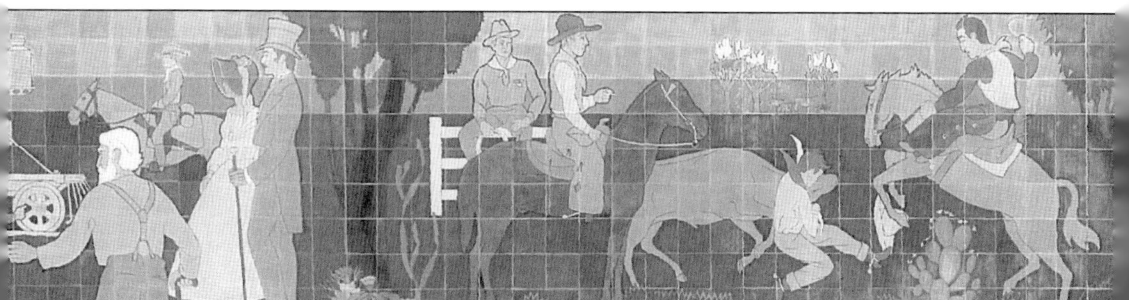

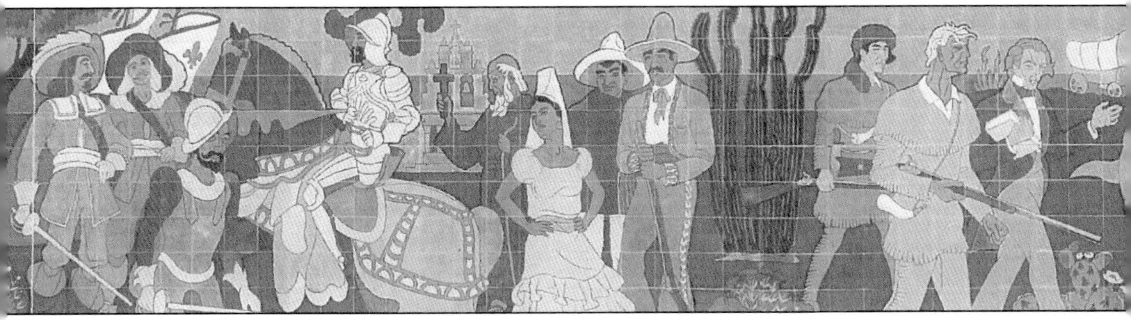

Zanesville was known as the Pottery Capital of the World because of all the manufacturers in the area. When the Mosaic Tile Company was selected for the job, many tile companies in the area had gone out of business due to the Depression. The Auditorium's frieze depicts, from left to right, (above) the Spanish and their early missions in Texas; Stephen F. Austin, Davy Crockett, James Bowie,

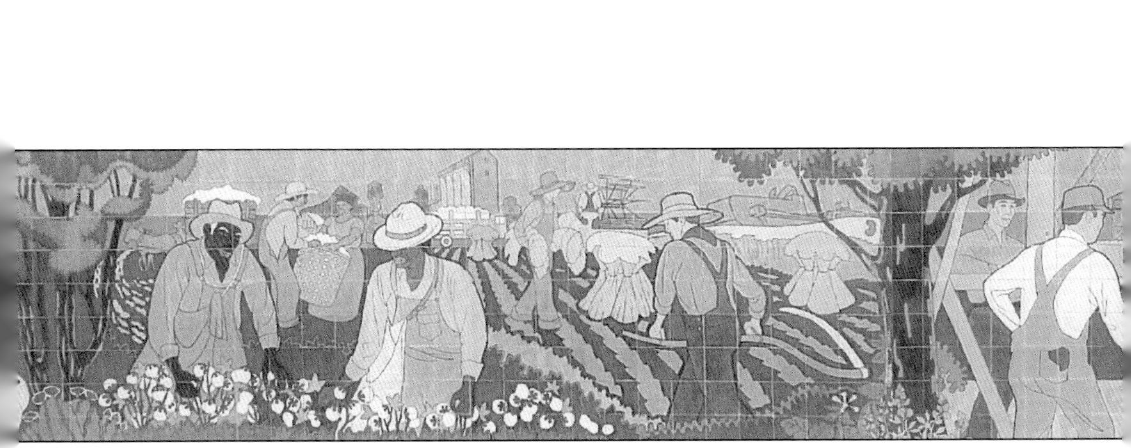

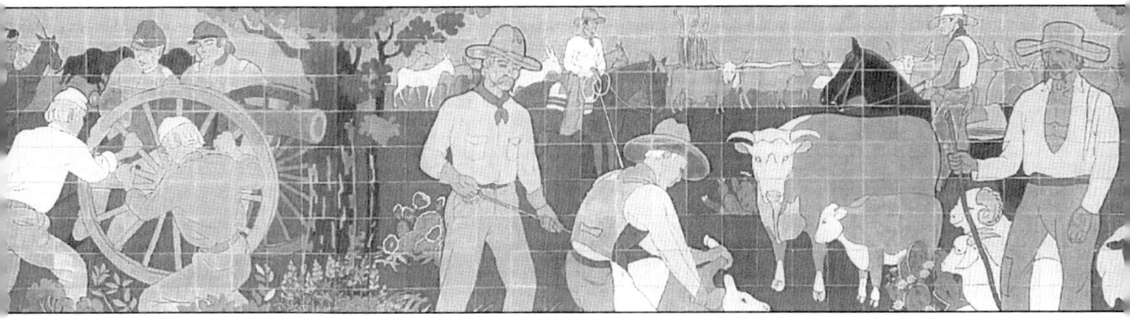

and Confederate soldiers; and ranchers branding and driving stock animals; (below) slaves working cotton and Anglo farmers working in the wheat fields; oil fields and refineries; and modern building and transportation. (Courtesy of Joe Jopling for Fort Worth Public Art.)

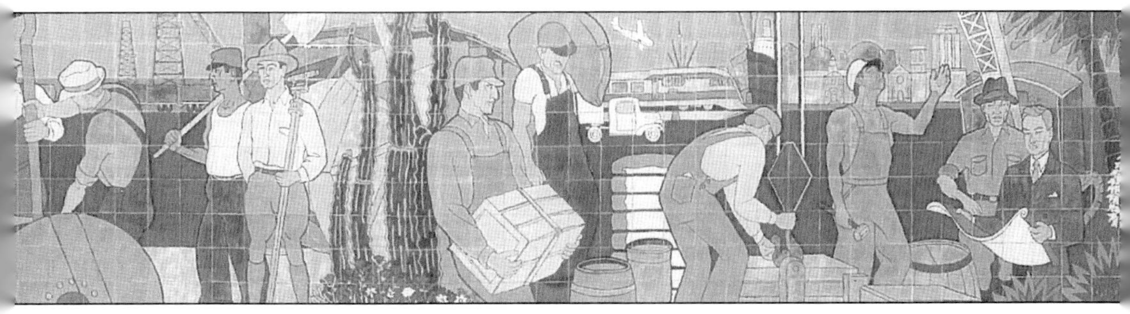

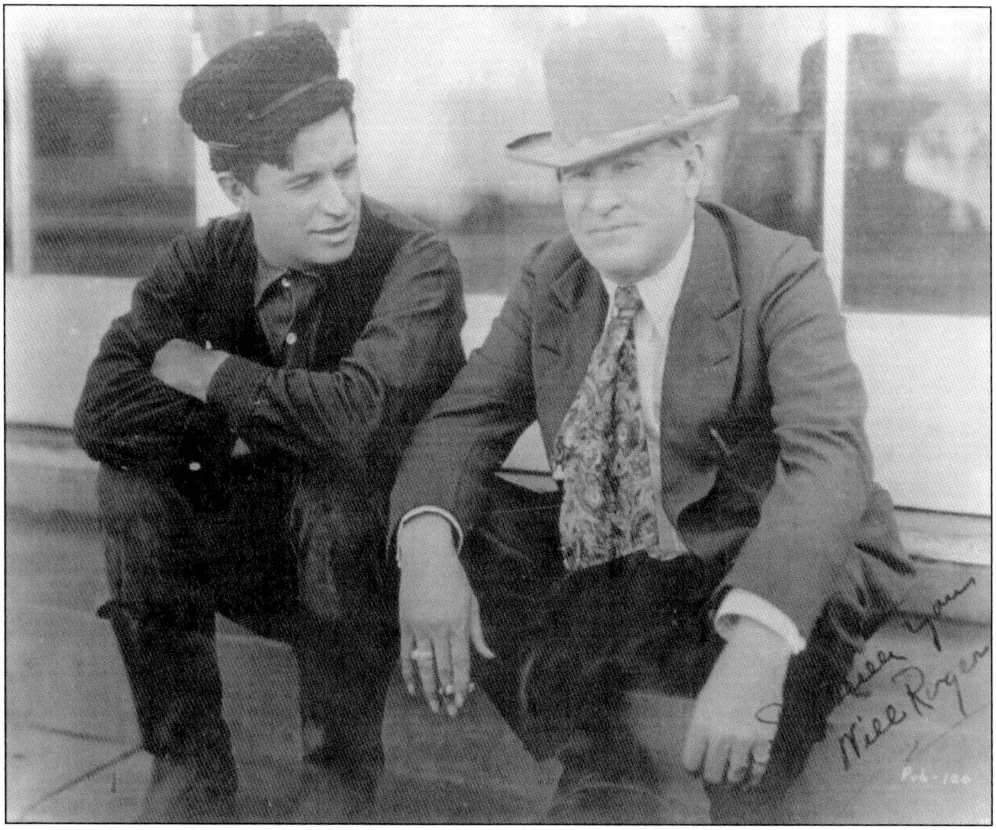

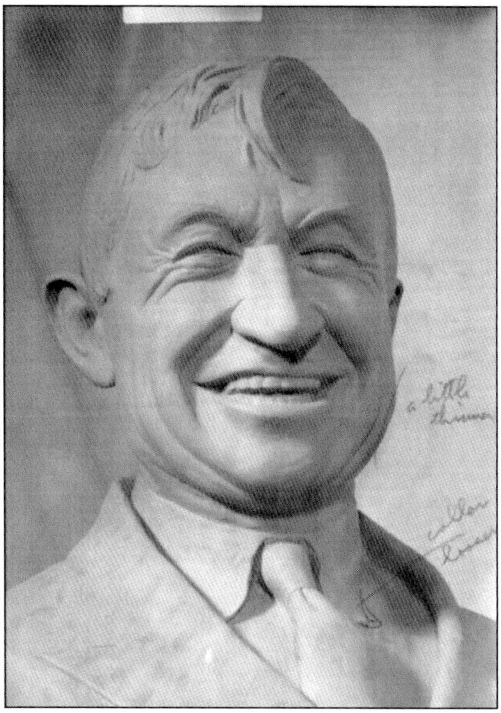

Amon Carter was enamored with Western art, due in part to his relationship with Will Rogers. Rogers had known Charles M. Russell and appreciated his work. He introduced it to Carter, who became one of the biggest collectors of Russell's work. Carter's collection of Western art can been seen at the Amon Carter Museum of American Art, across the street from the Will Rogers Memorial Complex. This photograph shows Russell and Rogers on Stage One at Goldwyn Studios during the filming of *A Poor Relation* in 1922. (ACM.)

The bust of Will Rogers sits on a pedestal in the Tower's rotunda. Created by Joseph Edward Lipe, it was cast by Roman Bronze Works in New York for $135 using the lost wax method. This is one of the photographs Lipe sent to get an estimate of how much it would cost to have the statue cast. It is likely that the writing on the photograph was Amon Carter's. (ACM.)

Joseph Lipe and his wife stand beside his first public commission on February 15, 1942. The life-size bust is 20.75 inches tall and 16 inches shoulder to shoulder and was donated by nine prominent citizens, including Amon Carter. Today, the bust's nose is shiny from all of the cowboys who rub it for luck. (FWST.)

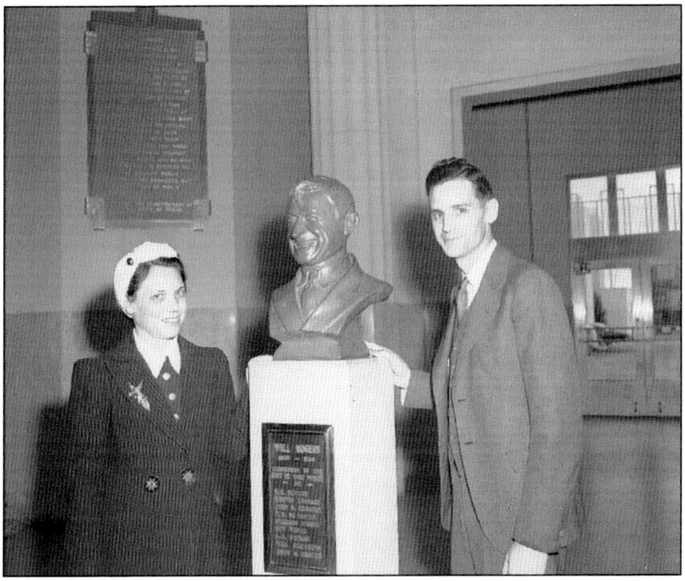

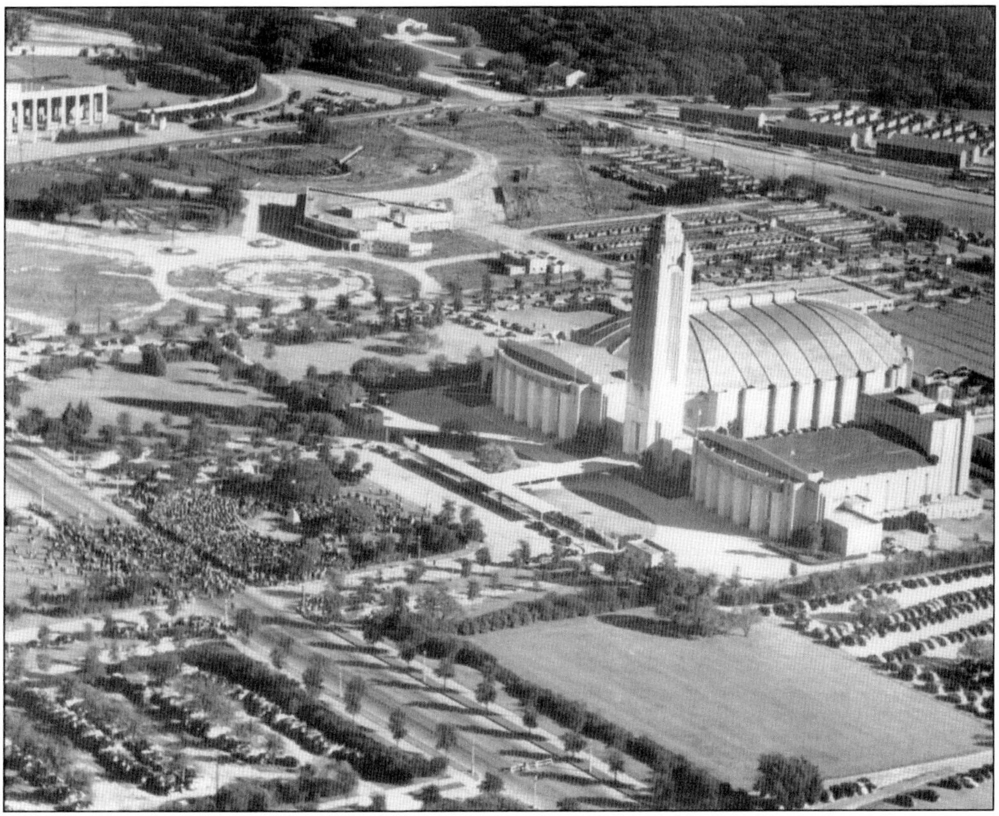

On November 4, 1947, Amon Carter officially donated two pieces of art to the city of Fort Worth and the Will Rogers Memorial Coliseum and Auditorium. Thousands came to witness the dedication ceremony. Present were Carter and his new wife, Minnie; Gen. Dwight D. Eisenhower and his wife, Mamie; and Margaret Truman, the president's daughter, who performed "Home on the Range," Will Rogers's favorite song. (TCU.)

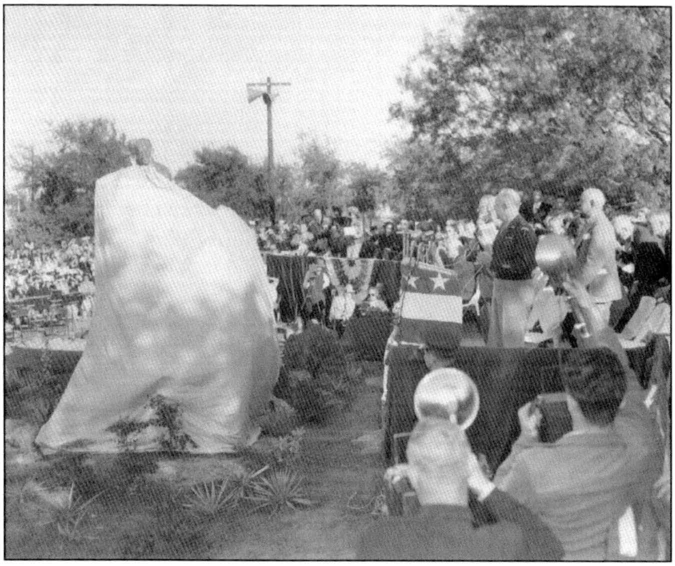

Thos. B. Byrne Construction built a wooden box around the bronze before it was unveiled, and then a drape was installed for the ceremony. On November 4, 1947, Gen. Dwight D. Eisenhower, chief of staff of the Army, pulled back the drape and unveiled Electra Biggs's sculpture *Will Rogers Riding into the Sunset.* Cast by Roman Bronze Works for $7,750, the statue was transported via the Pennsylvania Railroad Company to Fort Worth. (TCU.)

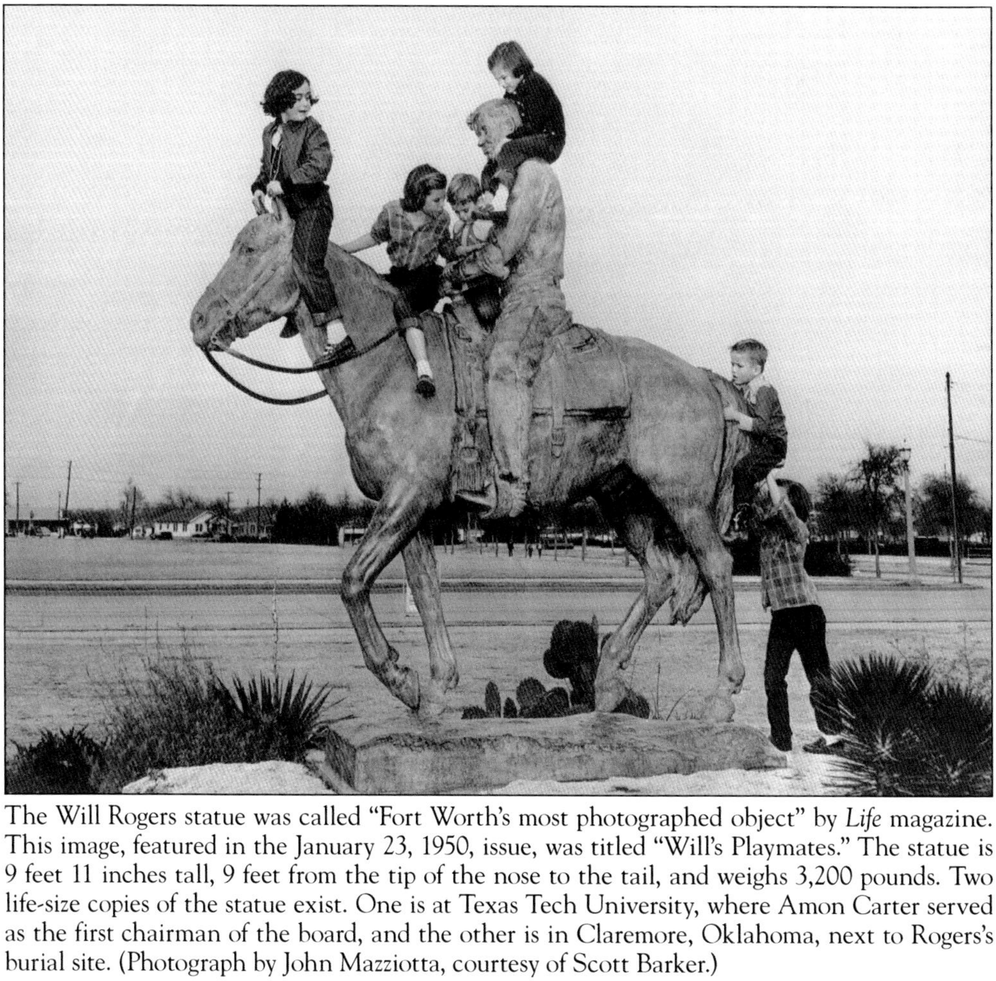

The Will Rogers statue was called "Fort Worth's most photographed object" by *Life* magazine. This image, featured in the January 23, 1950, issue, was titled "Will's Playmates." The statue is 9 feet 11 inches tall, 9 feet from the tip of the nose to the tail, and weighs 3,200 pounds. Two life-size copies of the statue exist. One is at Texas Tech University, where Amon Carter served as the first chairman of the board, and the other is in Claremore, Oklahoma, next to Rogers's burial site. (Photograph by John Mazziotta, courtesy of Scott Barker.)

Carter also donated a painting by well-known New York artist Seymour M. Stone the same day he donated the Biggs statue. Stone was known for his portraiture, painting John Nance Garner, Theodore Roosevelt, and others. This 12-foot-by-16-foot painting, also unveiled by Eisenhower (bottom left), depicts a smiling Will Rogers riding Soapsuds out on the range. (TCU.)

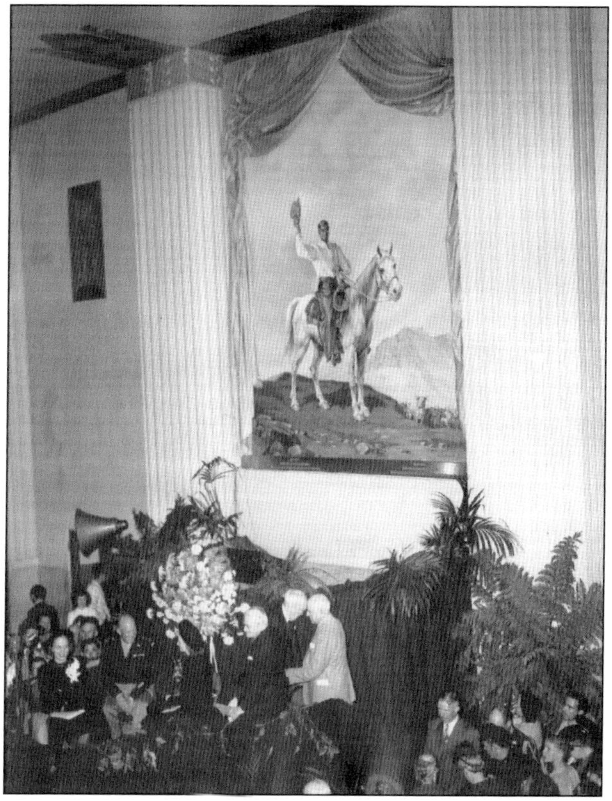

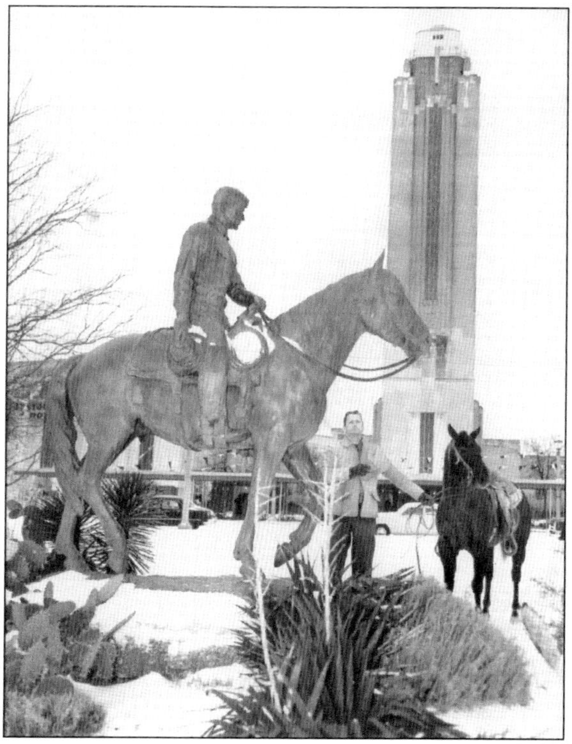

On January 31, 1960, during the Stock Show, Oklahoma lieutenant governor George Nigh placed a wreath at the statue of Will Rogers. Nigh and several hundred people from Texas and Oklahoma gathered to pay tribute to Rogers and to Amon G. Carter's efforts to have the center built and named after him. (TCU.)

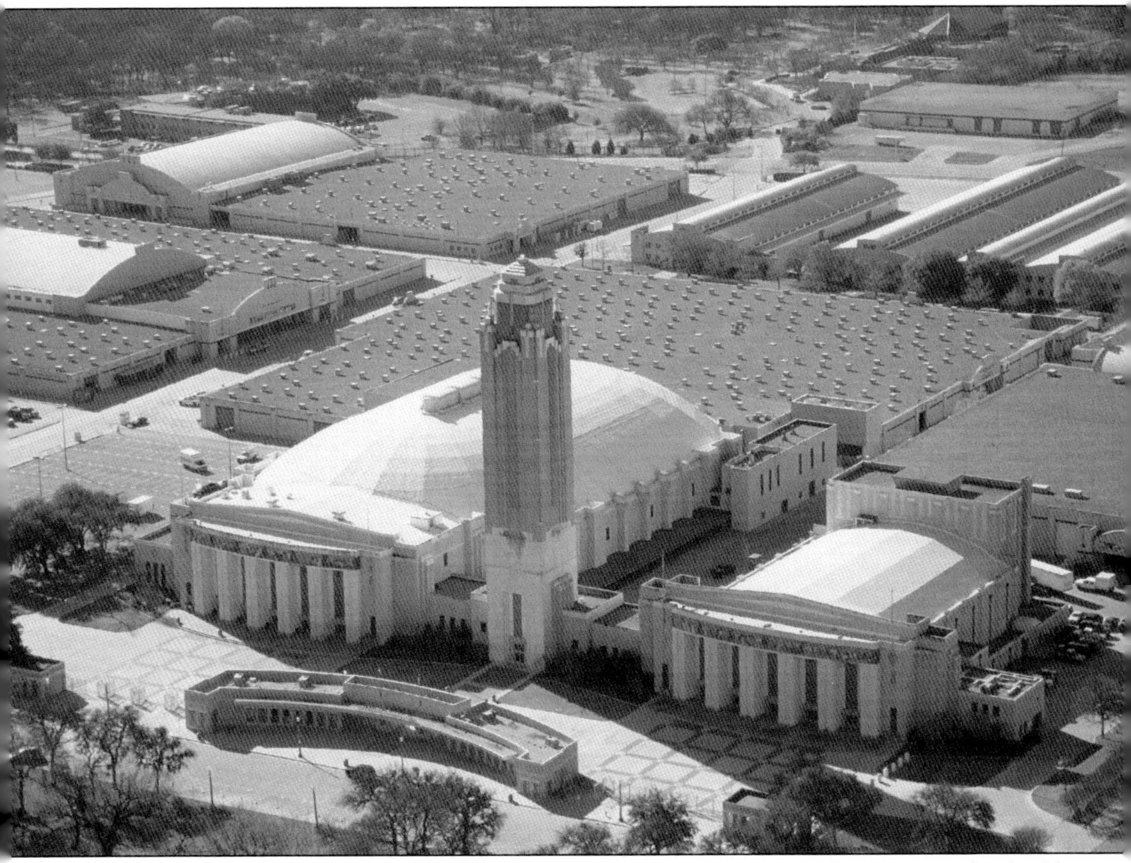

Will Rogers Coliseum and Auditorium are the history of Fort Worth. There are no other buildings in the city that embody the history they do. From their purpose-driven inception and their continued use, they have earned the right and privilege of protection and preservation. Amon Carter wanted to build a memorial to his friend, Will Rogers, but what he accomplished was far more: he built a city's legacy. (Courtesy of Jack W. Graves.)

Bibliography

Army Corps of Engineers. "History of Benbrook Lake." www.swf-wc.usace.army.mil/benbrook/Information/History.asp (accessed October 1, 2011).

Cowtown Memories: A History of Fort Worth. Television production. KERA Dallas/Fort Worth/Denton, 1994.

Flemmons, Jerry. *Amon: The Texan Who Played Cowboy For America*. Lubbock: Texas Tech University Press, 1998.

Fort Worth *Star-Telegram*.

Fort Worth Press.

Gearin, Joan. "Movie vs. Reality: The Real Story of the von Trapp Family." *Prologue* 37, no. 4 (Winter 2005). www.archives.gov/publications/prologue/2005/winter/von-trapps.html (accessed July 28, 2011).

"Gene Autry Tipped Stetson" www.willrogers.com/writers/stories/autry/autry.html (accessed July 28, 2011).

Hinckley, Herbert McDonald Jr., MD. *Under the Dome: A Biography of Herbert McDonald Hinckley Sr.* New York: Carlton Press, Inc., 1968.

Liles, Debbie. "Wyatt C. Hedrick: Builder of Cities." Master's thesis, University of North Texas, 2008.

Ragsdale, Kenneth B. *The Year America Discovered Texas: Centennial '36*. College Station: Texas A&M University, 1987.

Records of the Public Works Administration Projects in Fort Worth, Series 1. Will Rogers Memorial Complex, 1936.

Reynolds, Clay. *A Hundred Years of Heroes: A History of the Southwestern Exposition and Livestock Show*. Fort Worth: Texas Christian University Press, 1995.

Roark, Carol E. and Byrd Williams. *Fort Worth's Legendary Landmarks*. Fort Worth: Texas Christian University Press, 1997.

"Texas Military Forces Museum." www.texasmilitaryforcesmuseum.org/index.html (accessed October 27, 2011).

Winegarten, Ruthe, Janet G. Humphrey, and Frieda Werden. *Black Texas Women: 150 Years of Trial and Triumph*. Austin: University of Texas Press, 1995.